Oxford EAP

A course in English for Academic Purposes

PRE-INTERMEDIATE / B1

Paul Dummett & Jon Hird

OXFORD
UNIVERSITY PRESS

Contents

Introduction

Welcome to *Oxford English for Academic Purposes* – a complete course for anyone preparing to study in English at university level.

What is Oxford EAP?

Oxford EAP is designed to improve your ability to study effectively in English, whether you are planning to study on an undergraduate or postgraduate programme. Whatever your academic background, and whatever your chosen subject, *Oxford EAP* will help you develop your knowledge and skills in all of the following areas:

- reading and understanding authentic academic texts
- listening to lectures and presentations
- writing sentences, paragraphs, and different essay types
- participating in seminar and group discussions
- preparing and giving simple presentations
- improving your study skills such as note-taking, critical thinking, and working independently
- recognizing and using academic grammar and vocabulary.

What is in a unit?

Oxford EAP B1 has ten units. Each unit starts with a preview page which shows the learning objectives for that unit, plus a short discussion task to get you thinking about the unit theme.

The **academic focus** of each unit covers an important aspect of academic study relevant to all subject areas – for example, defining and explaining, describing, comparing and contrasting, cause and effect, and argument. This focus is maintained throughout the unit.

The units are divided into three main modules – Listening and Speaking, Reading, and Writing – plus one-page Vocabulary and Academic Language Check modules. Each module starts with a short list of learning objectives and includes a number of carefully sequenced tasks which help you to meet the objectives for that module.

Listening & Speaking focuses on both the receptive and productive skills needed to be successful in an academic environment. The initial part of the module focuses mainly on listening to lectures and presentations. It uses short video extracts from lectures to help you understand key information and language, as well as how the lecturer's material is organized. Note-taking is a key part of most modules, and the module usually features a critical thinking task which asks you to respond to the content of the lecture or presentation.

The Speaking focus of the module includes participating in seminars, discussions, and giving presentations. It covers communication strategies for these situations, and presents and practises useful language. Usually you will do a short listening task to introduce the context and present examples of useful language. At the end of the module there is normally an opportunity to think about and evaluate your own performance in the discussion or presentation task.

Reading uses extracts from authentic academic textbooks. It usually starts with a short task to get you thinking about the topic, or to predict the content of the text. Further tasks will help you to identify important features of the text, such as the main ideas or specific language, and demonstrate how you can read and understand an academic text even if you don't understand every word. This module often ends with a task where you respond critically to what you have read.

Writing focuses on some of the most important aspects of academic writing in the first four units, such as writing sentences, describing visuals, and simple paragraphs. Later in the book you move on to analyse paragraph structure, learn how to write summaries, and introductions and conclusions to essays. In the last three units, you will look at different types of academic writing tasks (e.g. describing a sequence or process, explaining cause and effect argument, and argument essays) looking at key aspects of organization, style, and use of language. You will also be helped to check and evaluate your writing.

Vocabulary looks at key aspects of academic vocabulary using the content of each unit, and covers useful vocabulary-learning strategies.

Academic Language Check provides the opportunity to further practise the academic language covered in the main modules.

What else is included?

Each unit includes:

- **Academic language** (grammar, vocabulary, and useful phrases) related to the academic focus of the unit, with examples taken from the texts or video / audio transcripts. Where necessary, there is a cross-reference to the Language reference.
- **Critical thinking** tasks encourage you to think about the content of each module, and about your own performance in writing and speaking tasks.
- **Independent study** tips suggesting how to transfer the skills from the course to your own studies.

At the front of the book there is:

- **Glossary** of grammatical and academic terms used in this book

At the back of the book there is:

- **Language reference** with more detailed information on the language covered in the units
- **Sample essays** and examples of academic writing
- **Answer key** for Vocabulary and Academic Languge Check sections
- **Video and audio transcripts**

Glossary

Words and phrases used to refer to grammar and other aspects of language in this book

Active voice the form of the verb which indicates something being done to the **object**, e.g. *Technology has made the growth of companies easier.*

Adjective a word which **modifies** a noun, e.g. *a **political** issue*, or functions as a **complement**, e.g. *This issue appears **political**.*

Adverb a word which **modifies** usually an adjective or verb, e.g. ***extremely** interesting*, or functions as an **adverbial** in a sentence, e.g. *However*

Adverbial a word / phrase that adds extra information, such as circumstance (how, where, when, why), e.g. *during the 20th century*; stance and perspective, e.g. *in terms of finance*; or linking, e.g. *however, in conclusion*

Affix the term used to cover both **prefix** and **suffix**

Argument a written or spoken discussion based on reason, logic, and evidence; an argument can be the main argument or a supporting argument

Article (1) the most frequent determiners: definite article *the*; indefinite article *a / an*

Article (2) a type of text which presents facts and argument

Aspect the form of the verb which expresses how an action or state is viewed: in progress (progressive), e.g. *is changing*, and / or completed (perfect), e.g. *has changed*

Auxiliary verb a verb which combines with another verb to indicate tense, e.g. *is / was changing*; voice, e.g. *is cleaned*; aspect, e.g. *has influenced*; or a modal verb, e.g. *can become*

Citation a **summary**, **paraphrase**, or **quotation** which is from a source text

Clause a grammatical unit which normally contains a **subject**, **verb**, and other parts of a sentence; a sentence may contain one clause, or two or more joined together using a **coordinator** or **subordinator**

Coherence how a text is connected in terms of meaning and ideas

Cohesion how a text is connected in terms of meaning and language

Collocation two words which frequently go together, e.g. *significant difference, influential decisions*

Complement the part of the sentence following verbs like *be* and *seem*, e.g. *It seems unlikely*

Compound noun two nouns put together to create one meaning, e.g. *radio journalist*; unlike adjective + noun combinations, the first noun is normally stressed in spoken language

Conclusion the part of a written or spoken text which sums up the main argument of the whole text; usually the end of the text

Conjunction the term used to cover both **coordinator** and **subordinator**

Content word a word which has real meaning rather than just grammatical meaning; nouns, verbs, adjectives, and adverbs are content words

Coordinator a word which joins two units of language: clauses, phrases, or words; the most frequent conjunctions in English are *and, but, or*

Definite article the determiner *the*, which specifies definite meaning

Determiner a word which specifies something about the **head noun**, e.g. *the, some, this*

Evaluation the writer's subjective, evidence-based response to an idea in the text, e.g. *This argument is **highly convincing**.*

Head noun the main noun in a noun phrase, e.g. *their social, emotional, and personal **development***

Hedge / hedging the language and academic practice of 'softening' statements, e.g. *This **may** result in failure.*

Indefinite article the determiner *a* (*an* before vowels), which specifies indefinite meaning

Infinitive the base form of the verb, with or without *to*, e.g. *consider, to consider*

Intransitive not taking an object, e.g. *They **cope** well in lessons.*

Introduction the part of a written or spoken text which introduces the topic, focus, aims, and limitations of the whole text

Modal verb an **auxiliary verb** such as *may* and *should*, which expresses objective meanings, e.g. *airborne pollution **may** result in lung damage*; or subjective meanings, e.g. *you **should** speak more slowly*

Modifier / modify a word such as *extremely* which adds to or limits the meaning of another word, e.g. ***extremely** significant*

Noun a word which can refer to anything concrete, e.g. *university*, or abstract, e.g. *success*

Object the part of a sentence, usually a noun phrase, which is affected by the action of the verb and which normally comes after the main verb; an object can become the **subject** in the **passive** form of the sentence, e.g. *The internet transformed **consumption habits**; **Consumption habits** were transformed by the internet.*

Paraphrase a piece of text which expresses similar ideas to another text of similar length but using different language

Participle the form of the verb which ends in *-ing* or *-ed*; used to form the progressive aspect (*-ing*), perfect aspect (*-ed*), and passive voice (*-ed*)

Particle a word, usually an **adverb** or **preposition** of one syllable, which is attached to another word, e.g. *look at*

Passive voice the form of the verb which is used to indicate something being done to the subject, e.g. *salt **is** then **added** to the mixture*

Perspective an essentially objective way of viewing something, e.g. *from a medical perspective*

Phrasal verb a verb which contains the base verb + an adverb particle, e.g. *put away*

Phrase a structure built round a **noun**, **verb**, **adjective**, **adverb**, or **preposition**, e.g. *a similar problem*

Prefix the first part of some words, which expresses a particular meaning or grammatical property, e.g. *un-, dis-, mega-*

Preposition / prepositional phrase a structure built round a preposition, e.g. ***despite** this difficulty*

Prepositional verb a verb which contains a base verb + a preposition, e.g. *look into*

Pronoun a word which takes the place of another noun or noun phrase, e.g. *he, it*

Quantifier a **determiner** which specifies the quantity or amount of the following noun, e.g. ***many** issues*

Quotation a **citation** which uses the exact words of the original source

Relative clause a structure in a longer **noun phrase** which follows the **head noun** and adds extra information, e.g. *the choices that are being voted upon*

Relative pronoun a word that links a **relative clause** to the **head noun**, i.e. *that, which, who, whom, whose*; the relative adverbs *when, where*, and *why* can also be used in a similar way, e.g. *the reason why flooding occurred*

Reporting the practice of informing and presenting information from another **source**

Source the original text from which a **citation** or reference is taken

Stance a way of viewing something which is essentially subjective but based on evidence, and connected to an **argument**

Subject the part of a sentence that normally comes first in a sentence, and which performs the action of the main verb, e.g. ***Capital cities in developed countries** often have a complex transport infrastructure.*

Subordinator a word which joins two clauses, e.g. *if, while, because*

Suffix the last part in some words, which expresses a particular meaning or grammatical property, e.g. *-tion, -ize, -ship*

Summary a short text which expresses the main argument(s) of a longer text

Tense the form of the verb which relates to time; English has two tenses: present, e.g. *this **occurs*** and past, e.g. *this **occurred***; future time is referred to by using **modal verbs**, e.g. *will, may*, and other expressions, e.g. *The price of oil **is likely to rise** dramatically over the next decade.*

Thesis statement the part of a text which briefly expresses some or all of the following: purpose, aims, rationale, limitations, organization

Topic sentence a sentence in a paragraph, often one of the first sentences, which expresses the topic of that paragraph

Transitive taking an **object**, e.g. ***make** a decision*

Verb the part of a sentence which typically comes between the **subject** and the **object**, and can be in the present or past tense, e.g. *Cultural differences **influence** the way firms in the East and West do business.*

Word class also known as 'part of speech'; the way a word is used in a particular context, e.g. the word *like* can function as different parts of speech: *situations **like** this* (prep); *she **likes** economics* (v); ***like** cases* (adj)

UNIT 1 Learning

ACADEMIC FOCUS: PRESENTING FACTUAL INFORMATION

LEARNING OBJECTIVES

This unit covers:

Listening and Speaking

- Understanding main ideas in a presentation
- Noting down key information
- Identifying questions asking for information
- Asking questions for further information

Reading

- Understanding a text
- Identifying factual information
- Identifying statistics and time references

Writing

- Identifying parts of a simple sentence
- Writing simple sentences
- Writing compound sentences using *and*, *but*, and *or*

Vocabulary

- Using academic vocabulary
- Vocabulary building: Identifying verbs and nouns

Academic Language Check

- Present and past simple and progressive forms
- Writing simple sentences
- Writing compound sentences

Discussion

1 Complete the steps in the process using the verbs.

accept apply attend complete enrol graduate

1 .... for a course → 2 .... a place on the course →
3 .... on the course → 4 .... the course →
5 .... the course → 6 .... from the university

2 Work in pairs. Explain where you are in this process.

3 Work in pairs. Respond to statements 1–4. State:

- whether you think it is a fact or an opinion
- what you think are the reasons for it.

1 More students in the UK apply for business courses than any other subject.
2 Seven of the top ten universities are in the USA.
3 Students who pay for their education study harder.
4 In China, 97% of university students complete their course. In the USA, over 50% drop out.

4 Work in pairs. Read three common reasons for going to university. Evaluate each reason. Is it good or bad?

1 To get a better paid job
2 To meet interesting people
3 To improve self-confidence

5 Explain your reasons for choosing to go to university. Use the following phrases to help you.

My main reason for choosing ... is that ...
I chose to go to university because ...

1A Listening & Speaking Presentations (1)

This module covers:

- Understanding main ideas in a presentation
- Noting down key information
- Identifying questions asking for information
- Asking questions for further information

TASK 1 Understanding the main idea

1 Read the definition. Discuss questions 1–3.

1 Who is a university orientation day for?
2 What kind of things happen on an orientation day?
3 What information do students receive?

> **orientation** (*n*)
> training or information that you are given before starting a new job, course, etc.

2 You are going to watch extracts from three short talks at an orientation day for international students. Match each speaker to the subject you think they will talk about.

Speaker 1: Clare Theakston, Head of Student Affairs
Speaker 2: Patrick O'Connor, 2nd-year student
Speaker 3: Sarah Wilkes, Programme Coordinator

a Giving details about the orientation day
b Welcoming the students
c Giving a personal view of university

3 1.1–1.3 Watch Extracts 1–3 and check your answers in 1.

TASK 2 Understanding key information

1 1.1 Watch Extract 1 again. Tick what the speaker does.

1 Welcomes the students ☐
2 Explains the programme for the day ☐
3 Explains what her department does ☐
4 Introduces all the members of her team ☐
5 Explains where students can find her ☐

2 1.2 Watch Extract 2 again and complete notes 1–3.

1 Most important aspect of the Orientation Week programme:
....
2 was nervous / unsure about: ....
3 New BCU students will find: ....

Speaker 1

Speaker 2

Speaker 3

TASK 3 Critical thinking – responding to the content of a talk

1 Work in pairs. Discuss questions 1–3.

1 Which speaker do you think provided the most useful information? Give reasons.

2 How did Speaker 2 make students feel less worried? Give examples.

3 How would you feel if you were a new student at this university? Explain your answer.

ACADEMIC LANGUAGE

Note-taking (1) Noting key information

In talks and lectures, you will often need to write down facts and figures (numbers) quickly. To do this:

- do not write complete sentences
- write only the content words (the words which carry the main meaning)
- do not include unnecessary words, such as determiners (*the*, *this*, etc.), and auxiliary verbs (*is*, *have*, etc.)
- use symbols instead of words or phrases (@ instead of *at*)
- use abbreviations (*p.m.* instead of *afternoon*).

Text: *'The talk on Life in the UK at 3 p.m. will be in room 7A, not 8A as advertised. That's room 7A.'*

Notes: *Talk – Life in the UK @ 3 p.m. Room 7A (not 8A)*

TASK 4 Noting key information

1 1.3 Watch Extract 3 again. Note down the changes to the programme.

Afternoon plenary session	1.30 p.m.	McDonald Theatre
Student Council presentation	2.30 p.m.	Lecture Hall 2
Sports societies meeting	2.30 p.m.	Byron House
Life in the UK	3.00 p.m.	Room 8A
Work and visas	4.00 p.m.	Lecture Hall 2
Walking tour	4.45 p.m.	meet in main reception

For advice on using study facilities, visit the Library information centre Monday–Friday 9 a.m. to 9 p.m.

2 Match sentences 1–4 with student notes a–d.

1 A lecture on the history of the university begins at 4.30 p.m. in Clarendon Hall. ....

2 The seminar on work opportunities during the vacation will be at 6 p.m., not 6.30 p.m. ....

3 The library will be closed for staff computer training on Wednesday morning. ....

4 All students who need a travel pass should register in office 3B from 9.00 a.m. onwards. ....

a Library closed Weds. a.m.

b Register for travel pass office 3B 9.00 →

c Lecture (History of Uni.) 4.30 p.m. Clarendon Hall

d Work opportunities seminar @ 6 p.m. not 6.30.

3 Work in pairs. In notes a–d:

1 identify the words from sentences 1–4 that are not used.

2 find examples of an abbreviation, a symbol, and a key content word.

TASK 5 Taking notes on factual information

1 1.4 Listen to a programme organizer giving four more pieces of information. Note down the key information.

1 Student Affairs offices ....

2 Library ....

3 Student travel discount cards ....

4 University Medical Service ....

2 Work in pairs. Explain why you noted down some words and not others.

TASK 6 Identifying questions asking for information

1 1.5 Listen to an extract from a question and answer session at the end of the orientation day talks. Note down key information about:

1 free internet access 2 journals 3 the university bus.

2 Complete the questions the students ask.

1 .... free internet access everywhere on the campus?

2 Where .... get more information about that?

3 How .... take books out of the library?

4 .... the last bus from town?

5 What .... you miss it?

6 And is the university bus free or .... have to pay?

3 1.5 Listen again and check your answers in 2.

ACADEMIC LANGUAGE ▸ Language reference page 150

Questions (1) Asking for further information

After lectures or talks, and in discussions, you will often need to ask questions to get further information. You can use a number of common types of question. For example:

Is there ...	*Is there internet access everywhere on campus?*
Where can I ...	*Where can I get more information about that?*
How can / do ...	*How do I take books out of the library?*
Can I / you ...	*Can you borrow them?*
Do I / you have to ...	*Do you have to pay?*
What happens if ...	*What happens if you miss it?*

Note that 'you' in these questions refers to people in general.

TASK 7 Asking questions to get further information

1 Work in pairs. You are going to take part in a question and answer session similar to the one in Task 6. Student A: turn to page 162. Student B: turn to page 164.

TASK 8 Critical thinking – evaluating information questions

1 Evaluate your partner's questions. Check that they have:

- used a correct question form ☐
- stressed the most important words ☐
- asked another question to get further information. ☐

INDEPENDENT STUDY

In talks and lectures, speakers often stress content words more strongly. These can help you to identify key information.

▸ Find a short lecture extract online on a topic that interests you. Listen and note down words that are stressed.

1B Reading Textbooks (1)

This module covers:

- Understanding a text
- Identifying factual information
- Identifying statistics and time references

TASK 1 Discussing the topic of a text

1 Work in groups. Discuss questions 1–3.

1. Approximately how many people from your country go abroad to study at university? Do people from other countries come to your country to study? If so, which countries?
2. Think of three reasons why people choose to study in a different country.
3. Think of three reasons why universities may want to attract international students.

2 Work in pairs. You are going to read a text called *The internationalization of higher education*. Before you read, discuss what you think the title means.

TASK 2 Understanding topic, purpose, and main idea

1 When reading any academic text, you need to understand the *topic*, *purpose*, and *main idea(s)*. Select the best description (a) or (b) for features 1–3.

1. The **topic** of a text is:
   a what the text is about
   b the style the text is written in.
2. The **purpose** of the text is:
   a who the text is written for
   b the reason for writing.
3. The **main idea** is:
   a the most important thing that the author wants to communicate
   b the most important thing that the reader understands in the text.

2 **Read the text quickly and identify (a) the topic, and (b) the purpose.**

3 **Read the text again and decide which statement 1–3 contains the main idea. Give reasons.**

1 Subjects taught in universities are more internationally relevant than in the past.
2 International cooperation between universities is stronger than in the past.
3 Universities have a greater international mix of students than in the past.

The internationalization of higher education

1 Tertiary education represents 34% of today's global market for education, and more students travel abroad for their university studies than ever before. Recent research suggests that in the region of four million tertiary-level students enrol each year in universities outside their native country. This number is steadily increasing. The largest numbers of international students are from China, the USA, and Western Europe.

2 International universities are not a new phenomenon. Nine hundred years ago, students from around Europe travelled to the first universities in Bologna, Paris, and Oxford. Over the centuries, this trend continued, creating strong academic networks, and helping information and research results to cross borders.

3 In the early part of the 20th century, the United States started to attract students and professors from around the world. American universities created a system where good teaching and first-class research took place under one roof. These universities were rich and had many of the best students, the best departments, and the most modern laboratories. Today, the vast majority of universities worldwide are following the US model.

4 Towards the end of the 20th century, universities in a number of other countries started to encourage more students from overseas. Today, many universities around the world have a large proportion of foreign students. For example, around 20% of the students at universities in the UK are now from another country. At the University of Oxford, students currently come from over 140 countries, and overseas students make up one-third of the student body. This broad international approach is mirrored in the teaching, as over 40% of the university's academic staff are citizens of foreign countries. Other countries which have a high proportion of foreign students include Australia, New Zealand, Japan, and some European countries, such as Luxembourg and Switzerland. The United States has over 20% of the world's international students, but this accounts for less than 5% of its total student numbers.

5 However, universities are not only attracting foreign students, they are also exporting their ideas abroad. By the 1990s, popular Western universities were becoming more financially-driven and were beginning to act more like businesses. They moved closer to their customers by establishing international branch campuses, particularly in Asia and the Middle East, or by making alliances with local universities. In this way they could offer a British, Australian, or American degree, for example, in the host country, so that the local student did not have to travel abroad. Overseas branch campuses are today a big part of the growing internationalization of higher education.

GLOSSARY

alliance *(n)* a union or partnership that helps both parties

financially-driven *(adj)* doing something because you want to make money

host *(n)* a person or place who receives other people as guests

tertiary *(adj)* the stage of education after primary and secondary

ACADEMIC LANGUAGE

Data (1) Identifying factual information

Academic texts often present and support key facts using statistics (information shown in numbers) and time references.

Tertiary education represents ***34%*** *of* ***today's*** *global market for education.* ***Over the centuries****, this trend continued, ...*

TASK 3 Identifying factual information in a text

1 Read the text again and identify the statistics and time references.

Example: *Tertiary education represents 34% of today's global market for education.*

2 Complete the student notes relating to the following dates.

1 900 years ago ....
2 During the early part of the 20th century ....
3 In the late 20th century ....
4 In the 1990s ....
5 Today ....

3 Note down what information statistics a–g refer to.

a 34% ....
b 4 million ....
c around 20% ....
d over 140 ....
e over 40% ....
f over 20% ....
g less than 5% ....

4 Identify the information that states which countries:

a are the most popular with foreign students
b provide the highest number of international students.

TASK 4 Critical thinking – extending the ideas in a text

1 Work in groups. Note down benefits of the internationalization of higher education for (a) individuals, (b) institutions, and (c) countries. Think about:

- programme of study
- knowledge of other cultures and languages
- preparation for the global labour market
- income for the institution
- benefits to the local and national economy.

ACADEMIC LANGUAGE

▸ Language reference page 150

Factual information Present and past simple and progressive

Use the **present simple** to talk about facts and situations which are generally true.

*Tertiary education **represents** 34% of today's global market for education.*

*Over 40% of the university's academic staff **are** citizens of foreign countries.*

Use the **past simple** to talk about events or completed situations in the past.

*Nine hundred years ago, students from around Europe **travelled** to the first universities in Bologna, Paris, and Oxford.*

*These universities **were** rich and had many of the best students, ...*

Use the **present progressive** to talk about something in progress now. This is often a changing situation.

*This number **is** steadily **increasing**.*

*Today, the vast majority of universities worldwide **are following** the US model.*

Use the **past progressive** to talk about something not complete at a time in the past.

*By the 1990s, popular Western universities **were becoming** more financially-driven and **were beginning** to act more like businesses.*

TASK 5 Using present and past simple and progressive forms

1 Put the verbs in brackets into the correct form – present or past simple or progressive.

1 From 1975 to 2010, the number of international students worldwide [1] .... (increase) by over 400% from fewer than one million to over four million. The figure [2] .... (double) to two million in the 25 years to 2000 and then [3] .... (double) again in the ten years from 2000 to 2010. Today, the figure [4] .... (increase) at an even faster rate. Latin America, Oceania, and Asia [5] .... (experience) the biggest increases in the number of overseas students.

2 Educational norms and values [6] .... (vary) between cultures. In some cultures there [7] .... (be) an emphasis on understanding and learning established facts. In other cultures, universities traditionally [8] .... (put) a strong emphasis on independent study and critical thinking. Today, attitudes [9] .... (change) and this more independent and critical approach to academic study [10] .... (become) more popular across the world.

3 Bill Gates [11] .... (study) at Harvard University when he [12] .... (start) the software company Microsoft with Paul Allen. Gates [13] .... (leave) the university before he [14] .... (finish) his studies. He [15] .... (become) one of the most influential and successful IT entrepreneurs in the world and today [16] .... (be) one of the richest people in the world. He [17] .... (leave) Microsoft in 2008 and now [18] .... (work) full-time for his charity.

2 Write at least four sentences about education in your country. Use the forms in Academic Language.

Example: *In the UK, compulsory education began in 1880.*
UK universities are accepting more and more international students.

3 Work in pairs. Compare sentences using the questions below.

1 Are the sentences clear and easy to understand?
2 Do the sentences accurately use the forms in Academic Language?
3 Is there anything that could be improved?

TASK 6 Critical thinking – responding to the content of a text

1 Read claims 1–3 from the text. Decide if each claim is a good thing or a bad thing.

1 The vast majority of universities worldwide are following the US model.
2 Many universities around the world have a large proportion of foreign students.
3 Popular Western universities were becoming more financially-driven and were beginning to act more like businesses.

2 Work in pairs and discuss your answers in 1. Give reasons.

3 Do you agree that the internationalization of higher education is a good thing? Give reasons.

INDEPENDENT STUDY

In your academic study you will read or hear a range of facts and statistics, and it's important to identify what these relate to.

▸ **Find a text from your own area of study, or a topic that interests you. Read it and note down the key statistics. Use these notes to write sentences about the main facts. Read the text again and check your sentences for factual accuracy.**

1C Writing (1) Simple sentences

This module covers:

- Identifying parts of a simple sentence
- Writing simple sentences

TASK 1 Understanding simple sentence structure

1 Read Paragraph 1 about higher education in China. Identify the subject, verb, and object in sentences 1–4.

Example: *Peking University has 30 colleges.*
subject verb object

Sentence	Subject	Verb	Object
1			
2			
3			
4			

Paragraph 1

[1]China has over 4,000 universities and colleges. [2]More than fifteen million students attend higher education institutions. [3]Chinese universities have varied teaching and research programmes. [4]Chinese higher education is expanding.

2 Work in pairs. Discuss questions 1 and 2.

1 Which sentence does not have an object?

2 Is the word order (subject + verb + object) the same or different in your language?

ACADEMIC LANGUAGE ▸Language reference page 150

Sentences (1) Subject + verb + object; Subject + verb + complement

Subject + verb + object

Simple sentences in English have a subject (s) and a verb (v).

Chinese higher education is expanding.
s v

Many sentences also include an object (o). Typically the subject and the object are nouns, (e.g. *university, students*) or noun phrases (e.g. *Chinese Universities, more than 15 million students*).

More than 15 million students attend higher education institutions.
s v o

Subject + verb + complement

A complement is a word or phrase that gives more information about the subject of the sentence. Some verbs (such as *appear, be, become,* and *seem*) are followed by a complement (c) instead of an object.

The university is modern.
s v c

Peking University is a teaching and research university.
s v c

TASK 2 Identifying parts of a simple sentence (1)

1 Identify the subject, verb, and object or complement in sentences 1–5.

1 Four hundred students studied law.
2 King Saud University has about 40,000 students.
3 Harvard and Yale are Ivy League universities.
4 Most universities offer a range of qualifications.
5 The University of Bologna was the world's first university.

Sentence	Subject	Verb	Object	Complement
1				
2				
3				
4				
5				

ACADEMIC LANGUAGE ▸ Language reference page 150

Sentences (2) Subject + verb + adverbial

Some simple sentences have an adverbial (a). An adverbial gives information about *when, where,* or *how* something happens. You can use an adverbial with or without an object or complement.

The university rejects over 20,000 applicants every year.
s v o a

Barack Obama studied at Harvard Law School.
s v a

TASK 3 Identifying parts of a simple sentence (2)

1 Identify the adverbial in sentences 1–4.

1 Over 40 British prime ministers studied at Oxbridge.
2 Riyadh University became King Saud University in 1982.
3 The number of higher education students in China is growing every year.
4 Harvard University is located in Cambridge, Massachusetts.

TASK 4 Writing simple sentences

1 Order the words and write simple sentences 1–6.

1 32 academic departments / Massachusetts Institute of Technology (MIT) / has
2 at UK universities / study / many international students
3 starts / in September / the US academic year
4 is / at UK universities / business and management studies / the most popular degree course
5 in the world / is / Princess Nora bint Abdulrahman University / the largest women-only university
6 its name / The Imperial University of Peking / in 1912 / changed / to Peking University

2 Write four simple sentences about higher education in your country. Write sentences that consist of a subject, a verb, and an object or complement and/or adverbial.

Example: *Turkey has about 150 universities and academies. Around 100 are state universities. Over one million people study at universities in Turkey. Turkish universities teach many different subjects.*

1C Writing (2) Compound sentences

This module covers:

- Writing compound sentences using *and*, *but*, and *or*

TASK 1 Recognizing compound sentences

1 Read Paragraph 2 and answer questions 1–3.

Paragraph 2

[1]In the UK, university students fund part of the cost of tuition and the government funds the other part. [2]Student tuition fees are up to £9,000 a year for EU students, but they are higher for non-EU students. [3]Students' parents or sponsors pay the fees or the students take out a loan.

GLOSSARY

EU *(n)* the European Union

fund *(v)* to pay for

tuition fees *(n)* the money you pay to study at university

1 Who funds the cost of university tuition?
2 How much are student tuition fees in the UK?
3 How do students pay the tuition fees?

2 Read the paragraph again. Identify the difference between sentences in Paragraph 2 and simple sentences.

ACADEMIC LANGUAGE ▸ Language reference page 150

Sentences (3) Writing compound sentences using coordinators

Two closely related simple sentences can be joined together to make a compound sentence. The most common words (or coordinators) for joining simple sentences together are *and*, *but*, and *or*.

*The university has three terms **and** these last ten weeks each.*
*In the past, some colleges were single-sex, **but** all colleges are mixed-sex today.*
*Students can live in their college **or** they can live outside college in rented accommodation.*

TASK 2 Writing compound sentences

1 Match each coordinator 1–3 with its function a–c.

1 and — a to connect alternatives
2 but — b to add information
3 or — c to introduce a contrast

2 Complete sentences 1–3 with *and*, *but*, or *or*. Use each coordinator only once.

1 The university is very popular .... it receives more than five applications for each available place.
2 A student must have a high IELTS score .... they must demonstrate their language level in a different way.
3 Last year, over 17,200 people applied for a place at the university, ... only 3,500 were accepted.

3 Read the pairs of sentences 1–6 about the University of Oxford's Department for Continuing Education. Rewrite them as compound sentences with the most appropriate coordinator, *and*, *but*, or *or*.

1 In the late 19th century, more and more adults wanted to continue their education. They didn't have the opportunity.
2 A new University Extension programme offered courses to the general public. People from many different backgrounds attended.
3 People could attend courses in Oxford. They could arrange for courses in their own towns.
4 The programme had several name changes. It became the Department for Continuing Education in 1990.
5 Today, the department runs over 800 courses. Over 15,000 students from 18 to 80 enrol on courses each year.
6 Students can take full-time courses. They can study part-time.

ACADEMIC LANGUAGE ▸ Language reference page 150

Sentences (4) Using compound sentences

Sometimes writers will express facts or ideas using **simple sentences**. For example:

In the UK, university students fund part of the cost of their tuition. The government funds the other part.

Student tuition fees are up to £9,000 a year for EU students. They are higher for non-EU students.

However, joining two ideas together in **compound sentences** shows the relationship between the ideas and makes your writing more fluent. For example:

In the UK, university students fund part of the cost of their tuition ***and*** *the government funds the other part.*

Student tuition fees are up to £9,000 a year for EU students, ***but*** *they are higher for non-EU students.*

TASK 3 Developing writing – from notes to compound sentences

1 Research the following information about your place of study or another institution.

- Number of students
- Courses / Programmes of study
- History

2 Use your notes from 1 to write simple sentences.

Example: *English department – biggest department in university. About 250 students.*
The English department is the biggest department in the university. It has about 250 students.

3 Connect some of your simple sentences from 2 to make compound sentences using *and*, *but*, and *or*. Use each coordinator at least once.

Example: *The English department is the biggest department in the university* ***and*** *it has about 250 students.*

TASK 4 Critical thinking – evaluating your writing

1 Read the sentences you wrote in Task 3. Check that you have:

- used only key information in your notes ☐
- expanded your notes to make simple sentences ☐
- joined simple sentences into compound sentences ☐
- used the coordinators *and*, *but*, and *or* at least once ☐
- used capital letters and the correct punctuation ☐
- checked your spelling. ☐

INDEPENDENT STUDY

It is important to check your writing for accuracy. Using correct punctuation helps readers to follow your ideas clearly. Remember to start your sentences with a capital letter and end them with a full stop.

▸ Refer to the Language Reference on page 151 about the use of commas before coordinators.

1D Vocabulary

TASK 1 Using academic vocabulary

1 Select an appropriate academic word to complete the text.

achieve institutions expand proportion available fund
phenomenon trend goal

Most countries would like to see a greater [1] .... of their population going to university and this indeed is the general [2] .... This growth in the higher education sector is now a worldwide [3] .... But as the number of students going to university increases and the [4] .... themselves [5] .... to accommodate them, governments are faced with a problem: how to [6] .... this expansion. Some politicians believe that asking the students to pay is the answer. They argue that people who have to invest their own money to [7] .... their [8] .... in life are more motivated. Others argue that this discourages people from poor backgrounds, and that a university education should be [9] .... to everyone despite their economic or social background.

2 Complete sentences 1–7 using your own ideas.

Example: *My goal in life to is to become a geologist.*

1 My goal in life is to ....
2 Only a small proportion of people in my country ....
3 .... is an important institution in my country.
4 A recent trend in my country is that more people are ....
5 The foreign languages that are available to study at school are ....
6 .... fund(s) university courses in my country.
7 .... is expanding all the time.

3 Work in pairs. Discuss your answers in 2.

TASK 2 Vocabulary-building: Identifying verbs and nouns

1 Read dialogues 1–7. Note down which words in bold are verbs (*v*) and which are nouns (*n*).

Example: *A: Did she* ***succeed*** *in her exam? (v)*
B: She got 68%, so I think it was a ***success****. (n)*

1 A: I hear they are going to **expand** the university campus again.
B: Yes, but the **expansion** will create many new jobs in the area.
2 A: He **achieved** many things in his life.
B: I think his greatest **achievements** were in the field of nanotechnology.
3 A: Can you give me some **advice** about studying abroad?
B: Well, I can **advise** you about studying in the UK.
4 A: My teacher **encouraged** me to study maths at university.
B: I didn't need any **encouragement** to study physics.
5 A: I want to **apply** for a course in medicine at London University.
B: Then you need to fill in an **application** form on the UCAS website.
6 A: Is your **research** about new metals?
B: No, we are **researching** new types of plastic.
7 A: What is the **attraction** of studying in another country?
B: It was the idea of a new culture that **attracted** me.

2 Write sentences about your own studies using the words in the list.

achieve advise encourage apply research attract

Example: *My high school teacher encouraged me to study medicine at university.*

INDEPENDENT STUDY

Try to be active in building your vocabulary. When you learn a new word, try to identify which word class it belongs to. Then note down related words of different classes: e.g. *educate* (v) *education* (n)

▸ **Read a short text related to your area of study. Write word families for at least four new words.**

1E Academic Language Check

TASK 1 Present and past simple and progressive forms

1 Read this extract from a presentation about Yale University. Put verbs 1–15 into the correct form: present or past simple or progressive.

Yale University in the USA [1] .... (be) one of the top universities in the world. Its history [2] .... (go) back over three hundred years. At that time, the colony of Connecticut [3] .... (try) to become more independent. However, it [4] .... (not / have) enough leaders or people who could govern. So, in 1701, Connecticut [5] .... (establish) Yale School to train its political leaders. The school [6] .... (become) Yale College in 1718 and then it [7] .... (change) its status and its name to Yale University in 1887. Today, the university [8] .... (enter) its fourth century and its goals [9] .... (be) very different from those of three hundred years ago. Yale [10] .... (be) now a truly global university and it [11] .... (attract) students from many different countries. But this globalization of the university [12] .... (be) not a new phenomenon. Yale first [13] .... (receive) students from outside the United States nearly two centuries ago. International issues [14] .... (be) at the centre of its curriculum and the university [15] .... (expand) its international collaborations all the time.

TASK 2 Writing simple sentences

1 Read sentences 1–5 about King Saud University. Identify the subject (S), verb (V), object (O) or complement (C), and/or adverbial (A) in each.

Example: *King Saud University is in Riyadh.*
S V A

1 King Saud University is the premier university in the Kingdom of Saudi Arabia.
2 It is the oldest university in Saudi Arabia.
3 The university has about 40,000 students.
4 It has students from a number of different countries.
5 Tuition is free at the university.

TASK 3 Writing compound sentences

1 Combine pairs of sentences 1–8 using a coordinator: *and*, *but*, or *or*.

1 The department has 15 teaching staff. There are three research fellows.

....

2 Steve Jobs studied at Reed College, Oregon. He dropped out after six months.

....

3 You can study on campus. You can study online.

....

4 I needed a score of 6.5 at IELTS. I only got 6.0.

....

5 Students can do a research project. They can do a literature review.

....

6 There are two semesters. Each semester is 14 weeks long.

....

7 We can eat in the refectory. We can eat in the café.

....

8 Internet access is free. You need a password from the office.

....

UNIT 2 Symbols

ACADEMIC FOCUS: DEFINING AND EXPLAINING

LEARNING OBJECTIVES

This unit covers:

Listening and Speaking
- Listening for the main and supporting ideas in a lecture
- Understanding spoken definitions
- Defining and explaining a simple concept in a seminar discussion

Reading
- Identifying definitions and explanations in a text
- Identifying the language of simple definitions and explanations
- Understanding meaning from context

Writing
- Writing simple definitions
- Writing definitions with relative clauses
- Writing definitions with prepositional phrases
- Writing extended definitions

Vocabulary
- Academic verbs
- Collocations (1): Verbs and nouns

Academic Language Check
- Definitions and explanations
- Definitions using defining words and phrases

Discussion

1 Read the definition of *concept*. Answer questions 1–4.

> **concept** (*n*) /ˈkɒnsept/ an idea or a principle that is connected with something abstract, e.g. *He can't understand the basic* ***concepts*** *of mathematics.*

1 What type of word is *concept*?
2 How do you pronounce it?
3 What is the definition of *concept*?
4 What example is given?

2 Work in pairs. Find these words in a dictionary.

Student A: *symbol*
Student B: *code*

3 Tell your partner your definition. Think of three more examples for each word.

4 Work in pairs. Discuss what you do if you don't know the meaning of a word. Give examples.

If I don't know the meaning of a new word, I ...
Usually I ... if I don't know the meaning of a new word.

2A Listening & Speaking Lectures (1)

This module covers:

- Listening for the main and supporting ideas in a lecture
- Understanding spoken definitions
- Defining and explaining a simple concept in a seminar discussion

TASK 1 Preparing for a lecture

1 Read the extract from an email sent by the lecturer. Complete the task in pairs.

> Next Tuesday's lecture is *A Brief History of Cryptography*. Before you attend the lecture, read the opening lines of this letter written in code to a man called David:
>
> *Efbs Ebwje, J ipqf zpv bsf xfmm.*
>
> a Decode what the letter says.
>
> b How does the code work?

2 Work in pairs. Read the words from the lecture and their definitions. Take turns to:

a define two or more components of a computer

b explain why a computer is a complex piece of equipment.

> **complex** (*adj*) with many different parts, not a simple structure
> **component** (*n*) one part or element of a structure or system

3 Work in pairs. Discuss which ideas 1–3 you would expect to be covered in the lecture.

1 A definition of cryptography

2 The people who contributed to its development

3 Famous spy films where codes are used

TASK 2 Understanding the main ideas in a lecture

1 2.1 **Watch Extract 1 and check your predictions in Task 1.3.**

2 Work in pairs. Predict other ideas which might be covered in the lecture.

3 2.2 **Watch Extract 2 and complete notes 1–4.**

1 Most basic type of code works by ....

2 Early example, Caesar cipher ....

3 Ciphertext became more complex when ....

4 Crib used to ....

TASK 3 Understanding definitions of technical terms

1 2.2 **Watch Extract 2 again. Match words or phrases 1–5 with definitions a–e.**

1 cipher — a an answer key

2 substitution cipher — b a code

3 key — c a code replacing each original letter with a different character

4 crib — d the coded message

5 ciphertext — e the component that tells you how to create the code

2 Note down the language which helped you match the definitions in 1.

3 2.3 **Watch Extract 3. Complete the notes on slides 2–4.**

Al-Kindi

- 9th century
- ....

Slide 2

Frequency Analysis

- letters appear with different frequency
- e.g. letter E = ...

Slide 3

The 'personality' of Q

- rare letter
- ....
- ....

Slide 4

4 Compare your notes. Help each other to complete the information.

ACADEMIC LANGUAGE ▸ Language reference page 151

Defining (1) Giving spoken definitions

When we explain how a particular device, system, or concept works, we often need to give definitions of key terms.

Giving definitions

A cipher ***is another word for*** *a code.*
A substitution cipher ***is when*** *you create a code by replacing text.*
The key is the component ***which*** *tells you ...*
A crib ***is a type of*** *answer key.*
Ciphertext ***means*** *the coded message.*

TASK 4 Practising spoken definitions

1 Match sentence halves 1–5 with a–e to make definitions.

1 A *cryptographer* is another word ......
2 *Breaking* a code is when ......
3 A *password* is a word which ......
4 *Morse* is a type of ......
5 *Substitute* means ......

a allows you to enter a protected area.
b for someone who makes and breaks codes.
c code used by sailors.
d you find a solution to it.
e to replace one thing with another.

2 Complete definitions 1–5 in your own words.

1 Taking notes is when ....
2 A lecturer is another word ....
3 A seminar is a type ....
4 History is a subject which ....
5 Self-study means ....

ACADEMIC LANGUAGE

▸ Language reference page 151

Defining (2) Asking for definitions and explanations

When we discuss systems, ideas, or concepts, we often need to ask for definitions and explanations of key terms.

What is *a substitution cipher?*

What does *ciphertext* ***mean****?*

Can you ***explain what*** *a key* ***is****?*

TASK 5 Understanding spoken definitions and explanations

1 2.4 Listen to an extract from a student conversation. Complete sentences 1–6 using the speaker's exact words.

1 A cipher .... a code.
2 A substitution cipher .... replace the original letters with other characters.
3 Can you .... what a key .... ?
4 The key .... the component .... tells you the operation to perform to create the code.
5 A crib .... answer key.
6 Ciphertext .... the coded message.

TASK 6 Explaining new terms and concepts

1 Work in pairs. Explain the concepts below. Student A: read the notes on page 162. Student B: read the notes on page 164.

A Speed reading
B Memorization

2 Work with someone who heard the same explanation as you. Evaluate your understanding of the concept.

The explanation was:

1 very clear ☐
2 quite clear ☐
3 not very clear ☐
4 difficult to understand. ☐

TASK 7 Defining and explaining in an informal discussion

1 Work in groups of three and hold a short discussion. Use guidelines 1–6.

1 Think of an object or concept in your area of study.
2 Make notes on how you can explain it.
3 Think about the terms which will be new to your audience.
4 Use the expressions in Academic Language to make definitions of these terms.
5 Present the object or concept to the group for no more than two minutes.
6 Make notes as you listen to their presentations. At the end, ask questions.

2 Evaluate your partners' presentations. Did they:

- give a clear explanation of the subject?
- explain the key technical terms?
- answer your questions?

INDEPENDENT STUDY

In seminars and discussions, you will often need to give explanations of new or technical terms.

▸ Practise doing this by giving an explanation of a specific term related to your subject to your partner. Then ask them to explain the term back to you.

2B Reading Textbooks (2)

This module covers:

- Identifying definitions and explanations in a text
- Identifying the language of simple definitions and explanations
- Understanding meaning from context

TASK 1 Previewing the topic of a text

1 Work in groups. Discuss questions 1–3.

1. Does your country or culture use Arabic numbers (1, 2, 3, 4, etc.) or does it have a different system of symbols? If it has more than one system, when is each used?
2. What are Roman numerals? When and where are Roman numerals usually used? Which numbers are represented by the Roman numerals in photographs 1–3?
3. Most ancient number systems began with simple bars such as I, II, and, III. Why do you think this is?

1

2

3

TASK 2 Reading for detail

1 Read Text 1. Complete the notes.

Numbers 1–3
Most civilizations used [1] ....
System used in three historical civilizations: [2] ...., ..., and .... System now used in [3] ....

Modern Arabic
Numerals 1, 2, and 3 come from [4] ....
But join when [5] ....
Number of bars humans see as separate without counting [6] ....
Effect on early written notation [7] ....

TEXT 1

1 A numeral is a sign or symbol that represents a number. People have for many years been interested in the origin of such symbols. Take Roman numerals for instance. The first three numerals (I, II and III) use bar notation. This means that they follow the simple rule of containing as many bars as there are units. The numeral for four, IV, however, breaks the rule. Roman numerals are not alone in using this system. Ifrah (1998), in his book on the history of numerical notations, shows that in all civilisations, the first three numbers were initially denoted by repeatedly writing down the symbol for 'one', usually a bar, as many times as necessary. In most civilizations, this was followed by a different symbol for four and beyond. Other examples of this are the Cuneiform numerals 𒁹, 𒈫, 𒐈 and 𒐉, used in ancient Mesopotamia, and ancient Indian numerals (–, =, □ and +). Today, the Chinese denote the numbers 1, 2 and 3 using one, two and three horizontal bars, yet they employ a different symbol for number 4. Even modern Arabic numerals (1, 2, 3 etc.) derive from the same principle. The numeral for one is a single bar and the numerals for 2 and 3 derive from two and three horizontal bars that became joined together when they were hand written.

2 One theory that explains the evolution of numerals is subitization. Subitization is defined as the ability to determine the number of something without actually counting. Research has shown that subitizing becomes much more difficult after the number 3. In other words, humans can easily distinguish between the numerals I, II and III but beyond this, bar notation becomes difficult and we are unable at a glance to accurately distinguish between, say, IIIIII and IIIIIII. This difficulty may explain the effect on early notation, as 'new' numerals were created to make it easier for us to tell the difference between the numbers denoted.

SOURCE: Dehaene, S. (2011). p.56. *The Number Sense: How the Mind Creates Mathematics.* Oxford: Oxford University Press.

GLOSSARY

at a glance *(idm)* with one look

denote *(v)* to mean or be a sign of something

derive (from) *(v)* to come from sth; have sth as its origin

notation *(n)* a system of signs or symbols used to represent something

TASK 3 Identifying definitions and explanations

1 Note down the definitions for terms 1 and 2 in Text 1.

1 *numeral* 2 *subitization*

2 Note down the explanations given in Text 1 of:

a what *bar notation* is b how *subitizing* can be difficult.

3 Identify the language in Text 1 that introduces definitions and explanations.

ACADEMIC LANGUAGE ▸ Language reference page 151

Defining (3) Identifying definitions and explanations in a text

Authors of academic texts often use certain typical phrases for giving definitions and explanations.

Definitions

A numeral ***is*** *a sign or symbol that ...*

Subitization ***is defined as*** *the ability to ...*

Explanations

This means that *they follow the simple rule of containing ...*

In other words, *humans can easily distinguish between ...*

TASK 4 Writing definitions and explanations

1 Complete sentences 1–5 with appropriate definitions or explanations. Use the words in the list.

define … as is another term for is defined as this means that in other words

1 Educators .... tertiary education .... post-secondary education at either a university or college.
2 University graduates are generally more employable. ...., they are more likely to get a job than non-graduates.
3 Colour blindness .... the inability to see colour or certain colour differences.
4 One in a hundred people is ambidextrous. .... they can use both left and right arms and/or legs equally well.
5 'Logograph' .... 'ideogram' – a picture or symbol which represents a word.

2 Link pairs of sentences 1–4 using appropriate definitions and explanations.

Example: Some poems are acrostic. The first word of each line gives a message.
Some poems are acrostic. ***This means that*** *the first word of each line gives a message.*

1 A few people are tri-lingual. They can speak three languages.
2 Some trees are deciduous. They lose their leaves in autumn.
3 Many people suffer from dyscalculia. They have difficulty with numbers and mathematics.
4 The numbers 2, 3, 5, 7, and 11 are prime numbers. They can only be divided by 1 and themselves.

TASK 5 Understanding meaning from context

1 Read Text 2. Match the researcher to the research process.

1 James McKeen Cattell
2 Bertrand Bourdon

a Tested time taken to count separate dots
b Tested ability to count separate dots

2 Read Text 2 again. Note down definitions for terms 1–5. Use phrases a–e and Academic Language to help you.

Example: *Subitization is the ability to determine the number of something without counting.*

1 ~~subitization~~
2 dot
3 enumeration
4 chronoscope
5 replication

a small round mark
b copying something exactly
c identifying the number of something
d device for measuring small amounts of time
e ~~ability to determine the number of something without counting~~

TEXT 2

James McKeen Cattell

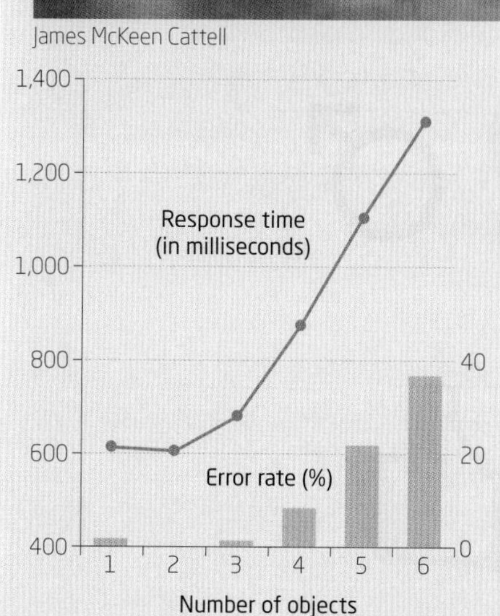

As noted, subitization is defined as the ability to determine the number of something without actually counting. Subitizing was first investigated more than a century ago, by psychologists who were interested in the way that people perceive and speak about numbers. In 1886, American psychologist James McKeen Cattell briefly showed cards to people and asked them to identify how many dots were on them. Test subjects could enumerate these dots accurately when there were small numbers. However, the greater the number, the more difficulty they experienced. Cattell demonstrated that correctly enumerating something becomes much more difficult after the number three. Subsequent studies investigated the precise time required to enumerate items. In 1908, Bertrand Bourdon, at the Sorbonne in Paris, using a chronoscope, showed that the time required to enumerate a number of dots increases gradually from one to three. However, after three, the time needed increases sharply. At the very same point, the number of errors also increases. It takes on average less than half a second to correctly enumerate up to three items but it takes almost a second for four items and over a second to enumerate five items. This result has been replicated hundreds of times and remains valid to this day.

SOURCE: Dehaene, S. (2011). p.56. *The Number Sense: How the Mind Creates Mathematics*. Oxford: Oxford University Press.

Chronoscope

3 Use your definitions and the information in Text 2 to complete notes 1–5.

Subitizing was first researched [1] ....

The first methods used were [2] ....

Average length of time to determine:

the number of three items [3] ....

the number of four items [4] ....

the number of five items [5] ....

TASK 6 Critical thinking – evaluating ideas in a text

1 Work in pairs. Discuss what you have learnt from Texts 1 and 2. Include the following points:

- ways of denoting number
- historic forms of numbering
- Modern Arabic numerals
- academics who worked in the field of psychology and number.

INDEPENDENT STUDY

Dictionaries are good sources for definitions of new words and terms.

▸ **Find words in a text that you can guess the meaning of and write a definition for them. Then look the word up in the dictionary and compare your definitions.**

2C Writing (1) Simple definitions

This module covers:

- Writing simple definitions
- Writing definitions with relative clauses

TASK 1 Completing simple definitions

1 Work in groups. Follow instructions 1–3.

1 Think of two symbols that you see or use in your studies.
2 Explain their meaning and use to the others in your group.
3 Ask follow-up questions after each explanation you hear.

Example: *'My subject is economics so I often use symbols for different currencies. This symbol US $ means United States dollars and ...'*
'That's interesting. What is the symbol for Chinese Yuan?'

2 Look at symbols 1–6 and complete simple definitions (a) and (b).

1

2

3
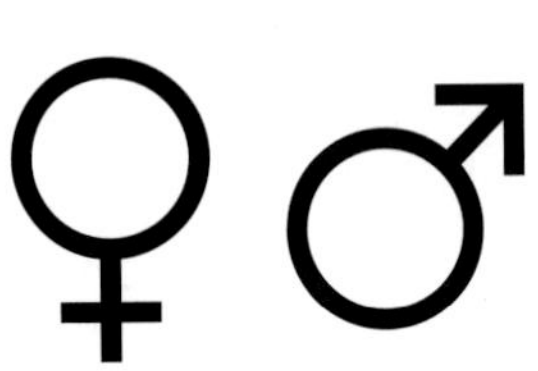

4

5

6

a Symbol 1 means ....
b You can find symbol 1 on ....

3 Work in pairs. Note down simple definitions for symbols 2–6.

TASK 2 Understanding simple definitions (1)

1 Complete statements 1–3 using the information in Paragraph 1.

1 An ideogram is a .... which .... an idea or concept.
2 馬 is an ideogram .... means .... in Chinese.
3 & .... a symbol .... is used in some letter-based languages to mean *and*.

Paragraph 1

Many languages use letters to represent certain sounds and these letters are put together to form words. However, other languages, such as Mandarin Chinese, use ideograms to represent words. An ideogram is a symbol which represents an idea or concept. An example of this is the symbol for horse in Figure 1. Ideograms also occur in letter-based languages, for example the symbol for *and* shown in Figure 2.

Figure 1

Figure 2

ACADEMIC LANGUAGE ▸ Language reference page 151

Defining (4) Relative clauses

In academic writing, relative clauses are often used in definitions.

For things and ideas use *which* or *that*. For people use *who* or *that*. For places use *where*.

Term being defined	Verb	General word	Relative clause
An ideogram	*is*	*a symbol*	*which represents an idea or concept.*
Emoticons	*are*	*symbols*	*that people use to show their emotions.*
A chronoscope	*is*	*an old device*	*which measures small periods of time.*
A cryptographer	*is*	*someone*	*who creates codes and ciphers.*
A laboratory	*is*	*a place*	*where people do scientific experiments.*

TASK 3 Writing simple definitions using relative clauses

1 Write definitions for items 1–7 using a relative clause.

Example: A phoneme a symbol represents a sound in a language.
A phoneme is a symbol which represents a sound in a language.

1 A degree a qualification you get from a university.

....

2 A carnivore an animal eats only meat.

....

3 A hierarchy a system organizes people / things into levels of importance.

....

4 A vegan a person doesn't eat animal products.

....

5 A logo a symbol a company uses as its special sign.

....

6 A thermometer a device measures temperature.

....

7 A settlement a place people live.

....

2 Think of an example for items 1–4. Write a definition for each using a relative clause.

Example: *A professor is someone who researches and teaches at a university.*

1 a person (e.g. a mathematician, an academic)

....
....
....

2 a place (e.g. a university, a reception area)

....
....
....

3 a device (e.g. a microscope, a sat-nav)

....
....
....

4 a process (e.g. photosynthesis, cultivation)

....
....
....

2C Writing (2) Extended definitions

This module covers:

- Writing definitions with prepositional phrases
- Writing extended definitions

TASK 1 Understanding simple definitions (2)

1 Read Paragraph 2 and note down:

a how a pictogram is different from an ideogram

b which of symbols 1–6 on page 030 are pictograms.

Paragraph 2

A pictogram is also a symbol which represents an idea or concept. However, it is different from an ideogram. Whereas an ideogram is a symbol which is used in place of a word, a pictogram is a pictorial representation of an idea. For example, Figure 1 shows a pictogram of an escalator and Figure 2 is a pictogram showing a warning sign for motorists.

Figure 1

Figure 2

2 Read Paragraph 2 again. Identify examples of relative clauses.

ACADEMIC LANGUAGE ▸Language reference page 151

Defining (5) Prepositional phrases

In academic writing, prepositional phrases are often used in definitions.

Term being defined	Verb	General word	Prepositional phrase
A pictogram	*is*	*a pictorial representation*	*of an idea.*
Cryptography	*is*	*the art*	*of writing and solving codes.*
An ammeter	*is*	*a device*	*for measuring electrical current.*

TASK 2 Writing simple definitions using prepositional phrases

1 Note an example for items 1–5. Write definitions using a prepositional phrase.

Example: *Astronomy is the scientific study of the universe.*

1 an area of study (e.g. astronomy, ecology, psychology)

2 an area / room in a building (e.g. a lecture hall, a cellar)

3 a device (e.g. a telescope, a memory stick)

4 a mode of transport (e.g. a bus, a plane)

5 a tool or implement (e.g. a drill, scissors)

2 Write a definition of something used in your own area of study. Use a prepositional phrase.

ACADEMIC LANGUAGE ▸Language reference page 151

Defining (6) Extended definitions

In academic texts, you often need to write extended definitions. Extended definitions can use a range of structures.

One or more prepositional phrases:

Democracy is a system [1]of government [2]with four key elements.

A prepositional phrase and a relative clause:

The circulatory system is a network of blood vessels which carries blood around the body.

TASK 3 Identifying extended definitions

1 Identify the prepositional phrases (P) and the relative clauses (R) in definitions 1–4.

Example: *A parallel processing system is a system of interconnected computers that work on the same application at the same time.*

1 Sign language is a system of communication that is used by deaf people.
2 A postcode is a group of letters and numbers which indicates an address.
3 A lynx is a species of wild cat with black spots and long pointed ears.
4 A bibliography is a list of sources which you put at the end of an essay.

TASK 4 Writing extended definitions

1 Write complete sentences to define items 1–5.

Example: **C.C.T.V.** / system of security cameras / linked to one monitoring system
C.C.T.V is a system of security cameras which are linked to one monitoring system.

1 **greenhouses** / buildings / glass roof and walls / people grow plants
2 **shorthand** / method / quick writing / uses symbols and abbreviations
3 **Uranium** / a chemical element / can produce large amounts of energy
4 **a stenographer** / an employee / a court of law / writes what is said in court
5 **a Dalmatian** / a breed of dog / black spotted coat / often kept as a pet

TASK 5 Writing sentences with a definition and/or explanation

1 Look at the diagram of a British car number plate. Complete the paragraph using the phrases in the list.

that the car is from ~~which distinguishes it from other cars~~
which give the car its unique identity for the area of manufacture of origin

A car number plate is a sign [1] *which distinguishes it from other cars*. It is attached to the front and back of a car. The letters on the far left (e.g. GB) show the country [2] .... The first two letters of the number (e.g. FE) are a code [3] .... [4] .... The two numbers (e.g. 07) indicate the year [5] .... The three letters at the end (e.g. GVX) are random letters [6] ....

Sample answer:
page 159

2 In each sentence of the paragraph, identify (a) the term being defined or explained, (b) the general word, and (c) the relative clause and/or prepositional phrase.

3 Select from items 1–4 and write a similar paragraph including a *definition* and *explanation*. Use at least one relative clause and/or a prepositional phrase.

1 a car number plate (or a property postcode or similar) in your country
2 a device or piece of equipment (e.g. a mobile phone, a calculator)
3 the information on the cover of a book (e.g. Oxford EAP B1)
4 an academic discipline (e.g. psychology)

INDEPENDENT STUDY

You can practise writing definitions with terms or words that you are already familiar with.

▸ **Work with a partner and write a definition of a word or term that you are both familiar with. Exchange definitions and compare them. Then compare these with a dictionary definition and see if you gave a clear definition.**

TASK 6 Evaluating your writing

1 Read the sentences you wrote in Task 5.3. Check that you have:

- simply but clearly described, explained, or defined the item ☐
- described, explained, or defined at least one of the component parts ☐
- used at least one relative clause and/or prepositional phrase. ☐

2D Vocabulary

TASK 1 Academic verbs

1 Select an appropriate academic verb to complete the text.

increased shown determine distinguish between occur derive from

Languages are not static; they change. For example, it is easy to [1] .... the English spoken in the 14th century and the 15th century. Languages also expand over time – English has [2] .... by 33% since the 1600s as new words, which often [3] .... other languages, have been added.

However, a recent study has [4] .... that in the last century the rate of change has slowed down. Researchers have been able to [5] .... this by analysing large amounts of text. Apart from a few specific words relating to new technology, such as 'live-stream', the study found that many expressions which [6] .... in everyday speech, such as 'at the end of the day', remain in common use for longer.

2 Complete questions 1–5 using your own ideas.

1 How do you distinguish between .... ?
2 How can we determine the age of .... ?
3 When does / do .... occur in your country?
4 Why has .... increased so much in the last 50 years?
5 Does research show that .... ?

3 Work in pairs. Ask each other your questions.

TASK 2 Collocations (1): Verbs and nouns

1 Collocations are words which commonly go together. Select the correct word to complete sentences 1–8.

Example: *No one was able to open / break / undo* **the code** *until an Arab mathematician, Al-Kindi, found a way.*

1 If you *follow / hold* **this rule**, you won't make a mistake.
2 Consider all options before you *do / give / make* **a decision**.
3 He *told / gave* **a talk** on the history of cryptography.
4 They *set / set up* **a target** of raising $100,000.
5 The **research** was *made / carried out* by a team at Harvard University.
6 The two countries *did / reached* **an agreement** on the ownership of the land.
7 It took scientists many years to *calculate / solve* **the answer**.
8 Al-Kindi *did / used* **a technique** called frequency analysis.

2 Select three collocations from 1 and write sentences of your own.

Example: *I gave a talk to my class last year about the science of climate change.*

1 ....
2 ....
3 ....

INDEPENDENT STUDY

When you learn a specific collocation, check which other verbs collocate with the noun, e.g. *follow* a rule, *break* a rule.

3 Work in pairs. Discuss your sentences. Remember to ask for:

- explanations of key terms
- definitions of new words
- more information to extend your discussion.

2E Academic Language Check

TASK 1 Definitions and explanations

1 Complete definitions 1–5 using one word. The first letter is provided for you.

1 Breaking a code m.................... solving it.
2 The fan is the component w.................... cools the computer.
3 Cryptography is a t.................... for code making.
4 Granite is a t.................... of rock.
5 Excavation is w.................... you dig in the ground for old buildings or objects.

2 Put the words in the correct order to complete conversations 1–4.

1 **A** is / cryptography / what ?
B the study / making and breaking / of / it's / codes
2 **A** does / what / auditorium / mean ?
B the place / it's / a theatre audience / sits / where
3 **A** what / is / you / a first draft / can / explain ?
B of something / it's / that you write, such as an essay / the first version
4 **A** what / mean / orca / does
B killer whale / it's / another / for / a / name

TASK 2 Definitions using defining words and phrases

1 Match words 1–6 with definitions a–f.

1 intelligence ....
2 a metre ....
3 a phoneme ....
4 obesity ....
5 Basic ....
6 ageing ....

a having excessive body fat that may damage health
b the ability to understand, learn, and think
c a symbol that represents one of the sounds of a language
d the distance travelled by light in 0.000000003335 of a second
e the process of physical deterioration of the body
f one of the earliest computer languages

2 Write full sentences defining the words in 1. Use at least three different defining words or phrases.

1 ....
2 ....
3 ....
4 ....
5 ....
6 ....

3 Work in pairs. Compare and evaluate your sentences. Did your partner:

- use a range of defining words or phrases?
- accurately define each word?

UNIT 3 Ethics

ACADEMIC FOCUS: DESCRIBING AND EXPLAINING

LEARNING OBJECTIVES

This unit covers:

Listening and Speaking

- Understanding the main idea and supporting details in a presentation
- Noting down examples in a presentation
- Describing a concept
- Asking for repetition and clarification

Reading

- Understanding a descriptive text
- Recognizing the use of description in a text
- Understanding noun phrases in descriptions

Writing

- Identifying the use of articles
- Using articles in sentences and in a short paragraph
- Identifying the use of determiners to give cohesion
- Adding descriptive detail to nouns
- Writing a short paragraph using noun phrases

Vocabulary

- Style: Academic vs informal vocabulary
- Collocations (2): Prepositions

Academic Language Check

- Noun phrases (1): Adjectives and nouns
- Noun phrases (2): Articles
- Noun phrases (3): Cohesive determiners

Discussion

1 Read the two definitions related to ethics. Complete alternative definitions 1 and 2.

> **ethical** (*adj*) connected with beliefs and principles about what is right and wrong
> **legal** (*adj*) connected with the law

1 .... describes things people *must* and *mustn't* do.
2 .... discusses things people *should* and *shouldn't* do.

2 Complete statements 1–4 using the words in the list.

agreement gifts respect rules

1 In sport, you should always follow the ....
2 In business, you should not give large .... to people you are doing business with.
3 In medical research, it is important to get the .... of the patient before testing a new drug on them.
4 In academic study, you should show .... for the work of other academics.

3 Work in pairs. Discuss whether you agree with the statements in 2. Give reasons.

4 Write one more ethical rule for each field.

1 Sportspeople shouldn't ....
2 In business, it is important to ....
3 Medical researchers should ....
4 In academic study, students shouldn't ....

5 Work in groups. Compare your ideas.

3A Listening & Speaking Presentations (2)

This module covers:

- Understanding the main idea and supporting details in a presentation
- Noting down examples in a presentation
- Describing a concept
- Asking for repetition and clarification

TASK 1 Preparing to listen to a presentation

1 Work in groups. Discuss examples of:
- three ethical actions in sport
- three unethical actions in sport.

TASK 2 Understanding the main idea

1 3.1 Watch Extract 1, part of a presentation on ethics in sport. Note down which concept, 1 or 2, represents an ethical approach to sport.

1 Sportsmanship 2 Gamesmanship

2 3.1 Watch Extract 1 again and complete the table.

	Gamesmanship	Sportsmanship
Definition	the principle that	the principle that ....
What sports it relates to	....	....
Why it happens	Some people believe	Some people believe ....

3 Work in pairs. Use your notes to describe the differences between sportsmanship and gamesmanship in your own words.

TASK 3 Understanding supporting details

1 3.2 Watch Extract 2. Tick the four principles of ethics in sport mentioned by the speaker.

fairness ☐	integrity ☐	responsibility ☐
honesty ☐	respect ☐	trust ☐

2 3.2 Watch Extract 2 again. Note down the speaker's definitions of principles 1–3.

1 Fairness ....
2 Integrity ....
3 Respect ....

3 3.2 If necessary, watch Extract 2 again. Note down:

1 why sportspeople have a responsibility to society
2 how society can affect sportspeople.

4 Work in pairs. Discuss questions 1 and 2.

1 Which of the four principles mentioned by the speaker do you think is most important? Give reasons.
2 Do you agree with the speaker's assessment of how society and sportspeople affect each other? Give reasons.

ACADEMIC LANGUAGE

Note-taking (2) Noting examples

When describing concepts or ideas, you can use examples which support and illustrate the points you make. When you make notes, you can replace these phrases with the abbreviation. For example:

Spoken examples	Note forms
An example of *a foul* ***is*** *touching the ball with your hand.*	*Foul, e.g. touching the ball with your hand*
In contact sports ***such as*** *rugby ...*	*Contact sports, e.g. rugby*
Unfair play, ***like*** *wasting time ...*	*Unfair play, e.g. wasting time*

TASK 4 Noting examples

1 3.3 **Watch Extract 3 and look at the notes. What phrase has the writer replaced with *e.g.*?**

Gamesmanship, e.g. deliberately injuring an opponent

2 3.3 **Watch Extract 3 again. Note down examples of gamesmanship and its effects.**

1 Gamesmanship, e.g. deliberately injuring an opponent ....

....

2 Lack of integrity can damage a sport, e.g. ....

....

3 Sportspeople = role models: negative behaviour affects ....

....

3 **Work in pairs. Use your notes in 2 and the information in Academic Language to give complete spoken examples.**

TASK 5 Critical thinking – responding to a presentation

1 **Work in groups. Discuss statements (a) and (b) and give examples.**

a The behaviour of sportspeople has a positive effect on others in society.

b The behaviour of sportspeople has a negative effect on others in society.

2 **Rank the positive and negative effects you discussed in 1 from the most to least significant. Give reasons for your selection.**

TASK 6 Identifying requests for repetition and clarification

1 3.4 **Listen to Extract 4, student questions from the end of the discussion. Match questions 1–5 with functions a–c.**

a asking for repetition b asking for clarification c checking understanding

1 You mentioned drugs, but there was a word which I didn't catch. Performance-something? ....

2 What does that mean? ....

3 I'm not sure I understood what you said about gamesmanship. ....

4 Could you just repeat the part about ... fairness? ....

5 And referees and officials are the same thing? Is that right? ....

2 3.5 **Watch Extract 5, the end of the discussion. Check your answers.**

ACADEMIC LANGUAGE

Repeating and clarifying information

In seminars and tutorials you will need to check your understanding of what you hear. You can do this by asking the speaker to repeat something or to explain it.

Asking for repetition

Could you just repeat ...?
There was a word I didn't catch ... something?

Asking for clarification

You mentioned ... What / How / Why ...?
I'm not sure I understood (what you said about) ...
What does ... mean (exactly)?
X ... Is that right?

TASK 7 Practising asking for repetition and clarification

1 Work in pairs. Student A: read the notes on page 162. Student B: read the notes on page 164.

2 Work in new pairs. Explain the concept your partner described.

TASK 8 Describing a concept

1 3.6 Listen to Extract 6, from a seminar where a student explains a concept. Complete the notes.

Name of concept:	Sustainability
Description:	Using resources to meet needs [1] ....
Example:	If you cut down a tree, then [2] ....
Relates to:	Environmental science and [3] ....
Reasons for importance:	[4] ....

2 You are going to present a concept from your area of study. Prepare for the presentation using stages 1-4.

1 State your area of study. *My area of study is ...*
2 Introduce the concept. *A very important concept is ...*
3 Explain the concept and give an example.
What is ...? It's the idea that ... It means, for example ...
4 Say what it relates to and why it is important.
... is a very important concept in ... because ...

3 Work in groups. Present your concepts to each other. Remember to:

1 invite questions from your audience
2 ask questions for repetition or clarification.

TASK 9 Critical thinking – evaluating a description of a concept

1 Evaluate each other's performance. Did the other students:

- explain the concept clearly?
- repeat or clarify any points?
- answer your questions effectively?

INDEPENDENT STUDY

In a discussion, people do not always give evidence or examples that clearly support their arguments.

▶ Listen to a discussion online or on television. Note down the main arguments of each speaker and the evidence or examples they provide. Decide whether the speaker provides relevant and strong evidence.

3B Reading Textbooks (3)

This module covers:

- Understanding a descriptive text
- Recognizing the use of description in a text
- Understanding noun phrases in descriptions

TASK 1 Preparing to read a text

1 The text, *Business Ethics*, is taken from a textbook. Look at the cover and quickly skim the text. Decide which text type a–d is presented here.

a A report on a piece of research.
b An explanation of a subject.
c An argument and the author's evaluation.
d A review of an article.

2 Before you read, complete definitions 1–4 using the words in the list.

beliefs law rules feel behave

1 A *code of conduct* is a set of .... that people follow. It tells them how they should act or .... in certain situations.
2 Your *principles* or *values* are your .... about what is right and wrong.
3 Your *attitude* is what you .... or think about something.
4 *Obligations* are the things that you must do either because the .... says you must or because society expects you to do them.

TASK 2 Understanding ideas in a text

1 Read the opening sentence of the text. Discuss what you think *ethics* means in the context of business.

> Ethics is the branch of philosophy which is concerned with principles and rules of human behaviour. It considers what is 'right' and 'wrong' and examines moral values.

2 Read ideas 1–5. Note down which ideas you think might be covered in the text.

1 Not every business agrees on what is defined as 'ethical.'
2 Companies have ethical codes to set out their basic principles of behaviour.
3 Codes of ethics deal with more than legal obligations.
4 Business ethics should be shared by all companies.
5 Unethical companies should be punished by the law.

3 Read the text and note which points in 2 the writer makes.

....

....

....

Business Ethics

Ethics is the branch of philosophy which is concerned with principles and rules of human behaviour. It considers what is 'right' and 'wrong' and examines moral values.

In business, the creation of a code of ethics is a way for organizations to establish basic principles about their behaviour. This covers all aspects of business conduct: the company's business strategy, its treatment of employees and suppliers, its sales practices and accounting practices. In fact, most business activities have an ethical aspect. In many ways this is determined by commercial objectives as unethical practices can have negative consequences for a business. More and more companies realize the value of ethics in today's crowded marketplace. Companies can benefit from promoting their ethical practice.

The ethical code of a company covers more than its basic legal obligations. It states what a company chooses to do rather than what it is forced to do by law. Business ethics concerns both the conduct of the organization as a whole and the conduct of the individuals within an organization.

The following questions are examples of ethical issues which business organizations are typically concerned with:

1 Is it ethical to reduce costs by using cheaper resources in less economically developed countries? For example, large Western multinational companies using child labour in some of their overseas factories.
2 Is it ethical to sell products that are legal, but could harm those who use them? For example, cigarettes and alcohol.
3 Is it ethical to advertise to children? For example, the use of thin models in clothes advertisements could discourage children from eating properly.
4 Is it ethical to look for loopholes in the law to avoid paying tax? For example, setting up offshore companies.

These are 'big' questions that elicit strong opinions and strong disagreements. But ethics also raises many smaller questions about individual employee behaviour. For example, "How do I manage my team?" and "Is it acceptable not to tell the whole truth when selling products or services to my customers?".

In theory, business ethics are a set of attitudes, morals and rules of behaviour that should be shared by all organizations. One company's ethical policy should be the same as another's. However, in practice, not all businesses agree on what is ethical and what is not. Individuals in everyday life have very different ethical standards, so why should we expect individuals in business organizations to be different? On the other hand, organizations often make very clear statements and promises about their values. For example, environmental concerns are central to most of today's businesses, so you would expect that a company with the slogan 'Making the world a better place' would be taking actions that were good for society or the environment. So anyone who voluntarily joins the organization is giving their agreement to the corporate culture and to the values attached.

SOURCE: Muchena, M., Lomine, L. & Pierce, R. (2014). p.30. *IB Business Management: Course companion*. Oxford: Oxford University Press.

GLOSSARY

child labour *(n)* workers who are still children, not yet adult working age

conduct *(n)* the way a person or business behaves in a particular situation

loophole *(n)* a way of avoiding something because the words of a rule or law are badly chosen

slogan *(n)* a short phrase that is easy to remember that is used in politics or advertising

TASK 3 Understanding the role of supporting detail

1 Academic texts often present a main idea and describe details that support this idea. Match statements 1–4 from the text with the main ideas you noted in Task 2.

1 It states what a company chooses to do rather than what it is forced to do by law.
2 One company's ethical policy should be the same as another's.
3 Individuals in everyday life have very different ethical standards, so why should we expect individuals in business organizations to be different?
4 This covers all aspects of business conduct: the company's business strategy, its treatment of employees and suppliers, its sales practices and accounting practices.

2 Read statements 5–7 from the text and note down your own supporting details for each statement.

Example: Most business activities have an ethical aspect – *employees given minimum wage; work in safe conditions*

5 Unethical practices can have negative consequences for a business.
6 Companies can benefit from promoting their ethical practice.
7 Environmental concerns are central to most of today's businesses.

3 Use your notes in 2 to write sentences including supporting details.

Example: Most business activities have an ethical aspect, *for example ensuring that employees are paid a minimum wage.*

4 Work in pairs. Compare sentences and decide which supporting detail is the most effective for each.

ACADEMIC LANGUAGE ▸Language reference page 151

Noun phrases (1) Using adjectives and nouns to modify nouns

In academic texts, noun phrases carry the main information. You can add description or detail to a noun (called the head noun) by combining it with other words to make a noun phrase. Two common ways of doing this are using adjectives and nouns.

Adjective + noun patterns

*These are **big questions** that elicit **strong opinions**.*

noun + noun patterns

*... the company's **business strategy**, its treatment of employees and suppliers, its **sales practices** ...*

TASK 4 Recognizing noun phrases using adjectives and nouns

1 Note down noun phrases in the text beginning with words 1–8.

1 moral ....
2 basic ....
3 legal ....
4 child ....
5 overseas ....
6 offshore ....
7 clear ....
8 corporate ....

2 Identify which of the noun phrases in 1 are adjective + noun and which are noun + noun.

3 Read the text again and note down:

a five noun phrases using *ethical*
b four noun phrases using *business*.

TASK 5 Using noun phrases in descriptions

1 Complete paragraphs 1 and 2 with the nouns and adjectives in the lists.

business international public

1 The Institute of Business Ethics (IBE) is an organization that aims to raise [1] .... awareness of the importance of doing business ethically. It collaborates with [2] .... organizations with interests and expertise in [3] .... ethics.

business (x2) corporate ethical high staff

2 The IBE helps organizations by encouraging [4] .... standards of [5] .... behaviour based on [6] .... values. It assists in the development and implementation of ethics and [7] .... responsibility. The IBE provides [8] .... training and gives guidance for building relationships of trust with the organization's [9] .... partners.

2 Rewrite phrases 1–10 as noun phrases (adjective + noun or noun + noun).

Example: a strategy for business *a business strategy*

1 partners in business
2 training for staff
3 a decision which is difficult
4 a workforce which is skilled
5 law which is international
6 art which is modern
7 work which is repetitive
8 issues concerning gender
9 a plan for business which is detailed
10 products which are eco-friendly

3 Rewrite sentences 1–8 to include more concise noun phrases.

Example: A business which is responsible must have a code which is ethical.
A responsible business must have an ethical code.

1 Some restaurants use food ingredients which are out of date.
2 Workers who are unskilled are usually cheaper to employ.
3 It is a good strategy of business to take care of the environment in the local area.
4 In most countries, the use of labour involving children is a practice which is illegal.
5 Law in the United Kingdom does not allow advertisements for cigarettes.
6 Many factories which make clothes are located where there is labour which is cheap.
7 Many directors of companies have to make decisions which are difficult.
8 Organizations which are big and international usually have values which are clear and codes of conduct which are ethical.

4 Write five sentences about your area of study. Use a noun phrase (adjective + noun or noun + noun) in each.

Example: *There are many* ***ethical issues*** *in the field of medicine.*
Environmental concerns *are becoming important for businesses.*

TASK 6 Critical thinking – reflecting on a text

1 Work in pairs. Discuss 1 and 2.

1 What are your views on the 'big' ethical questions 1–4 in the text?
2 Think of at least two more ethical issues a business has to deal with.

INDEPENDENT STUDY

When reading academic sentences it is important to identify the main parts of the sentence – Subject – Verb – Object or *who* or *what* does *what*.

▸ Find a short academic text and underline these key parts of the sentence: Subject – Verb – Object. Then look at how the other information relates to these parts.

3C Writing (1) Sentences using articles

This module covers:

- Identifying the use of articles
- Using articles in sentences and in a short paragraph

TASK 1 Previewing the theme of a writing task

1 Read the following essay title. Do you agree or disagree with the statement? Give reasons.

TITLE: *'Academic and scientific researchers should be ethical at all times. If they are not, then their work has little value.' Do you agree or disagree with the statement?*

2 Read this extract from a student essay. Does the writer agree or disagree with the statement in 1?

[1]All researchers need to follow a code of ethics. [2]Research ethics outlines the correct way to conduct research. [3]It protects the rights and the well-being of participants and informs them of any potential negative consequences. [4]Without a clear set of rules, many people may feel uncomfortable about getting involved in a research project. [5]An important aspect of research is the respect which is shown to the people who participate in a research project. [6]Research ethics is also an academic discipline, which studies the concept of ethics in research.

3 Note down the ideas and examples that the writer used to support his opinion.

ACADEMIC LANGUAGE ▸Language reference page 152

Noun phrases (2) Articles

Noun phrases (e.g. *a research project*) are an important part of academic texts. They usually carry a lot of important information. An article (*a, an, the*) is often the first word in a noun phrase.

Use *a* or *an* (the indefinite article) to refer to an indefinite or non-specific example of something.

An important aspect of research *is the respect which is shown to the people who participate in* ***a research project****.*

Use *the* (the definite article) to refer to a definite or specific example of something.

An important aspect of research is ***the respect*** *which is shown to* ***the people*** *who participate in a research project.*

Use no article (the zero article: ø) to refer to something in a general sense.

An important aspect of ***research*** *is the respect which is shown to the people who participate in a research project.*

TASK 2 Using articles

1 Read the extract in Task 1.2 again. Look at the underlined noun phrases and say why the indefinite, definite, and zero article are used.

Example: *'Research ethics outlines ...' uses the zero article because it is referring to research ethics in a general sense. Also, 'ethics' is an uncountable noun.*

2 **Complete paragraphs 1 and 2. Add the indefinite, definite, or zero article (ø).**

1 Central to research ethics is [1] .... idea that you must never invent or misrepresent [2] .... data. Additionally, you must not deceive [3] .... colleagues or [4] .... public. [5] .... research findings should be published solely to advance [6] .... field of research. They should not be published to advance [7] .... person's career or for [8] .... financial gain.

2 In [9] .... academic writing, when you refer to another person's work, [10] .... reference must be included in [11] .... body of [12] .... essay, e.g. (Smith, 2014). At [13] .... end of most assignments, there should be [14] .... list of [15] .... books and articles that have been referred to in [16] .... text.

3 **Read notes 1–6 about medical research trials in the UK. Expand them into full sentences by adding articles where needed.**

Example: research ethics is important issue in medical research
Research ethics is an important issue in medical research.

1 in UK, medical ethics committees protect rights of people in medical research trials

....

2 most hospitals have medical ethics committee

....

3 before starting medical trial, research team must submit detailed plan of research

....

4 research team must also prepare information leaflet for potential participants

....

5 leaflet needs to include information about possible risks involved

....

6 medical ethics committees are independent of both research team and organization which is funding research

....

TASK 3 Writing sentences using articles

1 **Write three sentences about your area of study or about a topic that interests you. Include the different uses of the indefinite, definite, and zero article.**

Example: ***The law** in most countries allows **research** that uses **animals**. However, this is only when there isn't **an alternative research technique**.*

1 ....

....

2 ....

....

3 ....

....

TASK 4 Critical thinking – responding to ideas

1 **Work in pairs. Discuss questions 1 and 2.**

1 Do you agree that the purpose of all research should be to improve the area of study instead of to advance the researcher's own career or to make money? Give reasons.

2 What possible risks might be involved in medical research?

3C Writing (2) Sentences using noun phrases

This module covers:

- Identifying the use of determiners to give cohesion
- Adding descriptive detail to nouns
- Writing sentences using noun phrases

TASK 1 Previewing the theme of a writing task

1 Work in pairs. Read the essay title and discuss the question it asks. Give reasons.

> **TITLE:** *'All academic writing must be original and plagiarism should be avoided at all times.' What is plagiarism and why is it unacceptable?*

2 Read this extract from a student essay. Compare the ideas with your own.

> Plagiarism is the act of copying other people's work or ideas in your own work without acknowledgement. All published and unpublished material is covered under this definition. Avoiding plagiarism means that authors of an original work are rightfully recognized and credited for the work they have produced. The term 'plagiarism' comes from the Latin word *plagiarius*, which means 'kidnapper'.

3 Read the extract again and complete notes 1–3.

1 Plagiarism (definition): ....

2 Plagiarism (coverage): ....

3 Plagiarism (origin of word): ....

ACADEMIC LANGUAGE ▸ Language reference page 152

Noun phrases (3) Determiners

Determiners help to connect parts of a text by referring to something that is known or understood, or that has previously been mentioned. Determiners that help give **cohesion** include:

Definite article (*the*)

__The__ term plagiarism comes from __the__ Latin word 'plagiarius', which means 'kidnapper'.

Demonstratives (*this, that, these, those*)

Ethics can concern moral standards and how we apply __these__ standards.

Plagiarism detection software is used and __this__ is standard procedure in most universities.

Possessive adjectives (*my, your,* etc.) and nouns (*Smith's, the writer's,* etc.)

Medical staff must not discuss __their__ patients outside work.

***Jones's** research was undertaken between 2005 and 2015.*

TASK 2 Using determiners

1 Complete the paragraph using the determiners in the list.

another person's a writer's their (x2) this these

Plagiarism by students is considered academic dishonesty or academic fraud. Today, academic institutions use plagiarism detection software. [1] .... software detects plagiarism and deters students from plagiarizing. Students who are guilty of plagiarism can be expelled from [2] .... institution. Plagiarism is defined in different ways. For example, the University of Oxford defines plagiarism as the use of '[3] .... ideas or phraseology without giving due credit.' Brown University defines plagiarism as using '[4] .... ideas or words without attributing [5] .... words or ideas to [6] .... true source.'

2 Rewrite sentences 1–6. Replace the words in italics with an appropriate demonstrative or possessive adjective.

1 The study of ethics concerns moral standards and how we apply *moral standards*. *The study of ethics* is common in most university philosophy departments.

2 Edward Jones (2014) claims that plagiarism has become more common. *Edward Jones's* findings were based on a study of over 100 institutions.

3 The law in most countries allows research that uses animals. However, *the use of animals* is only allowed when there isn't an alternative research technique.

4 'Declaration of Authorship' forms should be completed by all students. *The forms* should be attached to all essays or assignments.

5 Doctors sign an oath to declare that they will not discuss *the* patients *they treat*.

6 Students must not plagiarize other people's work. *Students* who do plagiarize may be expelled from *the* university *they attend*.

ACADEMIC LANGUAGE ▸Language reference page 152

Noun phrases (4) Using determiners, adjectives, and nouns

Use determiners, adjectives, and nouns to add descriptive detail to a **head noun**. Use some determiners (*the, these, this, their*, etc.) to refer to something known and/or to connect the noun with other parts of the text.

Students *generally undertake their research* ***projects*** *in their final* ***year*** *at university.*

Company ***directors*** *have to make difficult ethical* ***decisions****.*

The ***participants*** *in the online* ***studies*** *were post-graduate university* ***students****.*

TASK 3 Writing descriptive sentences

1 Write the notes 1–6 as full sentences by adding the words in brackets to the nouns in bold.

1 **Study** has revealed that **diplomats** owe **government** over £500,000 in **fines**. (the British, a recent, UK-based, foreign, unpaid parking)

2 **Diplomats** owe **largest proportion** of **fines**. (unpaid, the, these, Nigerian, Turkish, and Afghan)

3 **Staff** are trying to persuade **diplomats** to pay **debts**. (their, Foreign Office, the, guilty)

4 However, many of **diplomats** who were fined are no longer in **country**, which makes **task** almost impossible. (the, the, those)

5 Also, **immunity** means that no **diplomat** can face **prosecution**. (criminal, diplomatic, serving)

6 However, all **staff** are expected to obey **laws** of **country** they are in. (the, the, diplomatic)

2 Write a paragraph using the sentences from 1 and a range of determiners.

3 Write a few sentences or a short paragraph describing a study skill, or a topic which interests you. Include descriptive noun phrases and use determiners to connect ideas and to show cohesion.

Sample answer: page 159

INDEPENDENT STUDY

Using determiners incorrectly does not necessarily make it difficult for the reader to understand what you are saying but it can give a bad impression.

▸ **Find a short paragraph in English and underline all the nouns. Then look at the determiners (e.g. *the, a, this, his,* or no article) that are used before them. Decide which rule that you learned in this module the determiner follows. Then look back at the rules and check.**

TASK 4 Evaluating your writing

1 Read your paragraph from Task 3.3. Check that:

- you have added descriptive detail to some of the nouns ☐
- you have used determiners to connect ideas and give cohesion ☐
- the information you have added makes sense. ☐

3D Vocabulary

TASK 1 Style: Academic vs informal vocabulary

1 Replace the informal verbs / verb phrases 1–8 with the formal academic verbs taken from texts in Unit 3.

outlines covers state summarizes participate in
consider is concerned with examines

Bioethics is a subject that [1]**deals with** moral issues that arise from advances in biology and medicine. For example, it [2]**looks at** areas such as genetic engineering, which some people [3]**believe** to be morally wrong. It also [4]**includes** the everyday practice of doctors and biologists and the rights of those people who [5]**take part in** medical experiments and research. This chapter [6]**gives the main facts about** the challenges faced by bioethicists and [7]**sums up** the arguments on both sides of the genetic engineering debate. Traditional medical ethicists [8]**say** that a doctor must put the interest of each individual patient before the interests of society.

2 Select the correct form of a formal word from 1 to complete sentences 1–7.

Example: *The term 'earth sciences'* ***covers*** *all academic studies related to planet Earth.*

1 At the end of a talk it is a good idea to .... the main points you have presented.
2 It is important to .... the condition of the equipment before and after use.
3 The report doesn't go into detail, but it does .... the future direction of medical research.
4 They asked 25 students to .... the study.
5 What do you .... to be the best book on the subject?
6 The rules clearly .... that everyone needs the permission of the university to publish their work.
7 Psychology is not the only science to .... human behaviour.

TASK 2 Collocations (2): Prepositions

1 Select the appropriate preposition to complete sentences 1–8.

1 History **is concerned** *about* / *with* / *by* past events.
2 Newton's theory of gravity **was based** *in* / *with* / *on* the mass of objects.
3 Einstein's theory of relativity **is related** *to* / *with* / *for* Newton's theories.
4 A person's diet **has a** direct **effect** *for* / *with* / *on* their health.
5 Each player **is responsible** *for* / *to* / *of* their own conduct on the field.
6 The new evidence **raises questions** *on* / *about* / *of* the date of these events.
7 Aristotle **made a distinction** *between* / *about* / *with* the essential nature of things and their accidental nature.
8 It is important that everyone **participates** *for* / *in* / *with* the discussion.

2 Select three of the collocations in 1 and make sentences using your own ideas. Then read them to your partner.

Example: *I am not* ***responsible for*** *the mistakes in this report.*

1 ....
2 ....
3 ....

INDEPENDENT STUDY

Learning which preposition follows a verb will help you actively build your vocabulary.

▶ **When you read a new verb, check in a good dictionary to see if it is commonly followed by a particular preposition, or doesn't usually take a preposition, e.g.** ***be interested in a subject, join an organization.***

3E Academic Language Check

TASK 1 Noun phrases (1): Adjectives and nouns

1 Rewrite the sentences 1–5. Add the adjectives and nouns in brackets to the nouns in bold.

Example: WikiLeaks has a **database** of millions of **documents**. (sensitive, vast)
WikiLeaks has a vast database of many millions of sensitive documents.

1 WikiLeaks is an **organization** which publishes **information**.
(secret, international, non-profit, media)

2 The **website** was launched in 2006 by the **activist** Julian Assange.
(Australian, internet, WikiLeaks)

3 WikiLeaks publishes **information** from **sources**.
(anonymous, sensitive, publicly unavailable)

4 The organization has released a number of **documents** which have become **news items**.
(significant, front-page)

5 It always publishes **documents** to support any **information** it releases.
(new, original, unedited)

TASK 2 Noun phrases (2): Articles

1 Complete texts 1–3 with the correct article: *a* / *an*, *the*, or Ø (zero article).

1 [1]........ 'wiki' is [2]........ website developed by [3]........ community of users which allows [4]........ users to add and edit [5]........ content. [6]........ term 'wiki' comes from [7]........ Hawaiian word for 'quick'. [8]........ encyclopaedia project *Wikipedia* is [9]........ most popular wiki in terms of [10]........ page views.

2 Ethics is [11]........ branch of philosophy that involves analysing concepts of [12]........ right and wrong behaviour. [13]........ term comes from [14]........ Greek word *ethos*, which means 'character'.

3 Today, [15]........ term 'crime' does not have [16]........ universally accepted definition. However, one definition is that [17]........ crime is [18]........ act which is harmful to [19]........ individual, [20]........ community, or [21]........ state. [22]........ criminal acts are forbidden and punishable by [23]........ law.

TASK 3 Noun phrases (3): Cohesive determiners

1 Complete the text about the *Ethics Bowl* using the cohesive determiners in the list.

the (x3) the other team's this these their (x2)

The *Ethics Bowl* is an American intercollegiate tournament that combines a competitive quiz with a valuable educational experience. [1]........................ competitors are all undergraduate students who have been chosen by [2]........................ university.

There are preliminary tournaments at universities across the USA. [3]........................ results in the top 32 teams, who are invited to participate in the national finals.

Each round of [4]........................ tournament is between two teams, who have to answer several questions that pose an ethical problem. Each team also has a chance to challenge [5]........................ answers. The teams are then scored on [6]........................ responses and the winning team goes through to the next round. [7]........................ knock-out stages continue until there is an overall winner.

[8]........................ tournament takes place each year at the annual meeting of the Association for Practical and Professional Ethics.

2 Underline all the noun phrases in the text in 1. Circle the head noun.

Example: *The Ethics Bowl is an American intercollegiate tournament that combines a competitive quiz with a valuable educational experience.*

UNIT 4 Facts

ACADEMIC FOCUS: COMPARING AND CONTRASTING

LEARNING OBJECTIVES

This unit covers:

Listening and Speaking

- Understanding comparison and contrast in a lecture
- Giving a short presentation referring to visual information
- Comparing data in a short presentation

Reading

- Understanding the main idea and specific details in a text
- Identifying the language of comparison and contrast
- Understanding comparison and contrast in a text

Writing

- Identifying the language of comparison and contrast
- Writing connected sentences comparing and contrasting ideas
- Describing visual data using comparison and contrast

Vocabulary

- Vocabulary related to trends
- Prepositions in statistics
- Vocabulary-building: Antonyms

Academic Language Check

- Describing similarity and difference
- Comparative adjectives

Discussion

1 Compare your country and a neighbouring country. Tick one box for each option.

	Different	Same / Similar
the language	☐	☐
the size of the population	☐	☐
the main industries	☐	☐
the system of government	☐	☐
the weather	☐	☐
the national sport	☐	☐
the food	☐	☐

2 Work in pairs. Compare ideas.

Example: *I compared Argentina and Brazil. In Argentina, the main language is Spanish. This is different from Brazil, where people speak Portuguese.*

3 Work in pairs. Read the list of academic subjects and decide what people compare in each.

Example: *In economics, people compare the cost of living in different countries.*

economics	sociology
geography	biology and medicine
sports studies	business studies

4 Work in groups and share your ideas. Give examples.

4A Listening & Speaking Lectures (2)

This module covers:
- Understanding comparison and contrast in a lecture
- Giving a short presentation referring to visual information
- Comparing data in a short presentation

TASK 1 Predicting the content of a lecture

Where is all the food? The imbalance in world food distribution

Dr Anita Lane
Senior Lecturer
Department of
Environmental Studies

1 Read the lecture title. Predict what an imbalance in food distribution means.

2 Mark the areas of the world in Slide 1 which you think (a) consume the most food, (b) produce the most food, and (c) suffer most from hunger.

3 4.1 Watch Extract 1, the lecture's introduction. Note down which areas of the world are mentioned, and at least one thing the lecturer says about each.

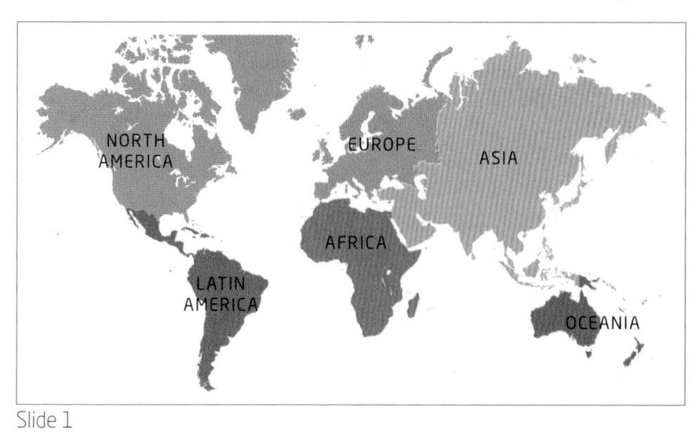

Slide 1

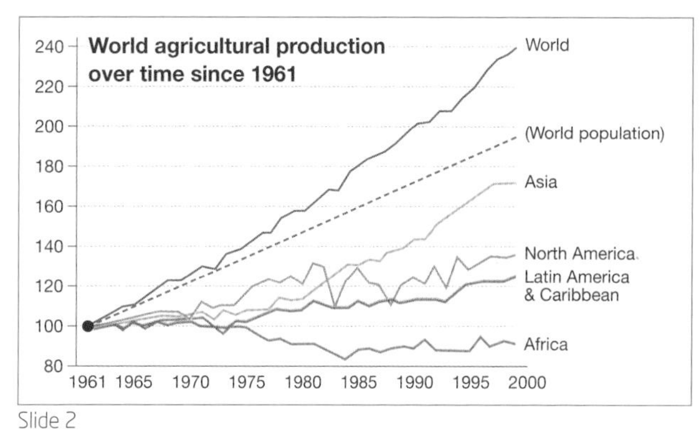

Slide 2

TASK 2 Noting down key facts and figures

1 4.2 Watch Extract 2. Which notes, (a) or (b), are the most accurate?

a 1961–2000: world population increased; food production also increased

b 1961–2000: world population increased; food production increased more

2 4.2 Watch Extract 2 again. Complete the summary.

In the 1960s, people thought the population would grow [1] .... food production. In fact the growth in food production was [2] .... the growth in the world population. This was because of [3] .... technology and because farming methods became [4] .... than in the past.

TASK 3 Identifying comparison in visuals

1 4.3 Watch Extract 3. Look at the graph in Slide 2, which compares world food production by continent. Use the phrases in the list to complete the notes.

higher than   not as high as   similar to

From the period 1961-2000

Asia food production .... Latin America

Latin American food production .... North America

Africa food production .... other parts of the world

2 4.3 **Watch Extract 3 again. Note down:**

a the reasons for Africa's poor food production

b the consequences of Africa's poor food production.

3 4.4 **Watch Extract 4. Complete the table.**

Country	Calorie consumption per capita
World average	2,940
USA	
Eritrea	

TASK 4 Critical thinking – responding to the content of a lecture

1 **Work in pairs. Use your notes from Task 3 to explain:**

1 why there might be differences in caloric consumption in the areas mentioned

2 how developing countries could solve food imbalance.

ACADEMIC LANGUAGE

▸ Language reference page 152

Comparison and contrast (1) Adjectives

Comparing (showing similarities) and contrasting (showing differences) often occurs in academic situations. Lecturers often make comparisons between objects and ideas. Many structures for comparing and contrasting use adjective patterns. For example:

comparative adjective with *-er* + *than*

In Asia, for example, food production was ***higher than*** *in Latin America.*

more **+ adjective +** ***than***

... Farming methods became ***more efficient than*** *in the past.*

not as **+ adjective +** ***as***

Africa was ***not as productive as*** *other countries during this period.*

Sentences which compare two objects or ideas do not always mention both.

This was because of ***better technology****.* (i.e. than in the past)

TASK 5 Using the language of comparison

1 **Underline the correct alternative in italics in sentences 1–5.**

1 Farming technology is more *good / advanced* than it was 50 years ago.

2 Many basic foods which use wheat are not *as cheap as / cheaper as* they were ten years ago.

3 Since 2010, European grain prices have been *higher than / more high than* US prices.

4 There are fewer problems with food distribution now than in the 20th century. This is because of *good / better* transportation systems.

5 Many modern farming methods are *more intensive than / more intensive as* in previous decades.

2 **Read notes 1–3 on key issues regarding food distribution. Use phrases from Academic Language to make comparisons.**

Example: Local food (cheap); imported food (expensive)
Local food is cheaper than imported food.

1 Ways of storing food: now (good); past (bad) – lots of waste

2 Fuel prices now (high) → transport of food (expensive)

3 Calorie consumption: 20th C (not big), 21st C (big)

TASK 6 Presenting information – referring to visuals

1 4.5 Listen to Extract 5, a student's presentation on food and fuel prices. Put stages a–d in order.

a introduce the topic ....
b describe what each line in the graph shows ....
c refer to the visual ....
d compare two trends ....

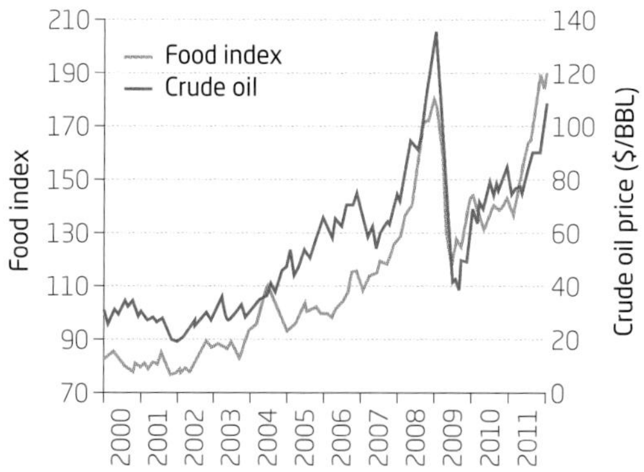

2 4.5 Listen to Extract 5 again. Note down the language used to introduce stages a–d.

3 Match sentence halves 1–4 with the correct endings a–d.

1 This chart compares ....
2 As you can see here ....
3 But if you look here ....
4 You will notice that ....

a you can see an increase in food prices.
b the two trends are similar.
c the relationship between oil and food prices.
d oil prices increased at a faster rate.

ACADEMIC LANGUAGE

Data (2) Referring to visuals

In academic lectures, visuals (graphs, charts, etc.) are often used to present facts. These factual presentations often follow the same stages.

Introducing the topic of the visual

Today I'm going to talk about ...
Today we are going to be looking at ...

Referring to a visual

This chart ***shows*** *Africa's exports and imports over the period 2000-2010.*
The table ***compares*** *life expectancy in four countries.*
If you ***look at*** *this graph / chart,* ***you will notice*** *...*

Describing and comparing trends

As you can see (from this graph), *imports rose over this period.*
As this next graph shows, *this trend was not the same for everyone.*
You will notice that *in some continents food production was higher than the world average.*

TASK 7 Comparing data in a short presentation

1 You are going to make a short presentation. Work in pairs. Student A: turn to page 163. Student B: turn to page 165.

TASK 8 Evaluating a presentation

1 Evaluate each other's presentations. Did your partner:

- introduce the topic of the visual?
- refer to the visual?
- describe trends?
- compare trends?

INDEPENDENT STUDY

Graphs and charts are good sources for comparison.

▶ Find a graph or chart on the internet where two items are compared or contrasted. Work with a partner and practise describing the facts or trends that the graph compares.

4B Reading Textbooks (4)

This module covers:

- Understanding the main idea and specific details in a text
- Identifying the language of comparison and contrast
- Understanding comparison and contrast in a text

TASK 1 Discussing the topic of a text

1 Name sports 1–5.

1 .... 2 .... 3 .... 4 .... 5 ....

2 Work in pairs. Discuss:

a which of the sports 1–5 are popular in your country

b their order in popularity from the most popular to the least popular.

3 Read the list of reasons why people take part in sports. Grade each reason as a (a major reason), or b (a minor reason).

to keep fit	....	for enjoyment	....
for competition	....	to be part of a team	....
for future fame and fortune	....	for a career	....
to impress people	....	to help focus on work or study	....

4 You are going to read the results of some research into sport in two different countries. Discuss whether people in different countries share the same reasons for doing sports. Give reasons.

TASK 2 Understanding main points of comparison

1 Read the text. Complete the notes about the study.

Author of the study: [1] ....

Date of publication: [2] ....

Focus of the study: [3] ....

Results of the study: In the USA, sport is [4] ....

In Malawi, sport is [5] ....

Method of collecting data: [6] ....

2 Which statement 1–3 contains the main idea of the text?

1 Different competitive sports are popular in different cultures.

2 Sport is more important in some cultures than in other cultures.

3 People from different cultures have different motivations for playing sport.

A comparative study of sport in the USA and Malawi

1 Guest (2007) carried out a study of two men's college soccer teams, one in the USA and the other in Malawi. The study involved observing and interviewing the participants. Analysis of the interviews produced interesting results. It showed that the reasons for doing sport are not the same in the USA and in Malawi. Competition was the main motivation for US players, at 70 per cent. In contrast, no Malawi players talked about competition as a motivation for doing sport. The US players saw sport as an opportunity to test themselves and to develop their abilities. The Malawians, however, talked about sport as a chance to display their abilities. In other words, the Malawi players were more interested in showing their abilities than being successful in competition.

2 In the USA, unlike in most other countries, sport is part of formal education. Physical education, it is believed, helps a person to compete and improve as an individual. In contrast, in Malawi sport is not an important part of the education system. Malawi, like many African countries, is a more collectivist society than the USA. Sports and other social activities often play a role in bringing people together. This can be seen in one Malawian's answer to one of Guest's questions about sport: 'It is a pastime activity. At the same time it is for physical fitness; it helps one's health. But it can also help to unite the nation too.'

3 The most significant Malawian answer was that sport is a pastime. This was defined in their answers as a way for a person to avoid trouble. The players said that sport gave an opportunity for people who were not as good at school as other students or who were not productive members of society. They talked a lot about how sport helps people to stay away from crime. This was similar to some US players' comments. However, the US players' cultural view was different from the Malawians'. The US players said that sport helps people to improve themselves and gives them an opportunity to be creative.

4 Guest concludes that understanding local variations in the meaning of sport is important for anyone interested in increasing the role and impact of sport. There are, for example, a growing number of humanitarian agencies who try to use sport to address social problems in different communities. Often these efforts assume that attitudes towards sport are the same across societies. Guest's research showed that this was not the case; people's attitudes differ around the world. As such, more detailed analysis is important when planning any sporting solution to a social problem.

SOURCE: Crane, J. & Hannibal, J. (2009). p.310. *IB Psychology: Course Companion.* Oxford: Oxford University Press.

GLOSSARY

collectivist society *(n)* a society that believes people must support each other and act as a group; the opposite is an individualistic society

motivation *(n)* a reason for wanting to do something

pastime *(n)* a hobby, something to do in your free time

3 Read Paragraph 1 again, and underline:

a the sentence that tells you the main idea

b the two key details that directly support this main idea.

TASK 3 Reading for specific details

1 **Note down (a) the Malawian and (b) the US athletes' reasons for doing sport.**

2 **Note down any additional reasons given.**

TASK 4 Critical thinking - responding to a text

1 **Work in pairs. Discuss questions 1 and 2.**
   1 Which view outlined in the text is most similar to your own? Give reasons.
   2 Which view of sport is most similar to the view in your country?

TASK 5 Identifying similarities and differences in a text

1 **Read the text again. For each paragraph, 1–4, identify which aspect of sport is being compared.**

a sport and education	Paragraph ....
b attitudes to sport around the world	Paragraph ....
c reasons for doing sport (motivation)	Paragraph ....
d sport and society	Paragraph ....

2 **Read extracts 1–5 from the text. Identify the language that expresses similarity or difference.**
   1 In the USA, unlike in most other countries, sport is part of formal education.
   2 Malawi, like many African countries, is more of a collectivist society than the USA.
   3 It showed that the reasons for doing sport are not the same in the USA and in Malawi.
   4 This was similar to some US players' comments.
   5 However, the US players' cultural view was different from the Malawians'.

ACADEMIC LANGUAGE

▸Language reference page 153

Comparison and contrast (2) Using different word classes

Academic texts often express similarities and differences between ideas. When reading, it is important to notice the language used to express similarities or differences.

like / unlike

*Malawi, **like** many African countries, is a more collectivist society than the USA.*
*In the USA, **unlike** in most other countries, sport is part of formal education.*

similar to / different from

*This **was similar to** some US players' comments.*
*However, the US players' cultural view was **different from** the Malawians'.*

are the same / differ

*Often these efforts assume that attitudes towards sport **are the same** across societies.*
*... People's attitudes **differ** around the world.*

TASK 6 Expressing similarities and differences

1 Complete the text using the words and phrases in the list.

differ different from like not the same similar to unlike

There are many similarities between the British and the Americans. But in terms of popular sports, the UK and the USA are very different. Football, rugby, and cricket, the most popular sports in the UK, are very [1] .... American football, basketball, and baseball, which are the most popular sports in the USA. Even though the actual games of American football and baseball are perhaps [2] .... rugby and cricket in some ways, as a complete sporting event they are [3] .... The British and US attitudes to watching sporting events [4] .... greatly. [5] .... the Americans, the British don't appreciate all the hype and showbusiness that is part of many American sporting events. On the other hand, the Americans, [6] .... many other nations, can't understand how a game like cricket can last five days.

2 Rewrite sentences 1–7 using the words in brackets.

Example: Both Pakistan and India are collectivist cultures. (like)
Pakistan, like India, is a collectivist culture.

1 Japan is a collectivist culture. The USA isn't. (unlike)
Unlike ....

2 Football today is not the same as football 100 years ago. (different from)
Football today ....

3 Sport and business have many similarities between them. (similar to)
Sport and business ....

4 Sporting ethical codes are not the same around the world. (differ)
Sporting ethical codes ....

5 There are some similarities between Malawi and its neighbour, Zambia. (similar to)
Malawi ....

6 American football is different from soccer. (not the same)
American football and ....

7 Professional sport and amateur sport is different. (not the same as)
Professional sport ....

3 Work in pairs. Write three sentences which show comparison and contrast.

Example: *Sport is more informal in the Saudi education system than in the USA.*

TASK 7 Critical thinking – responding to the content of a text

1 Research the role of sport in the education system in your country. Note down how your country compares to the USA and Malawi in areas 1 and 2.

1 Sport as a part of formal education

2 Sporting ability and/or sporting success

INDEPENDENT STUDY

Many arguments in academic texts rely on comparing one set of facts with another.

▸ **Find a text that uses a comparison of two or more things to present a particular argument. Note down the main comparisons and contrasts that are made in the text. Then explain the argument and the evidence that supports it to your partner.**

4C Writing (1) Writing connected sentences

This module covers:

- Identifying the language of comparison and contrast
- Writing connected sentences comparing and contrasting ideas

TASK 1 Identifying comparison and contrast

1 Work in pairs. Discuss whether the following have changed in your country in recent years.

life expectancy popular sports temperature unemployment

Example: *Life expectancy in Thailand is higher today than it was in 2006.*

2 Read sentences 1–4. Underline the language of comparison and contrast.

Example: *Compulsory education is from 6 to 16 in Italy. This is also true in France. In contrast, in England it is from 5 to 18.*

1 In Saudi Arabia, football is the most popular sport. Volleyball, cricket, and basketball are also popular.

2 Both Sweden and Switzerland have a life expectancy of 81.1 years. In contrast, life expectancy in Swaziland is just 32 years.

3 In the UK, unemployment is highest in the under-25s. However, it is lowest in the 50 to 60 age range. This is also the case in most European countries.

4 The average global temperature in 1860 was 13.5 degrees Celsius. By comparison, today's average is 14.5 degrees Celsius.

ACADEMIC LANGUAGE ▸ Language reference page 153

Comparison and contrast (3) Showing similarities and differences

In academic writing, it is often necessary to compare and contrast ideas or data. You can use a range of linking adverbials to show similarities or differences.

Similarities

*Volleyball, cricket, and basketball are **also** popular.*

*10–15% of people are left-handed. **Similarly**, about 15% of the population is left-footed.*

Differences

*Sri Lanka has two official languages. **By comparison / In contrast**, India has over 20.*

*Cycling is one of the fastest-growing sports in the UK. **However**, in many other countries the number of bikes on the road is in decline.*

TASK 2 Using language to show similarity and difference

1 Complete sentences 1–4 with an appropriate word or phrase from the list.

Example: *Soccer is played around the world by about 250 million people. In contrast, only about 5 million people regularly play rugby.*

also by comparison however in contrast similarly

1 In 2013, the global average birth rate was 2.47 children per family. ...., in Singapore the figure was much lower, at 0.79.

2 The original research involved over a thousand participants. ...., a more recent study interviewed only fifty individuals.

3 65% of Koreans have attended higher education. ...., less than 10% of the Chinese population goes on to higher education.

4 Low-lying areas of Bangladesh regularly flood. ...., flooding .... occurs in neighbouring West Bengal in India.

2 Match sentences 1–4 with sentences a–d.

1 Research has shown that about one-third of the male adult global population smokes. ....

2 According to United Nations statistics, the worldwide average life expectancy for males is 65.7 years. ....

3 There are about 6.5 million land species. ....

4 Poland ended its communist rule in 1989. ....

a Approximately 2.2 million species live in the seas and oceans.

b Only about a quarter of adult women smoke.

c Communism was abandoned in a number of European countries in the early 1990s.

d The worldwide average life expectancy for females is 70.1 years.

3 Rewrite the sentences from 2 using a word or phrase from the list.

by comparison   however   in contrast   similarly

1 ....

....

2 ....

....

3 ....

....

4 ....

....

TASK 3 Writing comparison and contrast sentences

1 Write notes 1–4 as two full sentences using appropriate linking adverbials.

Example: average temperatures in Saudi Arabia: winter 15°C, summer 42°C
In Saudi Arabia, the average winter temperature is 15°C. In contrast, the average summer temperature is 42°C.

1 number of universities: India 8,400, China 1,050

....

2 working in administrative jobs in the UK: 22% of females, 5% of males

....

3 optimum temperature for growth: bacteria A 20°C, bacteria B 35°C

....

4 population: Australia 23.2 million, Ivory Coast 23.2 million

....

2 Note down six facts relating to your area of study. Write at least three sentences to compare and contrast the information. Use appropriate linking adverbials.

Example: *Fossil fuels are a major source of air pollution. In contrast, nuclear energy does not directly produce airborne pollutants.*

1 ....

....

2 ....

....

3 ....

....

4C Writing (2) Describing visual data

This module covers:

- Describing visual data using comparison and contrast

TASK 1 Using visual information in writing

1 Look at Figure 1. Select the most appropriate summary of the bar chart.

a The bar chart shows an overall population increase in seven major European countries from 1997 to 2007.

b The bar chart compares the changing populations in seven major European countries from 1997 to 2007.

2 Read a student's description of Figure 1. Put stages a–e in order 1–5.

The bar chart compares population growth in selected major European countries between 1997 and 2007. It shows that the population was higher in all countries in 2007 compared to 1997. While the populations of France, Italy, and Spain increased by around 5%, in contrast there was an increase of almost 15% in Turkey. During the ten-year period, there was very little change in population size in Germany. This was also true in Poland, where the population remained just over 38 million.

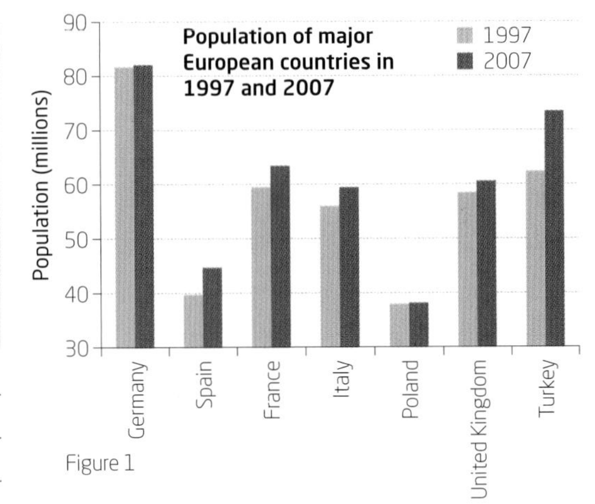

Figure 1

a Compare similar population growth ....

b Contrast overall pattern and pattern with no change ....

c Refer to the visual and say what the chart is comparing ....

d Contrast very different population growth ....

e State what the chart shows overall ....

3 Read the description again. Note down the words / phrases used to compare and contrast information.

ACADEMIC LANGUAGE ▸ Language reference page 154

Data (3) Approximation

In academic writing, you often summarize information or data. When talking about large numbers, it is usual to use approximation.

The populations of France, Italy, and Spain increased by ***around*** *5%.*

There was an increase of ***almost*** *15% in Turkey.*

The population remained ***just over*** *38 million.*

TASK 2 Presenting numbers

1 Work in pairs. Identify the numbers used in Figure 1.

2 Practise presenting the information in Figure 1 using approximation.

Example: *In 1996, the population of Germany was just over 80 million.*

TASK 3 **Completing a description of visual information**

1 Look at the bar chart in Figure 2. Note down:

1 what data the chart is comparing
2 what overall statement you can make about the data
3 which data are very similar, and could be compared
4 which data are very different, and could be contrasted.

2 Complete the description of Figure 2 using the words / phrases in the list.

also compares compared to in contrast shows

Figure 2 [1] .... participation in five different leisure activities by two different age groups: 16–24 year olds and 35–44 year olds. It [2] .... that 88% of both age groups watched TV, making it the most popular leisure activity. However, there are large differences depending on age for other activities. Going to the cinema is more popular with the younger age group. This is [3] .... true of listening to music, where there is nearly a 15% difference in participation. [4] ...., gardening is more popular with the older age group. Just over 50% of 35–44 year olds do some gardening [5] .... only 16% of 16–24 year olds.

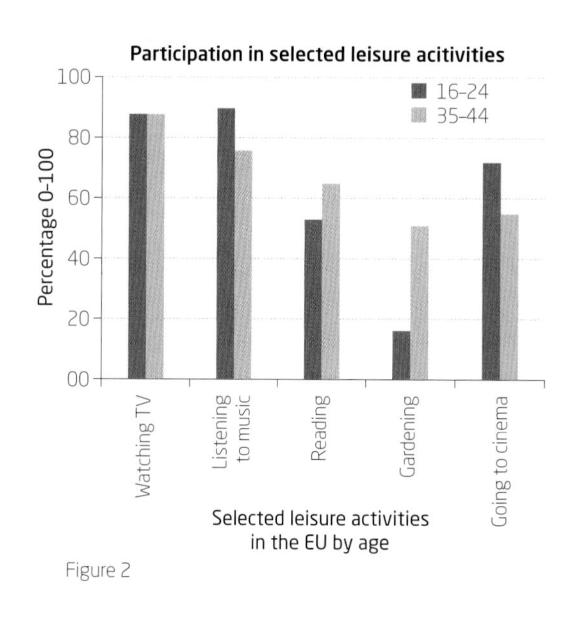

Figure 2

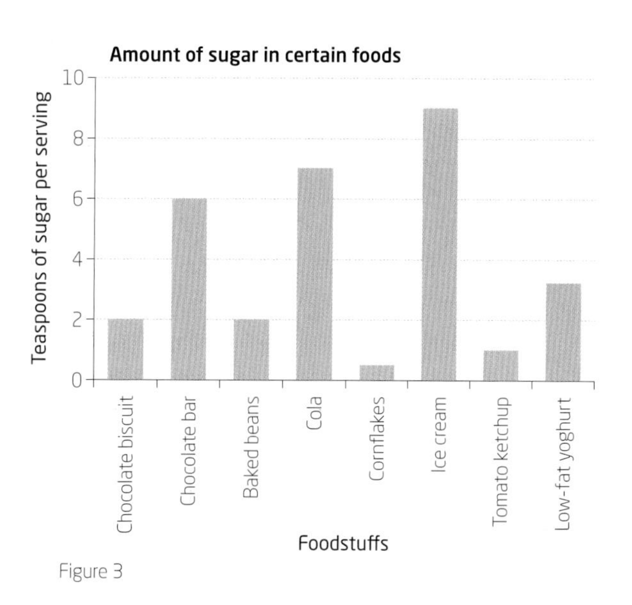

Figure 3

TASK 4 **Writing a description of visually-presented information**

Sample answer:
page 159

1 Write a description of the information presented in Figure 3. Note down:

1 what data the chart is comparing
2 what overall statement you can make about the data
3 which data are very similar, and could be compared
4 which data are very different, and could be contrasted.

TASK 5 **Evaluating writing**

1 Read the paragraph you wrote in Task 4. Does the paragraph include:

- language to refer to the visual?
- linking adverbials to signal differences and similarities?
- approximation?

INDEPENDENT STUDY

You can practise writing simple comparisons by writing single sentences that compare one thing with another.

▶ **Think of some simple facts relating to how your country is different now from how it was in the past. Write three sentences comparing past and present and then exchange ideas with your partner.**

4D Vocabulary

TASK 1 Vocabulary related to trends

1 Complete the text using the correct word from each pair.

Since 2000 there has been a [1]*significant* / *greatly* rise in world oil production. Most of this [2]*grow* / *growth* – an extra two million barrels a day – has come from the United States and Canada. Although the price of oil has [3]*varied* / *difference* from one month to another, overall there has been a sharp [4]*decline* / *increase*, from $40 a barrel to approximately $110. Analysts are divided about whether this [5]*trend* / *rate* of increase will continue or not in the coming years. If it does, we can also expect to see a [6]*little* / *dramatic* increase in the cost of other goods.

2 Work in pairs. Tell each other about something that:

a *varies greatly* from one place to another

b has had a *dramatic decline* in quality in recent years

c is *growing in popularity* at the moment

d is a *significant trend*.

TASK 2 Prepositions in statistics

1 Complete sentences 1–5 with the correct preposition from the list.

at over in of (x2) to ~~from~~

1 Winter temperatures in the region vary *from* one country .... another.

2 There was an increase in youth unemployment .... 3.2%, but only a small increase .... general unemployment.

3 .... 40% of the population take exercise at least once a week.

4 .... the end of 2013, the economy started to show some signs of growth.

5 18% .... females work in administrative jobs compared with only 8% of males.

TASK 3 Vocabulary-building: Antonyms

1 Antonyms are words with opposite meanings, for example *easy* / *difficult*, *popular* / *unpopular*. Read the adjectives below and note down:

1 six adjectives whose antonyms are formed with the prefix *un-*

2 two adjectives whose antonyms are formed with the prefix *in-*

3 two adjectives whose antonyms are completely different words.

competitive high productive creative efficient different
popular interested formal successful

2 Complete questions 1–7 using an appropriate antonym.

Example: Are you a competitive or *uncompetitive* person?

1 What are the most popular and .... subjects at university in your country?

2 Is there a subject you were .... in at school that interests you now?

3 Do you find that using the internet when you are studying makes you more productive or more ....? Does it make you more creative or more ....?

4 As well as formal, organized sports, what .... games or sports do people in your country play?

5 How high does the temperature get in your country in summer? How .... does it fall in winter? Does it reach minus figures?

6 Are your national teams successful? In which sports are they ....?

7 Are your educational aims the .... as a few years ago or are they different?

3 Work in groups. Ask each other questions from 2.

4E Academic Language Check

TASK 1 Describing similarity and difference

1 Read the results of a study about attitudes to PE (physical education) in three regions in the world. Complete the summary using the words in the list.

	Number who answered YES		
	Middle East	Asia	USA
Is PE a useful subject at school?	30%	27%	13%
Do parents think PE is important for their children?	60%	11%	75%
Are you happy with the school PE facilities?	37%	12%	40%
Are you happy with the number of specialist PE teachers?	94%	59%	96%

both ~~differ~~ differences different same similar similarities unlike

Attitudes towards PE in schools [1] *differ* around the world. A recent study compared attitudes in the Middle East, Asia, and the USA. While there are some [2] .... between the countries, there are also a number of [3] ....

One key finding is that, [4] .... in Asia and the Middle East, not many students in the USA think PE is a useful subject at school. On the other hand, the parents of schoolchildren in [5] .... the USA and the Middle East think that PE is important. This is very [6] .... in Asia, where only 11% of parents think that PE is an important school subject.

Satisfaction with PE facilities and with PE teachers is not the [7] .... in the three regions. Attitudes in the USA are [8] .... to the Middle East and are generally positive.

TASK 2 Comparative adjectives

1 Complete sentences 1–6 with the comparative form of the adjective or noun. Add any other necessary words.

Example: The world's most popular non-competitive sports are swimming and cycling. A recent study suggests that swimming is marginally *more popular than* (popular) cycling.

1 Research suggests that, globally, volleyball has the most players of any team sport. It is .... (popular) both basketball and football. However, the sport is not .... (popular) football among men aged 18–25.

2 Statistically, powerboat racing is five times .... (dangerous) motor racing.

3 Sumo wrestler Konishiki is .... (heavy) any other sportsman or woman in history. In 1994, he weighed 267 kg.

4 According to a recent survey, as a brand Bayern Munich is .... (valuable) any other football club. However, financially it is not .... (valuable) Real Madrid.

5 In terms of Olympic medals, Russia's women gymnasts have not been .... (successful) the Soviet Union's were. The latter won team gold at all but one Olympics from 1952 to 1988.

6 Analysis has shown that when Usain Bolt set the 100m world record of 9.58 seconds in 2009, he momentarily ran at 44.7 km/h. This was 0.8 km/h .... (fast) Bolt's previous record, achieved at the 2008 Olympics. To date, no human has run .... (fast) this.

UNIT 5 Environment

ACADEMIC FOCUS: EXPRESSING STANCE

LEARNING OBJECTIVES

This unit covers:

Listening and Speaking
- Identifying stance in a lecture
- Expressing stance with supporting evidence
- Asking for and responding to stance in a discussion

Reading
- Identifying the main arguments in a text
- Recognizing stance in a text

Writing
- Writing sentences expressing stance
- Writing a paragraph expressing stance
- Using hedging language to express stance

Vocabulary
- Vocabulary related to research
- Vocabulary-building: Noun suffixes
- Nouns and verbs with the same form

Academic Language Check
- Expressing stance
- Agreeing and disagreeing
- Hedging

Discussion

1 Read the definition of *stance*.

stance (*n*) a way of viewing something subjectively but based on evidence

2 Work in pairs. Decide which statements a–e express a positive or negative view of environmental change.

a A few decades ago, no one believed that renewable energy could solve our energy problems. Now, the public attitude is changing.

b According to the UN Report on Climate Change 2013, new technologies to fight climate change might offer some hope.

c Environmental problems are the responsibility of governments. There is nothing individuals can do.

d Public opinion is that environmental change is important, and requires more political attention.

e According to many governments, economic growth is more important than protecting the environment.

3 Whose stance is expressed in each statement a–e?

1 the writer

2 people in general

3 another person or source

4 Work in pairs. State whether you agree with the stances in a–e. Give reasons.

5A Listening & Speaking Lectures (3)

This module covers:

- Identifying stance in a lecture
- Expressing stance with supporting evidence
- Asking for and responding to stance in a discussion

TASK 1 Previewing vocabulary in a lecture

1 You are going to watch part of a lecture about the effects of the environment on past civilizations. Discuss what you know about civilizations 1–3.

Easter Island, Pacific Ocean

Mayan civilization, Mexico

Norse settlement in Greenland

2 Read sentences 1–3 from the lecture. Match the definitions to the words in bold.

1 Several environmental factors contributed to the **collapse** of early civilizations.
2 If there is a **shortage** of food or energy resources, people often look for a technological solution.
3 As the civilizations became more established, and the population grew, there was increased demand for **resources**.

.... (*n*) a situation when there is not enough of something
.... (*n*) the things people have or can use
.... (*n*) a sudden or complete failure of something

3 Work in pairs. Predict what the lecturer will say about civilizations 1–3.

TASK 2 Identifying a main argument

1 5.1 Watch Extract 1. Complete the notes.

Environmental Change

- Success of civilization linked to [1] ....
- Failed past civilizations reflect this, e.g. Easter Islanders, Mayans, Norse in Greenland
- Environmental factors which contributed to collapse – problems with soil, water management, introducing non-native [2] ....
- Growing civilizations = increased demand → overhunting or [3] ....

2 5.1 Watch Extract 1 again. Select which statement, (a) or (b), best expresses the speaker's argument.

a Past civilizations collapsed when people tried to change their environment.
b Different environmental factors can contribute to the collapse of a civilization.

3 5.2 **Watch Extract 2. Work in pairs. Use the lecturer's visuals to explain what happened on Easter Island.**

4 5.2 **Watch Extract 2 again. Note down the evidence the lecturer gives to support his main argument.**

5 **Match stances (a) and (b) to the people who expressed it.**

Early researchers   Modern archaeologists

a Easter Island's environment was affected by human actions.
b Easter Island's environment was most affected by animals.

ACADEMIC LANGUAGE ▸Language reference page 154

Stance (1) Referring to someone else's views

Speakers in lectures and seminars often present other people's stance as well as their own. It is important to recognize when the speaker is referring to someone else's views.

__The__ ecocentric __view is that__ the Earth is here for all species.
Modern archaeologists __believe that__ the rats also contributed ...
__According to__ early researchers, the people who settled there changed the environment.
__In their opinion__, economic growth is a good thing.

Early settlers destroyed palm trees

Early settlers cleared land

Early settlers introduced new species

TASK 3 Understanding different stances

1 5.3 **Watch Extract 3. Match stances (a) and (b) to the people who expressed them.**

Ecocentric thinkers   Technocentric thinkers

a Technological solutions help economic growth.
b We need to protect nature and preserve ecosystems.

2 5.3 **Watch Extract 3 again. Complete the description of the technocentric and ecocentric stances using appropriate words or phrases.**

The technocentric [1] .... is that nature is there to benefit mankind. [2] .... technocentric thinkers, if humans face food or energy shortages, they will find a technological solution. [3] .... economic growth is a good thing.

The ecocentric [4] .... is that humans share the Earth's resources with other species. Ecocentric thinkers [5] .... it is a mistake to think that we can manage nature. [6] ...., nature is complex and we still don't fully understand it.

3 **Rewrite sentences 1–4 expressing the stance using the words in brackets.**

1 Ecocentrics say that we must only use resources that can be replaced. (view)

....

2 According to technocentrics, economic growth is a good thing. (believe)

....

3 The ecocentric view is that the Earth is here for all species. (opinion)

....

4 Technocentrics believe that human beings will find a technological solution to shortages of resources. (according to)

....

4 **Discuss which stance, technocentric or ecocentric, you agree with more. Give reasons.**

TASK 4 Identifying stance and supporting evidence

1 5.4 Listen to a group of students discussing the content of the lecture. Tick the view each student agrees with.

	The technocentric view	The ecocentric view	Language used
1 Sarah	☐	☐	
2 Joel	☐	☐	
3 Hasan	☐	☐	

2 Note down the language that each speaker uses to give their opinion, agree, or disagree.

3 5.4 Listen again and complete the notes on the reasons they give to support their opinion.

Sarah: ....

Joel: ....

Hasan: ....

ACADEMIC LANGUAGE Language reference page 154

Stance (2) Giving an opinion, agreeing, and disagreeing

In seminars and tutorials, you will often be asked to express your opinion or to say whether or not you agree with other speakers.

Giving an opinion

It seems to me that *the technocentric view is probably right.*
I think that *we're going to see a lot more use of technology ...*
I would argue that *you have to balance economic growth with use of resources.*

Agreeing	**Disagreeing**
I agree with that.	*No, I don't agree.*
Yes, and ...	*Yes, but ...*

TASK 5 Expressing stance with supporting evidence

1 Work in pairs. Note down one piece of evidence for each statement 1–4.

Example: It is possible to use natural resources carefully.
For example, you can save water by taking a shower. Showers use 70% less water than baths.

1 Man-made pollution is changing the Earth's climate.
2 Population growth puts pressure on resources.
3 Technology can solve environmental problems.
4 Nature can repair the damage that humans do to the Earth.

2 Work in groups. Discuss the statements in 1. Use the phrases in Academic Language to help you express your opinion, agree, or disagree.

3 Evaluate your performance in the discussion. Did you:

- clearly express your stance on each subject?
- give supporting evidence for your stance?
- use agreeing and disagreeing language correctly?

INDEPENDENT STUDY

In talks and lectures, speakers often express others' views as well as their own. It is important to be able to distinguish whose view is being expressed.

Find an online talk on a subject that interests you. Listen and note down what the speaker's stance is and what other views he or she refers to.

5B Reading Journals

This module covers:

- Identifying the main arguments in a text
- Recognizing stance in a text

TASK 1 Preparing to read about a new topic

1 You are going to read a journal article about a ban on public smoking on a university campus. Note down possible stances for (a) smokers, (b) non-smokers, and (c) university employees.

2 Work in pairs. Read paragraph 1 of the text. Select the most suitable purpose 1–3 for the journal article. Give reasons.

1 a medical study 2 an environmental study 3 a social study

TASK 2 Identifying the main arguments in a text

1 Read the whole text. Tick the findings that are included in the report.

The smoking ban created the problem of people smoking near the entrances to buildings. ☐

No one felt sympathy for the smokers who had to smoke outside. ☐

Most people thought that allowing people to smoke inside the building again was a bad solution. ☐

2 Identify the sentences in the text where you found each answer.

3 Read the text again. Complete the notes in the table.

Positive effect of the smoking ban
Many people [1] ....
Negative effects of the smoking ban
People started to smoke near entrances, causing smoke [2] .... and a negative [3] .... impact
Solutions suggested by staff
1 [4] .... people smoking around entrances
2 put smokers [5] ....
3 encourage smokers to [6] ....
Action taken by University
Giving smokers [7] ....
Conclusion
Give smokers somewhere to smoke [8] ....

Environmental Tobacco Smoke – a study

In this paper we focus upon the relocation of smokers from inside University buildings to outside, and consider some implications for smokers and non-smokers among University staff.

The smoking ban in University buildings significantly reduced smoking at work. However, it did not eradicate the problem of Environmental Tobacco Smoke (ETS). Research data showed that the problem of smoke pollution was moved to the entrances and exits of University buildings, affecting individuals as they entered and left the workplace. The ban also had a visual impact. One of the first sights that met visitors to the University was groups of smokers congregating outside buildings to smoke. Staff were questioned about this and invited to suggest possible solutions.

In considering how to deal with the problems resulting from the relocation of smokers to University entrances, staff opinion was divided. A minority view was that there should be stricter measures to 'eradicate' smoking. This group placed the health interests of the non-smoking members of staff above the interests of the smaller number of smokers. Many were unsympathetic to smokers being allowed to smoke near entrances. A typical response came from staff member X who commented that there should certainly be a ban on 'smokers who congregate around building entrances'. According to staff member Y, smokers should be put in 'a pen in the middle of the car park'.

The majority view, however, was that smokers should be helped to quit. These respondents described smoking as 'addictive' and smokers as 'dependent' individuals who should be encouraged to stop smoking. Many non-smokers noted positively that the University had tried to help smokers with such advice. Staff member Z expressed the view that it was wrong to force people to smoke outside in very cold weather. Others also felt that this sent a very negative message to smokers.

The relocation of smoking to the entrances of buildings or even further away is clearly not a satisfactory solution. It simply shifts the problem to another place. Perhaps then the most obvious solution is to provide designated smoking areas within buildings. No doubt changing this approach could be considered a backwards step, but over half of all respondents favoured this solution.

SOURCE: Parry, O., Platt, S. & Tomson, C. (2000). p.125-133. *Health Promotion International*. Vol 15 (2). Oxford: Oxford University Press.

GLOSSARY

ban *(n)* a rule that says that something is not allowed

congregate *(v)* to gather together

designated *(adj)* officially chosen for a particular purpose

eradicate *(v)* to destroy or get rid of something completely

unsympathetic *(adj)* without any feelings for, not in agreement with

TASK 3 Recognizing stance in a text

1 ***Stance*** **is the position that a person takes on an idea or situation. Work in pairs. Complete the table with the correct stance a–e for each person.**

Person	Stance
The minority of staff	
Staff members X and Y	
The majority of staff	
Staff member Z	
The author	

a It is not right to make people smoke outside in poor weather.
b Smokers have a problem and need to be helped.
c Since relocation outside does not work, smokers should be given a space to smoke inside.
d The university needs to have stricter measures to stop people smoking.
e People should not be allowed to smoke near building entrances.

2 Work in pairs. Note down the phrases in the text used to introduce the stance of 1–5.

Example: The minority of staff: *A minority view was that ...*

1 Staff member X: ....

2 Staff member Y: ....

3 The majority view: ....

4 Staff member Z: ....

5 The author: ....

ACADEMIC LANGUAGE

Stance (3) Author's stance; other people's stance

Authors will often present other people's stance as well as their own. It is important to recognize whose stance is being presented.

Reporting other people's stance using key phrases

__According to__ staff member Y, smokers should be put in 'a pen in the middle of the car park'.
__A__ minority __view was that__ there should be stricter measures to 'eradicate' smoking.
__The__ majority __view__, however, __was that__ smokers should be helped to quit.

Reporting other people's stance using reporting verbs

Many non-smokers __noted positively that__ the university had tried to help smokers.
Staff member X __commented that__ there should certainly be a ban.

Expressing the author's own stance

The relocation of smoking to the entrances of buildings ... is __clearly__ not a satisfactory solution.
__Perhaps__ then the most obvious solution is to provide designated smoking areas within buildings.

TASK 4 Expressing stance

1 Complete sentences 1–5 with a word from the list.

clearly commented notes perhaps view

1 One .... of the IQ test is that it is not a good measure of intelligence.
2 Vygotsky .... that written language differs from spoken language in several respects.
3 The ability to make decisions is .... the most important expression of leadership.
4 A leading environmentalist .... that average global temperatures have increased by two degrees.
5 It is .... wrong to think that humans have had no impact on the environment.

2 Rewrite statements 1–6 using the words in brackets.

1 According to Harper, the results of the experiment were inconclusive.
Harper .... (noted that)
2 Mathau states that there is insufficient evidence that ETS is harmful.
According to Mathau, there is .... (clearly)
3 Most people felt that there wasn't enough evidence to change the policy.
The .... (majority view)
4 Some people think that the opinions of non-smokers are given too much weight.
.... (one view)
5 Others say that their opinions are not considered enough.
.... (another view)
6 The change in the attitude of the smokers themselves is the most significant fact.
.... (perhaps)

TASK 5 Discussing stances expressed in a text

1 Work in groups. Discuss what the article concludes is a good solution to the problem of smoking in office buildings.

2 Do you agree with this solution? Give reasons.

3 Work in pairs. Choose one of topics 1–3 OR a topic connected with your field of study or interests. Write two sentences expressing stance: one expressing another person's stance and one expressing your own stance.

Example: Climate change and the rise in global temperatures
According to one group of researchers at the University of East Anglia, world temperatures are falling, not rising.
But climate change can clearly be seen in the increasing number of extreme weather events, like floods and hurricanes.

1 People smoking in public
2 Standards in education in your country
3 The increase in food allergies

4 Work in groups. Read out your sentences and evaluate the stances given.

INDEPENDENT STUDY

In academic writing, writers often express their stance by using words and phrases such as *clearly*, *perhaps*, or *no doubt*.

▸ Find a short academic text and note down any similar expressions. Decide whose view is expressed in each case.

5C Writing (1) Sentences expressing stance

This module covers:

- Writing sentences expressing stance

TASK 1 Previewing a writing task

1 Read Paragraph 1. Note down what evidence of human activity in the high slopes of the French Alps has been discovered.

2 Note down what the evidence in 1 tells us about (a) the Alpine environment and (b) early humans.

Paragraph 1

In 2013, archaeologists uncovered relics of human activity in the high slopes of the French Alps which date back over 8,000 years. The archaeologists found what are thought to be Stone Age camps and other dwellings. They also found areas where trees were cleared to create new grazing land. It is likely that the landscape was occupied over many centuries. The discovery indicates that people, as well as climate, influenced the Alpine landscape. This also suggests that early humans lived in a wider range of environments than was previously thought.

GLOSSARY

dwelling *(n)* the place where a person lives

grazing *(n)* (used about cows, sheep, etc.) eating grass in a field

relic *(n)* an object from the past that still survives today

ACADEMIC LANGUAGE ▸ Language reference page 154

Hedging (1)

In academic writing, writers often use hedging language to avoid expressing things as absolute facts and to make it clear they are expressing a claim or opinion. For example:

Verbs

The archaeologists found what ***are thought to be*** *Stone Age camps ...*
The discovery ***indicates*** *that people, as well as climate, influenced the landscape.*
This also ***suggests*** *that early humans lived in a wider range of environments than was previously thought.*

It ... that ...

It is probable / likely that *the landscape was occupied over many centuries.*
It is possible that *the environment was too extreme for year-round habitation.*

TASK 2 Using hedging language

1 Underline the phrases in Paragraph 1 that show that something is a claim or an opinion, rather than a fact.

Example: *The archaeologists found what* <u>*are thought to be*</u> *Stone Age camps ...*

2 Select the most appropriate hedging language to complete the paragraph about the environment of Antarctica.

Tremors up to 40 kilometres under the surface of west Antarctica [1]*indicate / are thought to be* the presence of an active volcano under the ice sheet. Volcanoes in Antarctica, both above and below ground, [2]*suggest / were always thought to be* inactive, but the new discovery [3]*suggests / is thought to be* this is not the case. [4]*It indicates / It is possible that* the heat from the volcano may speed up the melting of the Antarctic ice sheet.

In a separate survey, the discovery of a layer of ash trapped in the ice [5]*is thought to be / indicates* previous volcanic activity in the Antarctic. Based on its depth, [6]*it is likely that / suggests* the ash is at least 8,000 years old, which [7]*it is likely that / indicates* the time of the last volcanic activity in the region.

3 Complete sentences 1–5 by adding appropriate words / phrases. Try to use a different word for each sentence.

Example: *It is* <u>*probable*</u> *that there was once water on Mars.*

1 It is .... that plants evolved from green algae.
2 Research .... that the Amazon rainforest will one day disappear.
3 The Earth's temperature is .... to be increasing at a rate of about 1°C per fifty years.
4 It is .... that there will be a 50% increase in nuclear energy.
5 The discovery of a five million-year-old leopard skull in Tibet .... that big cats originated in Asia and not in Africa.

4 Rewrite statements 1–6 using the hedging words / phrases in brackets.

Example: Desertification will be a major environmental problem in the future. (it/thought)
It is thought that desertification will be a major environmental problem in the future.

1 The universe began to exist about 15 billion years ago. (it / probable)
....
2 There are around a million insect species on Earth. (thought / be)
There are ....
3 Many dinosaurs had feathers, according to a recent discovery. (suggests)
A recent discovery ....
4 Recent research into personality states genetic factors have more influence than environmental factors. (indicates)
Recent research ....
5 By the end of the century, many homes will produce their own electricity. (it / likely)
....
6 The Japanese giant spider crab lives for up to 100 years. (thought / live)
The Japanese giant spider crab ....

5 Think of key facts in your field of study or in topics you are interested in. Write a sentence for each using hedging language. Write at least five sentences.

Example: *There are thought to be about 300,000 species of plants on Earth.*
It is likely that Machu Picchu was built in the mid-15th century.

5C Writing (2) Writing a stance paragraph

This module covers:

- Writing a paragraph expressing stance
- Using hedging language to express stance

TASK 1 Identifying stance

1 Read Paragraph 2, an extract from a student's essay based on the following title. Decide whether the writer (a) agrees or (b) disagrees with the statement.

TITLE: *'The only solution to over-population and limited resources is for humans to exploit new environments beyond the Earth.' Do you agree or disagree with this statement?*

Paragraph 2

There is evidence that Mars could support human life if there were long-term missions to the planet in the future. This idea has been put forward by technocentric thinkers, such as Elon Musk. Liquid water cannot exist on the surface of Mars due to the planet's low atmospheric pressure and temperature. However, the two polar ice caps appear to be made largely of frozen water and there may also be a very small amount of water vapour in the atmosphere. Recent missions to the planet indicate that there is also liquid water in the soil. It appears that about 2% of Martian soil is water. It seems that this is the same all over the planet. This could mean that there is a permanent water supply for any future human exploration of the planet.

2 Evaluate the paragraph using questions 1 and 2.

1 Is the writer's stance clear?
2 Are the supporting examples appropriate?

TASK 2 Identifying hedging language

1 Read Paragraph 2 again. Identify which information in sentences 1–7 is not presented as fact.

1 Liquid water cannot exist on the surface of Mars.
2 Mars has low atmospheric pressure and temperature.
3 The two polar ice caps are made of frozen water.
4 There is a small amount of water vapour in the atmosphere.
5 About 2% of Martian soil is water.
6 Martian soil contains water all over the planet.
7 There is a permanent water supply for any future human exploration of the planet.

2 Underline the language in Paragraph 2 used to avoid expressing something as an absolute fact.

Example: *However, the two polar ice caps appear to be made largely of frozen water ...*

ACADEMIC LANGUAGE ▸ Language reference page 154

Hedging (2) *appear* and *seem*; modal verbs

In academic writing, we often use *seem* and *appear* and the modal verbs *can, could,* and *may* to avoid expressing things as absolute facts.

appear* and *seem

*However, the two polar ice caps **appear** to be made largely of frozen water ...*
***It seems that** this is the same all over the planet.*

Modal verbs: *can, could,* and *may*

*... There **may** also be a very small amount of water vapour in the atmosphere.*
*This **could** mean that there is a permanent water supply for any future human exploration of the planet.*

TASK 3 Using hedging verbs and modal verbs

1 Rewrite statements 1–7 to avoid expressing them as absolute facts. Use the hedging language in brackets.

Example: The Arctic Ocean is emitting substantial amounts of methane. (seems to)
The Arctic Ocean seems to be emitting substantial amounts of methane.

1 A volcanic eruption in the Antarctic will cause sea levels to rise considerably. (could)
2 Drought is the major problem in parts of sub-Saharan Africa. (seems to)
3 The surface of the planet Mercury is covered in craters. (appears to)
4 The first tools used by humans are over 2.5 million years old. (may)
5 The brain uses up to about a fifth of the body's total energy consumption. (can)
6 University applications are increasing. (it appears)
7 Population growth in China is slowing down. (it seems)

TASK 4 Writing a paragraph expressing stance

1 Read Paragraph 3, based on the essay title below. Note down which stance the writer takes.

TITLE: *'Due to limited resources, and an environment that is changing for the worse, humans need to make bold technological decisions to survive.' Do you agree or disagree with the statement?*

Sample answer: page 160

Paragraph 3

New research shows that widespread flooding will be a consequence of global warming in Europe by as soon as 2050. Tens of millions of people are at risk and dozens of cities across Europe will have to build defences to protect against rising sea levels. This kind of construction will only be possible if we use new technologies to our advantage. During previous floods, traditional methods of dealing with the problems have completely failed.

2 Underline the words / phrases in Paragraph 3 that could be hedged.

Example: *New research shows that widespread flooding will be a consequence of global warming in Europe by as soon as 2050.*

3 Rewrite Paragraph 3 using appropriate hedging language.

Example: *New research suggests widespread flooding could be a consequence of global warming in Europe by as soon as 2050.*

4 Read the essay title again. Note down three examples to support a stance that (a) agrees and (b) disagrees with the statement.

Example: *Agree – building more nuclear power stations will help generate more energy.*
Disagree – we need to limit pollution by using solar power, etc.

5 Write a paragraph of about 80 words using your notes. Make sure it includes:

1 your stance
2 an example with supporting evidence
3 at least three examples of hedging language.

INDEPENDENT STUDY

It is important that you become familiar with a range of language for expressing stance.

▶ **Think about your own stance on a current issue in the news. Write two sentences that express this stance. Then exchange your sentences with a partner and compare your ideas.**

TASK 5 Evaluating writing

1 Work in pairs. Read your partner's paragraph. Check that they have:

- expressed their stance ☐
- used appropriate hedging language. ☐

5D Vocabulary

TASK 1 Vocabulary related to research

1 All the words in the list come from Unit 5. Select an appropriate word to complete the paragraphs.

contributed range conduct factor effects conditions measure existing

The aim of the study was to examine the [1] .... of air pollution on the local environment. Since the [2] .... data was out of date, having been recorded in 2006, the researchers decided to [3] .... new experiments. They used a [4] .... of tools to [5] .... air pollution in the city.

Car use was found to be the main [6] .... that [7] .... to increased air pollution. However, the researchers also found that levels of air pollution varied according to the weather [8] ....

TASK 2 Vocabulary-building: Noun suffixes

Noun suffixes

A noun suffix can be added to an adjective or verb to change it to a noun. The adjective or verb is the *root word*. Some common noun suffixes are ***-ity***, ***-tion***, ***-ment***.

The suffix *-ity* can be added to some adjectives, e.g. *practical* → *practical**ity***

The form of some adjectives changes when *-ity* is added, e.g. *able* → *abil**ity***, *possible* → *possibil**ity***

The suffix *-tion* can be added to some verbs. With *-tion* the final *-e* of the verb is usually dropped, e.g. *complete* → *comple**tion***

The suffix *-ment* can be added to some verbs. With *-ment* the final *-e* of the verb is not usually dropped, e.g. *move* → *move**ment***

1 Look at the nouns below. Identify:

a which part is the root word

b which part is the noun suffix

Example: *encouragement*

relocation majority agreement activity suggestion statement

2 Complete sentences 1–5 by adding the correct suffix to each root word.

1 The scientists found that a small (minor) .... of subjects did not respond to the treatment.

2 The study investigated the .... (contribute) of parents in children's .... (educate).

3 Over a period of two months, they observed an (improve) .... in the participants' behaviour.

4 There was no difference between the (able) .... of the two groups.

5 The low level of productivity was a result of poor (manage) ....

TASK 3 Noun and verbs with the same form

1 Some nouns have the same form as the verb, e.g. *to change* and *a change*. Read sentence pairs 1–3. Note whether the words in bold are nouns or verbs.

1 a The experiments had a great **influence** on social scientists.
b The experiments still **influence** the way research is conducted today.

2 a The wells **supply** water to all the neighbouring villages.
b The villages have secured their water **supply** for the future.

3 a There was no **change** in the participants' behaviour.
b The researchers wanted to know if the participants' behaviour would **change**.

INDEPENDENT STUDY

When you learn a noun, make sure you learn words that naturally go before and after it, e.g. *a majority of*, *an improvement in*.

▸ **As you read academic texts, start making a list of these combinations in a notebook.**

5E Academic Language Check

TASK 1 Expressing stance

1 Put the words into the correct order to make sentences that express stance.

1 just 10,000 blue whales worldwide / says / Greenpeace / may / there / be / that
2 that / deforestation / view / must / is / Most experts' / slow down
3 believes / Evans (2014) / many species / may / that / soon become extinct
4 Peterson / humans must one day / to / According / another planet / colonize
5 the research findings / that / notes / Smith (2012) / inconsistent / are
6 not reliable / claim / are / the survey findings / that / Harris and Jones
7 research / perhaps / that of Roberts and Hick / The most important / was
8 risk losing / clearly / their habitats / A number of species

TASK 2 Agreeing and disagreeing

1 Complete dialogues 1 and 2 using the words in the list.

don't agree think don't think seems

1 **A** I [1] .... an open-plan working environment is best. You know, when all the desks are in one big, open room.
B I [2] .... I could never work in a place like that. It [3] .... to me that people are afraid to talk to each other. I [4] .... it's very relaxing at all.

agree and but right to me think (x2)

2 **A** It seems [5] .... that shale gas could be the solution to some countries' energy challenges in the future.
B Yes, I [6] .... you're [7] .... But there's a lot of opposition to it in some countries. Extracting the gas can be dangerous to the local environment.
A Yes, [8] .... the risk is very small.
B I [9] .... Personally, I [10] .... it's worth the risk.
A Yes, [11] .... it produces less pollution, too.

TASK 3 Hedging

1 Rewrite statements 1–8 to avoid expressing them as absolute facts. Begin with the word given and use the hedging word in brackets.

1 Average life expectancy will soon be over 100. (could)
Average ....
2 The number of different natural habitats is decreasing. (seems)
It ....
3 The results of the study are inconclusive. (appear)
The ....
4 Many of the world's rainforests will one day disappear completely. (may)
Many ....
5 The physical workplace greatly affects a worker's performance. (appears)
It ....
6 Humans are destroying much of the planet. (seem)
Humans ....
7 There will be a manned trip to Mars before 2050. (likely)
It ....
8 Global temperatures are rising faster than ever. (thought)
Global ....

UNIT 6 Science

ACADEMIC FOCUS: PERSPECTIVE

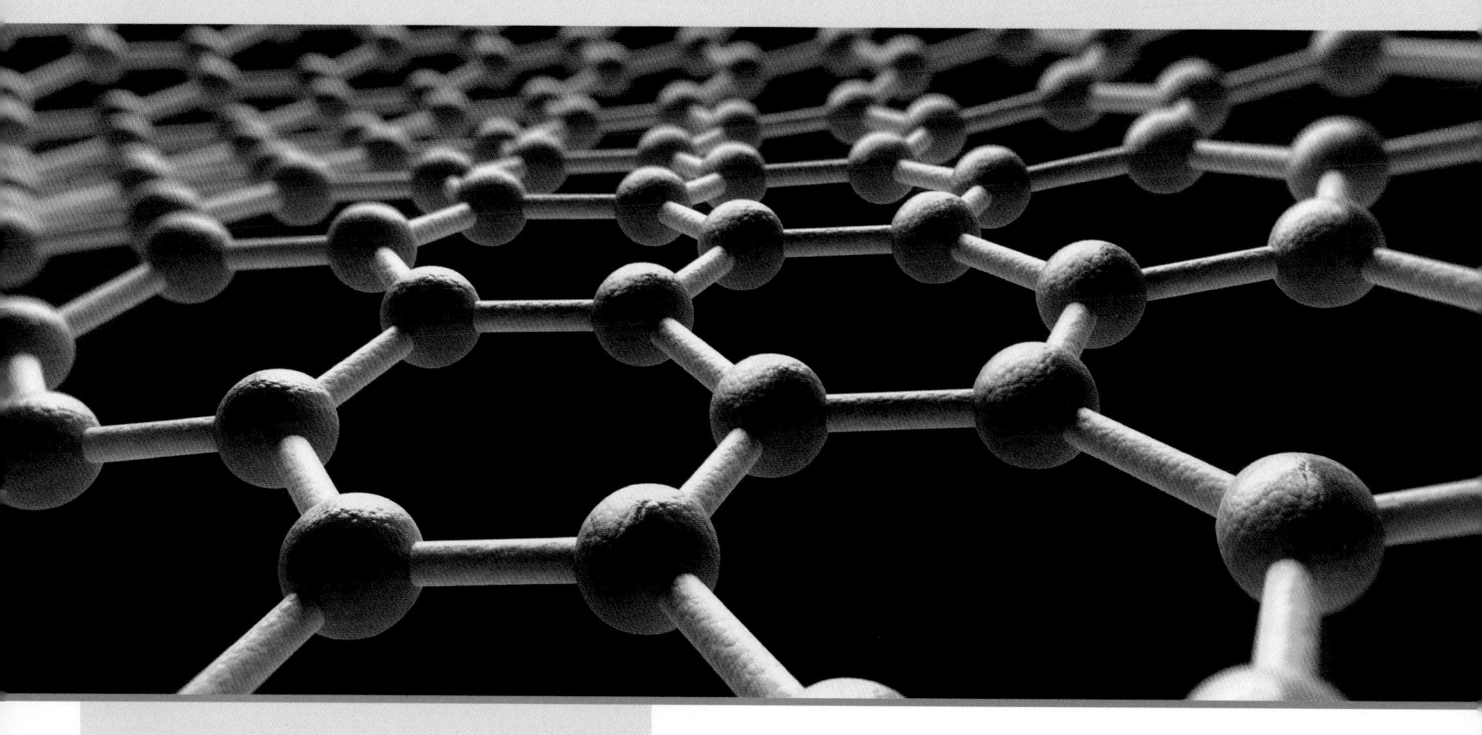

LEARNING OBJECTIVES

This unit covers:

Listening and Speaking
- Recognizing perspectives in a lecture
- Using abbreviations to take notes
- Identifying perspectives in a presentation
- Presenting an idea from a range of perspectives

Reading
- Identifying perspectives in a text
- Using perspectives to understand a text

Writing
- Identifying topic sentences in a paragraph
- Writing topic sentences
- Identifying concluding sentences
- Writing a paragraph with topic and concluding sentences

Vocabulary
- Vocabulary-building: Adjective and adverb formation
- Vocabulary-building: Multi-part verbs

Academic Language Check
- Abbreviations in note-taking
- Expressing perspective
- Topic and concluding sentences

Discussion

1 Read the definition of *perspective* and note down three more perspectives.

> **perspective** (*n*) the direction from which you view or approach an idea, fact, or situation, e.g. political, medical, economic, geographical

2 Complete statements 1–5 with the correct adjective.

economic industrial medical social environmental

1 Science is important from an .... perspective because it helps countries to develop and become richer.
2 From a .... perspective, science has allowed us to overcome disease and to live longer.
3 Some people blame science and technology for causing pollution. But science has also helped the world from an .... perspective by creating cleaner fuels.
4 From an .... perspective, science and technology have allowed us to mass produce goods.
5 Science is important from a .... perspective because it has changed the way we live and interact.

3 Work in pairs. Select which of statements 1–5 you most agree with. Give reasons.

4 Work in groups. Explain why your own area of study is important. Use the perspectives below.

Example: *The study of chemistry is important from an economic perspective because ...*

economic industrial health social environmental

6A Listening & Speaking Lectures (4)

This module covers:

- Recognizing perspectives in a lecture
- Using abbreviations to take notes
- Identifying perspectives in a presentation
- Presenting an idea from a range of perspectives

TASK 1 Preparing for a lecture

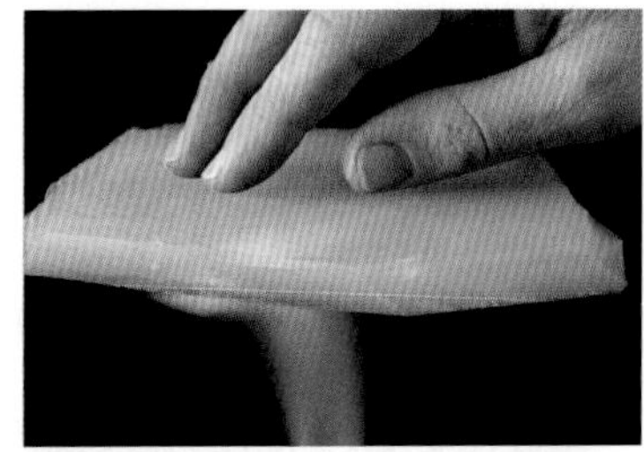

Aerogel an extremely light and strong material which stops heat getting through it

1 You are going to watch part of a lecture on new materials. The words in bold in sentences 1–4 are key terms. Match them with the definitions.

1 Copper is a highly **conductive** metal.
2 The radioactive elements like uranium are the least **stable**.
3 The cover of the book is made with a **flexible** plastic coating.
4 Researchers were unable to **isolate** the virus from the surrounding cells.

.... (*v*) separate sth physically from other things
.... (*adj*) able to conduct electricity, heat, etc.
.... (*adj*) steady, firm, and unlikely to change
.... (*adj*) able to bend easily without breaking

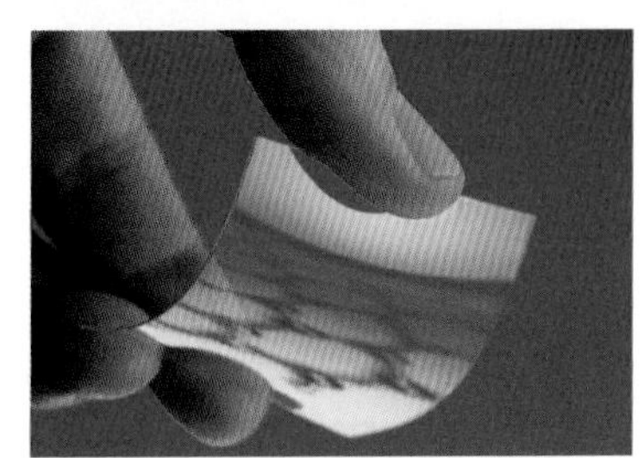

Graphene a very thin, lightweight, and flexible material which is highly conductive

2 Read the notes on three recently discovered materials. Match each material with a use a–c.

a used as a material to make car tyres grip roads better
b used as a cover for equipment during space exploration
c used as a material to make flexible smartphones and tablets

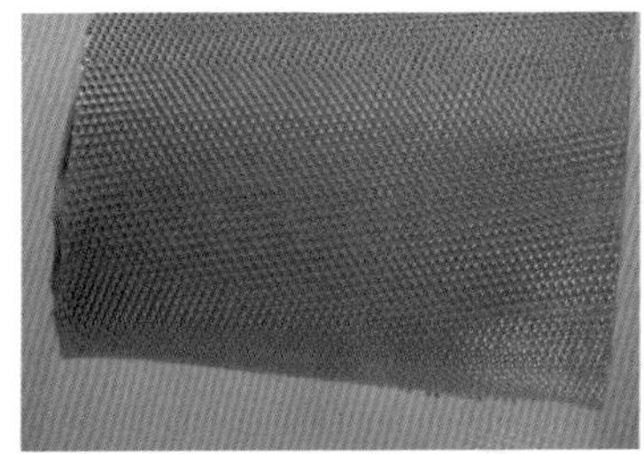

Gecko tape a thin, flexible material which can stick to most surfaces

3 Work in pairs. Discuss possible benefits of each material from perspectives a–d.

a industry b fashion c safety d transport

Example: *Products made from graphene will be cheaper for businesses to transport, because they are light.*

TASK 2 Noting down the main ideas in a lecture

1 6.1 Watch Extract 1 of the lecture. Complete the notes.

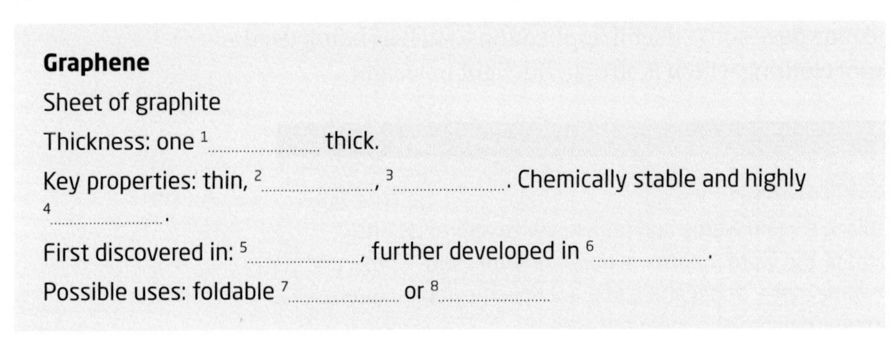

Graphene
Sheet of graphite
Thickness: one [1].................. thick.
Key properties: thin, [2].................., [3].................. . Chemically stable and highly [4].................. .
First discovered in: [5].................., further developed in [6].................. .
Possible uses: foldable [7].................. or [8]..................

2 Work in groups. Think of three more uses of graphene from a commercial perspective.

3 6.2 **Watch Extract 2 and complete Diagram 1.**

TASK 3 Recognizing different perspectives in a lecture

1 6.3 **Watch Extract 3. Tick three perspectives mentioned by the lecturer.**

chemical ☐
commercial ☐
physical ☐
historical ☐
industrial ☐

2 6.3 **Watch Extract 3 again. Note down what the lecturer says about graphene from each perspective you ticked in 1.**

ACADEMIC LANGUAGE ▸ Language reference page 155

Perspective (1) Expressing spoken perspective

Often in lectures (and in texts) you will find words that tell you the perspective from which something is being described. To provide the context when talking about perspectives, use adverbs and adverbial phrases. For example:

Graphene is also extremely strong and ***chemically*** *stable.*
Historically*, graphene was difficult to isolate.*
From a commercial perspective*, this represents a much better solution.*
In practical terms*, it just takes too long to produce graphene in this way.*

Geim's technique: mechanical exfoliation

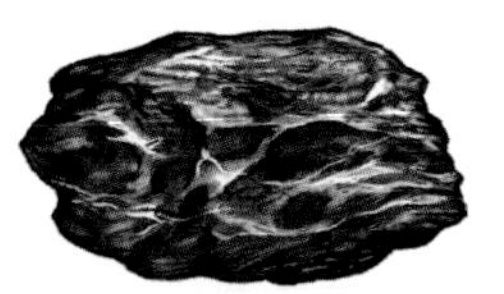

begins with 25mm graphite

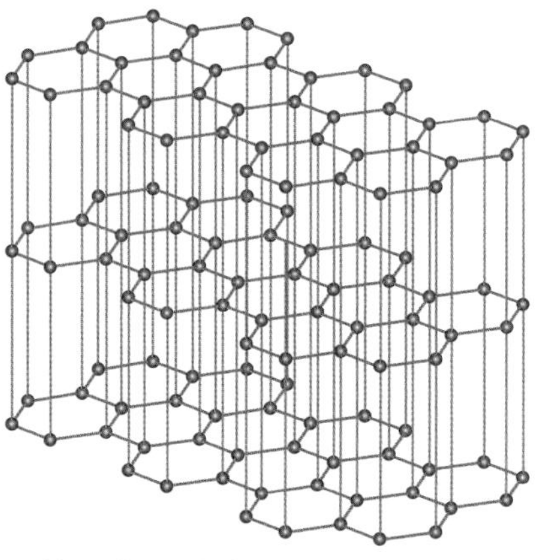

graphite split to make [1] ....

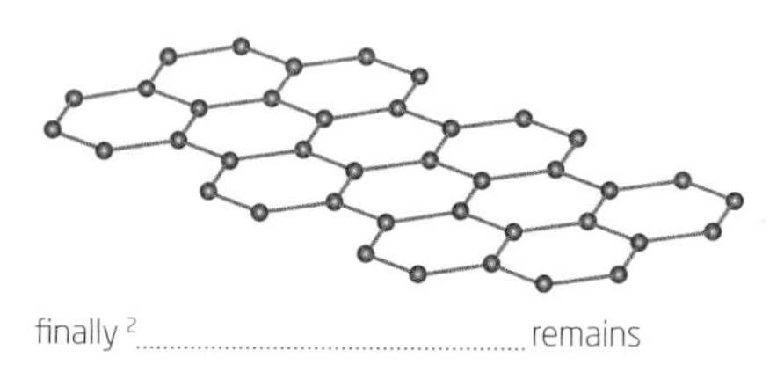

finally [2] .... remains

Diagram 1

TASK 4 Expressing perspectives

1 **Complete statements 1–4 using the words / phrases from the list.**

environmentally   industrially   in political terms   militarily

1 Graphene production has not made a real difference .... because the process of making it on a large scale has not been perfected.
2 Graphene has become important ...., because each government wants its own country to be the first to develop it.
3 ...., graphene should have great benefits, because lighter materials generally mean less energy use.
4 ...., graphene may have some useful applications, such as being used to make protective or bulletproof clothing which is strong, but light in weight.

ACADEMIC LANGUAGE

Note-taking (3) Abbreviations and symbols

When you make notes, you can replace certain words and phrases with abbreviations. Some of these are a shortened form of the word (*approx. = approximately, diff = different, uni = university, yrs = years, lge = large, sm = small*) and some are specific abbreviations (*e.g. = for example*). Some of the more common abbreviations are:

Abbreviation	Meaning	Example
i.e.	that is / in other words	*Foldable screens for mobile devices, i.e. computers + tablets*
etc.	et cetera, and so on	*Industrial metals: iron, steel, etc.*

TASK 5 Using abbreviations

1 Rewrite sentences 1–5 as notes using abbreviations.

1 Research was led by a large team from Durham University.
2 Approximately three hundred people were interviewed.
3 The three US west coast states, that is, Washington, Oregon, and California are ...
4 The study in Seattle tested twenty different metals.
5 The roman alphabet is not used in certain languages, for example Arabic, Russian, Japanese, and so on.

2 6.4 Listen to Extract 4. Complete the notes using abbreviations.

1 Aim of study: ....
2 Professor Shackelford ....
3 Most students ....

TASK 6 Taking notes on key perspectives

1 6.3 Watch Extract 3 again and complete the notes using abbreviations.

Northwestern [1] .... developed [2] .... process of graphene production, [3] .... putting graphite in solution – produces graphene flakes. Mixed with ink and printed on plastic, clothing, [4] .... Uses [5] .... foldable screens.

TASK 7 Recognizing perspectives in a presentation

1 6.5 Watch Extract 5, a student presentation about concrete. Tick the perspectives which are discussed.

☐	chemical	☐	historical	☐	commercial	☐	industrial
☐	visual	☐	environmental	☐	practical	☐	scientific

2 Note down which perspectives in 1 view concrete positively.

3 6.5 Watch Extract 5 again and complete sentences 1–5.

1 .... , it has been the main building material for large-scale construction.
2 The largest sector of the concrete market, ready-mix, is worth approximately $100 billion. So, in that respect, it's been .... very successful.
3 In .... terms, concrete is a versatile substance – you can build quickly with it, it's strong, and it lasts a long time.
4 There are, however, some .... impacts. Producing and transporting concrete uses a lot of energy.
5 A lot of people who would say that, ... , concrete isn't very attractive.

4 Work in pairs. Practise presenting a substance from different perspectives. Student A: turn to page 163. Student B: turn to page 165.

TASK 8 Presenting using perspectives

1 Work in pairs. Prepare to make a short presentation. Use steps 1–3.

1 Note down a material that is used in your area of study, or one you are familiar with.
2 Note down at least four perspectives to use in your presentation.
3 Decide if each perspective is mostly positive or negative.

2 Listen to your partner's presentation and evaluate it. Did they:

- present their topic using a range of perspectives?
- use the language of perspectives correctly?

INDEPENDENT STUDY

It is important to consider the perspective from which you are arguing a particular point: *economic, historical, technical*, etc.

▶ **Think about a recent decision that has been made. Describe to your partner whether you think it is a good or a bad decision. Note down the perspectives from which you think it is good or bad.**

6B Reading Textbooks (5)

This module covers:

- Identifying perspectives in a text
- Using perspectives to understand a text

TASK 1 Previewing the theme of a text

1 Work in pairs and discuss the questions.

- What are the three major branches of scientific study? Which of them have you studied?
- Which branches of scientific study do images A–C represent?

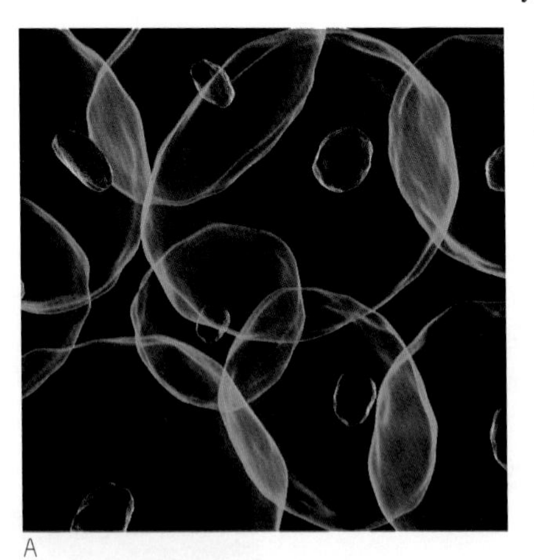
A

B

C

TASK 2 Understanding the main ideas of a text

1 You are going to read the introduction to a chemistry textbook. Decide which of the following topics you expect the introduction to include.

a a definition of chemistry ☐
b a description of a chemical element ☐
c profiles of some important chemists ☐
d a historical perspective of the study of chemistry ☐
e a description of some important chemical processes ☐
f positive and negative uses of chemistry knowledge ☐
g the importance of ethics in chemistry ☐

2 Read Text 1. Tick the topics in 1 that are included.

3 Match five of topics a–g with Paragraphs 1–5 in Text 1.

Para 1 .... Para 2 .... Para 3 .... Para 4 .... Para 5 ....

TASK 3 Identifying perspective language

1 Text 1 considers chemistry from a number of different perspectives. Identify the paragraphs that discuss perspectives 1–5.

1 historical 2 health 3 environmental 4 global 5 ethical

2 Note down the words / phrases in Text 1 that introduce perspectives 1–5.

Example: *Historically, chemistry is one of the oldest scientific disciplines.*

TEXT 1

Studying the Elements

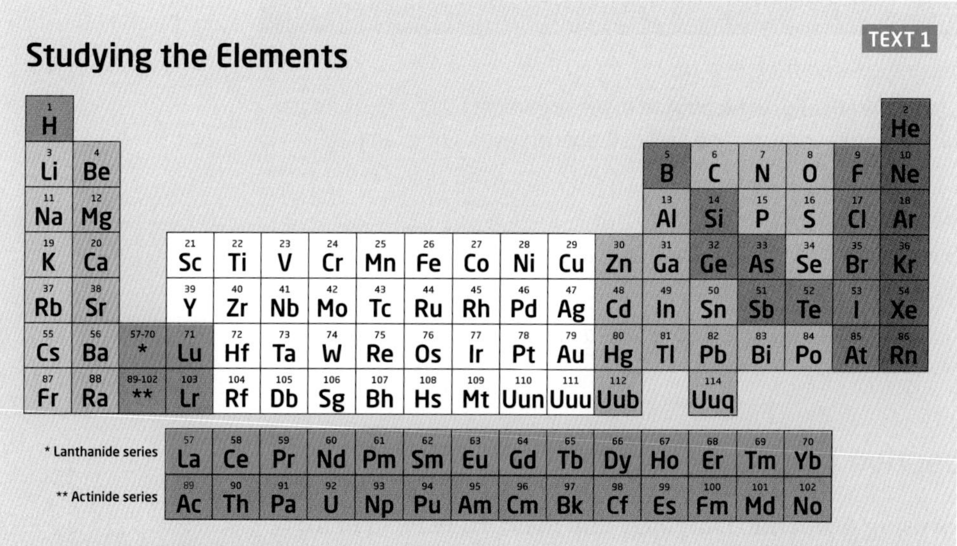

1 Elements are the simplest form of matter. They cannot be chemically broken down into anything simpler. There are over 100 elements and everything on Earth - the rocks beneath our feet, the air we breathe, the water we drink, the clothes we wear, even our own bodies - is made up of some combination of these chemical elements. They are the building blocks of the physical world and of all life in it.

2 The study of the elements - their individual properties, the reactions between them and the compounds they form - is what constitutes the subject of Chemistry.

3 Historically, chemistry is one of the oldest scientific disciplines. In terms of our understanding of the elements, some of the less reactive elements, such as copper and gold, have been analysed and made use of for centuries. Others, such as the artificial elements copernicum and ununseptium, have been discovered only in the last few years and relatively little is known about them.

4 The study of chemistry has had an enormous impact on society. Much of this is positive. As far as our health is concerned, we now enjoy longer life expectancy and a better quality of life. Reasons for this include the chemical treatment of water to produce safe drinking water, the synthesis of antibiotics and other drugs to combat previously lethal diseases, and the use of chemical fertilizers to grow more food. At the same time, we face the challenges caused by the negative influences of chemistry and the manipulation of the elements. In terms of the environment, the pollution of water, air, and the ground, particularly in less developed countries where environmental controls are less strict, is a major problem. From a more global point of view, the increase in carbon dioxide emissions, leading to global warming, is an increasingly important issue.

5 From an ethical perspective, there are many other issues resulting from the negative impact of advances in our understanding of chemistry. For example, should the commercialization of chemistry allow pharmaceutical companies to charge high prices for medicines which many people need but not everyone can afford? And should our knowledge of chemistry be used to produce harmful weapons and explosives?

SOURCE: Neuss, G. (2007). p.006. *IB Chemistry: Course Companion*. Oxford: Oxford University Press.

GLOSSARY

artificial *(adj)* created by people, not occurring naturally

building blocks *(n)* parts that are joined together in order to form a larger thing

combat *(v)* to fight against something

compound *(n)* a substance formed by a chemical reaction between two or more elements

lethal *(adj)* causing death

matter *(n)* a physical substance

TASK 4 Using perspectives to understand the content of a text

1 Read Paragraphs 3–5 of Text 1 again. Note down in column A of the table whether the author's view of chemistry is mostly: (a) positive, (b) negative, or (c) neutral.

Paragraph	Perspective	Column A Positive / Negative / Neutral	Column B Supporting idea / Example
3	Historical		
4	Social (health, environment, etc.)		
5	Ethical		

2 Note down supporting ideas and examples in column B of the table.

ACADEMIC LANGUAGE

▸ Language reference page 155

Perspective (2) Expressing perspective in a text

As well as using adverbs (e.g. **chemically**, **ethically**) to express perspectives, nouns and adjectives can be used with adverbial clauses and prepositional phrases. For example:

Adverbial clauses

From an *ethical* ***perspective****, there are many other issues ...*

As far as *our health* ***is concerned****, we now enjoy longer life expectancy ...*

Prepositional phrases

In terms of *the environment, the pollution of water ... is a major problem.*

TASK 5 Using perspective language

1 Complete the sentences using Academic Language and the correct form of the word in brackets.

1 .... perspective, it is likely that coins were first used as an expression of thanks. (historical)

2 .... is concerned, there needs to be a number of changes to the device. (safety)

3 In ...., the software delivers excellent performance. (value)

4 ...., laser eye surgery is a relatively simple procedure. (technical)

5 The film is .... inaccurate in a number of instances. (factual)

6 .... perspective, research demonstrates that girls and boys do equally well in co-educational institutions. (education)

2 Complete the student text with the perspective language from the list.

environmentally   in ethical terms   historically   from a social perspective
in terms of engineering   physically

Text 2

[1] ...., gold is one of the most significant elements known to mankind. For many thousands of years it has been exchanged and traded for goods, and used for jewellery and decoration. The first gold coins were made in Asia Minor in 600 BCE, and from the 13th century gold became a way for most European economies to measure their strength.

[2] ...., gold is a very dense material. However, it is also very soft. This means it can easily be made into many different forms – a gram of gold can be beaten into a thin 1m² sheet. Gold is also able to reflect infrared light. Due to these qualities, gold has many uses [3] .... NASA use gold coating on their space telescopes and spacesuit sun-visors to protect from the damaging rays of infrared radiation. This same principle is used in many modern buildings. Gold plating in windows reflects heat radiation, helping to keep buildings cool in summer and warm in winter. [4] .... this is beneficial, as it lowers energy costs and reduces carbon emissions.

[5] ...., gold is considered a luxury item in most parts of the world, and owning it gives people a lot of status. This has meant that the price of gold has stayed high while other materials change price quite dramatically over time.

[6] .... gold, and gold mining in particular, has faced a lot of criticism. Many of the people who mine gold in central Africa are badly affected by the chemicals used to extract gold, and the pollution that comes from mines. This has led many NGOs (Non-Governmental Organizations) to call for better working conditions for the labourers. The gold mining industry hopes that these initiatives will move the focus from morality, and back to an appreciation of a mineral that has changed so many lives.

GLOSSARY

appreciation *(n)* pleasure in the good qualities of sth

extract *(v)* to remove or take out

initiatives *(n)* new plans for dealing with a problem

significant *(adj)* important enough to have an effect or be noticed

Gold bullion

Modern gold miners

3 Work in pairs. Discuss which perspectives in Text 2 view gold (a) positively or (b) negatively.

4 Note down the ideas used to support each perspective in 3.

TASK 6 Critical thinking – reflecting on perspectives in a text

1 Work in pairs. Read the student notes on four other elements. Discuss the importance of each element from at least two perspectives.

Example: *Aluminium is used to build most kinds of vehicles. From a cultural perspective this allows people to travel the world, and to interact with each other. From a social perspective it means that people can travel further for work, and have more opportunities...*

Element	Symbol	Main uses
Aluminium	Al	transportation – cars, trains, planes, etc. all made using aluminium packaging for food – cans, aluminium foil, etc.
Copper	Cu	wires and cables – power supply, telecommunications
Iron	Fe	engineering – building bridges + large structures like skyscrapers
Silicon	Si	design – clay, ceramic, stone for building electronics – circuits in computers and other electronic devices

2 Work with another pair. Compare your ideas.

3 Work in groups. Look back at Text 1 on page 083. Do you agree with statements 1 and 2? Give reasons.

1 Drug companies should be allowed to charge high prices for life-saving medicines. They are private businesses, and have a right to be commercially successful.

2 It is acceptable for highly skilled scientists to use their knowledge to make weapons.

INDEPENDENT STUDY

Perspective may be expressed in different ways and it is important to recognize these when reading a text.

▸ Find a text that describes a recent action or event and identify the perspectives which the writer uses to describe it.

6C Writing (1) Topic sentences

This module covers:

- Identifying topic sentences in a paragraph
- Writing topic sentences

TASK 1 Identifying topic sentences

1 A topic sentence is often the first sentence in a paragraph, and expresses the topic of that paragraph. Read Paragraph 1 and identify the topic sentence.

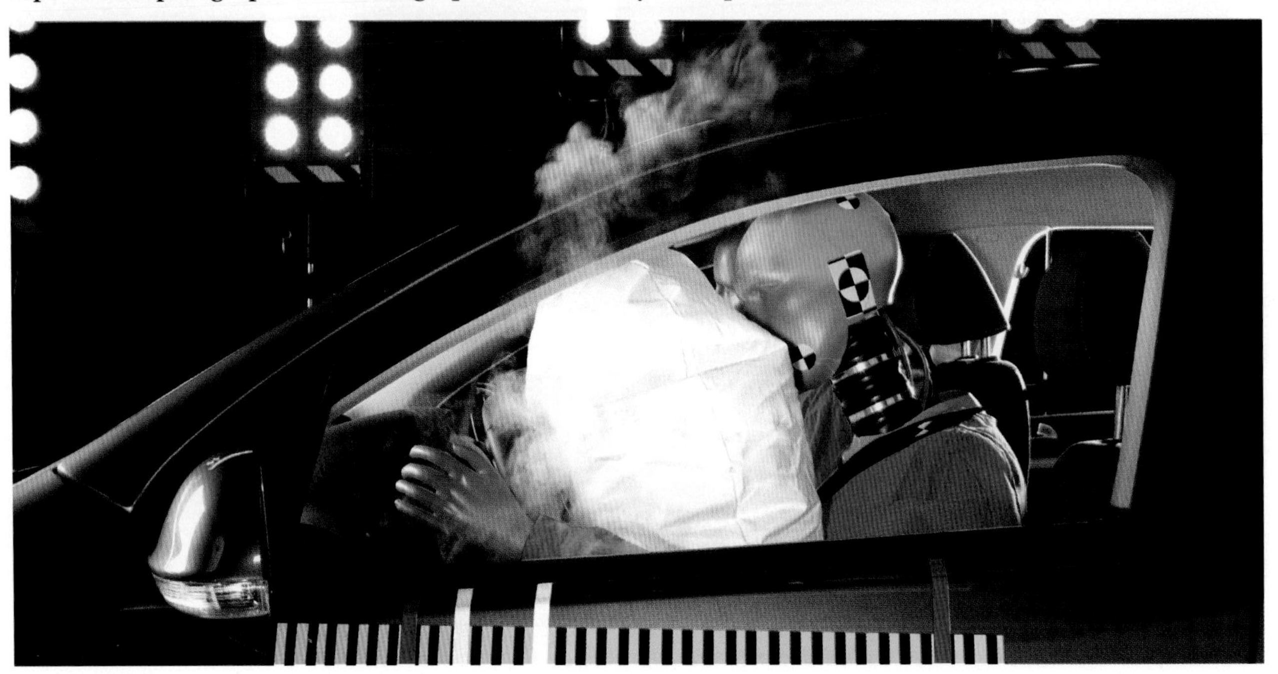

Paragraph 1

[1]Chemical reactions and processes occur at different speeds. [2]An example of a very fast reaction is the rapid inflation of airbags used in automobiles. [3]Sodium azide and potassium nitrate react to produce nitrogen gas, which inflates the bag instantly, before the driver can hit the steering wheel. [4]Other reactions are much slower. [5]For instance, the reaction to produce ethyl ethanoate, which is used to make artificial smells and flavours, usually takes several days.

GLOSSARY

inflate *(v)* to fill something with air or gas

reaction *(n)* a chemical change produced by two or more substances coming into contact with each other

2 Read Paragraph 1 again. Note down:

1 two examples of types of chemical reaction
2 the words / phrases used to introduce the example.

3 Read Paragraph 2, a later paragraph from the same text. Complete it with the most appropriate topic sentence a–c.

Paragraph 2

[1]Chemists often wish to speed reactions up so that they can make products faster.
[2] ....
[3]They do this by using 'inhibitors'. [4]Inhibitors are substances that slow down or prevent a chemical reaction. [5]An example is the antioxidants used in the food industry to extend the life of food sold in supermarkets.

a But first it is necessary to understand what is meant by the rate of reaction.
b However, there are some reactions that chemists deliberately try to slow down.
c There are often strong commercial reasons for doing this.

4 **Sentences 3–5 in Paragraph 2 support the topic sentence. Select which sentence gives:**

a an example to illustrate the main idea

b an explanation of how chemists do something

c a definition of a key term.

5 **Read sentences a–d. Identify the topic sentence and decide on the best order for the four sentences.**

a This is when molecules are given less space to move in, and collide more often.

b Most of these faster reactions involve gases.

c There are several ways to make a reaction faster.

d One way is to increase the pressure around the reactants.

TASK 2 Writing topic sentences

1 **Read Paragraph 3, then use the prompts to write a topic sentence.**

Paragraph 3

(one / common / example reaction / oxidation) ....

Oxidation occurs when substances react to oxygen in the air. Oxidation can be seen with metals which rust over time. Another familiar example is aging fruit, which becomes brown and decays very quickly when its protective skin is broken.

2 **Read Paragraph 4 and complete the topic sentence.**

Paragraph 4

It is important ....

The chemicals in household cleaning products may be safe when they are used independently, but can be very dangerous in combination with other chemicals. An example of this is mixing vinegar and bleach. When these two substances react, toxic chlorine gas is released. Therefore, people should always read the labels on household products to avoid such accidents.

3 **Work in pairs. Compare your topic sentences in 1 and 2. Note down similarities and differences.**

6C Writing (2) Topic and concluding sentences

This module covers:

- Identifying concluding sentences
- Writing a paragraph with topic and concluding sentences

TASK 1 Recognizing topic and concluding sentences

1 Read Paragraph 5. Select the sentence a–c that best describes the main idea of the paragraph.

Paragraph 5

[1]There seem to be significant individual differences in people's awareness of the smells around them. [2]Whereas some individuals comment frequently on the smell of food or the smell of the flowers in the garden, others only notice these features when they are pointed out to them. [3]This characteristic is called 'odour awareness'. [4]Individual differences in odour awareness are related either to an individual's ability to smell or to an individual's sensitivity to smells compared to other stimuli, such as sights and sounds.

a Some people are more sensitive to certain smells than other people are.
b Some people are particularly sensitive to different stimuli, e.g. smells, sights, sounds.
c Some people are more conscious of smells in the environment than others.

2 Identify the topic sentence in Paragraph 5.

3 Sentence 4 is the concluding sentence of the paragraph. Match it to a function a–c.

The concluding sentence:

a repeats the main idea exactly
b repeats and develops the main idea
c questions the main idea.

TASK 2 Understanding paragraph structure

1 Read Paragraph 6. Match sentences 1–4 with features a–d.

Paragraph 6

[1]Being able to measure a person's level of odour awareness may be useful in a number of ways. [2]Doing this may, for example, help to reduce the bad effects that certain negative smells have on people. [3]From a commercial perspective, it may help businesses to understand how people notice and react to different smells. [4]As the value of odour awareness becomes more obvious, researchers are spending more time exploring the area – in fact a team at Utrecht University have developed a questionnaire, the Odour Awareness Scale (OAS), that could be used by health organizations and businesses to measure differences in odour awareness.

a development: to develop the main point with an example ....
b topic sentence: to introduce the topic of the paragraph ....
c development: to develop the main point with reference to a perspective ....
d concluding sentence: to restate the main point and offer brief evaluation ....

2 Which extra information does the concluding sentence give to develop the main idea?

TASK 3 Writing concluding sentences

1 Read Paragraph 7. Choose the best concluding sentence: (a), (b), or (c).

Paragraph 7

In terms of scientific research, there are a number of existing questionnaires about the effects of smell. Most of these tend to focus on psychological rather than physiological effects. For example, the Affective Impact of Odour Scale (Wrzesniewski et al. 1999) considers how our memories are affected by smells. ....

a By focusing on physiological effects, however, the OAS questionnaire provides a new range of data.
b However, the data from the OAS questionnaire is more reliable.
c However, the data from the OAS questionnaire looks at physiology.

2 Complete the concluding sentence for Paragraph 8.

Paragraph 8

The study also looked at the relationship between people with a high level of odour awareness and general health. When the researchers analysed data from employees in a chemical factory, it found a higher incidence of illness in those employees who were found to be sensitive to bad smells. The same was true for people who lived in the area around the factory. From such analysis it seems that

....

TASK 4 Writing a paragraph using topic and concluding sentences

1 Number sentences a–d in order to make a paragraph.

a Testing is a key stage in the construction of a good questionnaire. *1*
b Once the testing is completed, the questionnaire can then be sent to all the participants. ....
c Any 'bad' questions can then be removed. ....
d When questions have been written, they are tested on a small sample of participants to see if the results are consistent. ....

2 Write a paragraph of about 80 words, including at least four sentences. Use guidelines 1–4 to help you plan the paragraph.

1 Begin your paragraph with topic sentence (a) or (b):
   a Studying abroad can give you valuable experience in your future life.
   b Studying a science can help you to contribute to a better society.
2 Include an example to develop the main point.
3 Include a perspective to develop the main point.
4 Include a conclusion to restate the main point and offer brief evaluation.

Sample answer: page 160

INDEPENDENT STUDY

The main points in paragraphs are often indicated by the use of topic sentences and concluding sentences.

▶ Look at two or more paragraphs in a textbook that you are using at the moment. Try to identify topic sentences and concluding sentences.

TASK 5 Evaluating your writing

1 Read your paragraph from Task 4. Check that you have:

- provided an example to develop the main point ☐
- referred to a perspective to develop the main point ☐
- provided a conclusion restating the main point and offering brief evaluations. ☐

6D Vocabulary

TASK 1 Vocabulary-building: Adjective and adverb formation

1 Complete the table.

Noun	Adjective	Adverb
commerce	....	commercially
emotion	....	....
politics	....	....
....	historical	....
industry	....	....
psychology	....	....
technology	....	technologically
chemistry	....	....
machine	mechanical	....

2 Use the correct form of the word given to complete sentences 1–8.

1 From a .... point of view, graphene has enormous potential. (commerce)
2 ...., failing an exam can be very damaging. (psychology)
3 In its ...., a lipid is similar to a carbohydrate. (chemistry)
4 From a .... perspective, the moon landing was a great success. (politics)
5 The discovery of shale gas gave a great boost to .... (industry)
6 ...., the Rhine is the most important river for trade in Europe. (history)
7 ...., Japan is one of the most advanced nations on Earth. (technology)
8 From a .... point of view, mountain formation is a simple process. (mechanics)

3 Write four sentences describing a topic from perspectives in 2.

INDEPENDENT STUDY

When you look up a word in the dictionary, look at the words related to it in different word classes, e.g. *electrical* (a.), *electric* (a.), *electricity* (n.), *electrically* (adv.)

TASK 2 Vocabulary-building: Multi-part verbs

Multi-part verbs

A multi-part verb is a verb + particle which combine to give a meaning different from the meaning of the verb and the particle taken separately. For example:

Elements are the simplest form of matter. They cannot be chemically broken down into anything simpler. Here *broken down* means *separated.*

1 Replace the verbs in bold in sentences 1–6 with the correct form of a multi-part verb in the list. Use a dictionary to help you if necessary.

break down find out look at look into make up set up

1 NASA scientists are hoping to **discover** .... more about why water disappeared from the surface of Mars.
2 Currently 118 elements **constitute** .... the periodic table.
3 Researchers at Harvard University are **investigating** .... 'smart' drugs that respond to patients' specific physiology.
4 Normal cells produce proteins called enzymes which **separate into smaller parts** .... cells and other tissue.
5 The European Organization for Nuclear Research (CERN) was **established** .... in 1952.
6 Scientists are **studying** .... new ways of turning plant material into fuel.

INDEPENDENT STUDY

When you come across an unfamiliar multi-part verb, try to work out the meaning from the context. Then check in a dictionary. Make a note of any new multi-part verbs.

6E Academic Language Check

TASK 1 Abbreviations in note-taking

1 Make notes on this extract from a speech by (a) deleting unnecessary words and (b) replacing underlined words with abbreviations.

'The study at Heidelberg University investigated lucid dreaming (LD), that is to say dreams which the dreamer is aware of. Approximately 300 participants were questioned. It was found that they used lucid dreaming for different reasons, for example solving problems, getting new ideas, and also increasing performance. It seems lucid dreaming is very useful in sports training: learning new techniques, or making small improvements in athletic performance.'

TASK 2 Expressing perspective

1 Reorder the words to make sentences expressing perspective. Begin with the words given.

1 perspective / from / a physics / 'light' /, / is a series of particles moving through air
From ....

2 successful / *Pong* was / the world's first / commercially / video game
Pong was ....

3 in / safety / , / of / *Finnair* / terms / is the number one airline
In ....

4 speaking / scientifically /, / the experiment / was a great success
Scientifically ....

5 solar energy / concerned / far / , /cost / as / as / is / is / the most economical method
As ....

TASK 3 Topic and concluding sentences

1 Complete the paragraph by adding the topic, main body, and concluding sentences a–f.

a Sources of uranium may one day run out.

b It is therefore a much cleaner and more reliable alternative to conventional fossil fuel energy.

c There are also concerns about nuclear power.

d There are a number of points in favour of nuclear power.

e Until these issues are resolved, reservations about the use of nuclear energy will continue to exist.

f Currently, the nuclear industry stores the waste inside concrete structures.

1 .... It does not use fossil fuels, releases less radioactivity than coal-fired power plants, and it is not affected by changes in oil and gas prices. 2 ....
3 ....
One unanswered problem of nuclear power is what to do with nuclear waste. About 2,000 tons is produced yearly, with nowhere safe to put it.
4 .... In addition, nuclear power relies on uranium, which is not a renewable source of energy.
5 .... Also, nuclear incidents such as Chernobyl in 1986 and Fukushima in 2011 are always a possibility.
6 ....

UNIT 7 Language

ACADEMIC FOCUS: SUMMARIZING AND PARAPHRASING

LEARNING OBJECTIVES

This unit covers:

Listening and Speaking
- Understanding signposting language
- Note-taking (4): Organizing notes into summaries
- Using signposting language
- Giving a summary of a talk

Reading
- Identifying key features of a summary
- Understanding references in a text
- Summarizing information in a text

Writing
- Paraphrasing sentences
- Paraphrasing a paragraph
- Recognizing citation

Vocabulary
- Collocations (3): More verb and noun collocations
- Using synonyms in paraphrasing

Academic Language Check
- Signposting language
- Referring back in a text
- Paraphrasing
- Citation

Discussion

1 Work in pairs. Discuss which of statements 1–3 you most agree with. Give reasons.

1 Powerful people are often good language users.
2 It is very difficult to express emotions using language.
3 You can learn more from people's body language than from the words they use.

2 Work with another pair. Compare your ideas giving examples.

3 Work in groups. Discuss to what extent you agree with the following statement.

'You can only understand a different culture if you can understand its language.'

4 Form new groups. Explain your initial group's main ideas. Use the following phrases.

The main points we discussed were ...

We felt that ...

To sum up, we agree / disagree with the statement because ...

7A Listening & Speaking Lectures (5)

This module covers:

- Understanding signposting language
- Note-taking (4): Organizing notes into summaries
- Using signposting language
- Giving a summary of a talk

TASK 1 Previewing the topic of a lecture

1 Work in pairs. Read the lecture title. Then discuss questions 1 and 2.

> **The significance of names and naming traditions**
>
> **Dr Sam Jarvis**
> Department of Social Sciences
>
> Lecture Hall B9
> 12 October 12.00 – 13.00

1 Where do your first name and surname come from? What is their meaning?
2 How important are names in your country? Do they tell you anything about a person?

2 Read sentences 1–4. Match the definitions to the words in bold.

1 Is your first name from an **ancient** tradition or is it quite modern?
2 What do the letters 'Dr' before a person's name **denote**?
3 Can you think of a name that describes a **trait** in someone's character?
4 Do you think the names you choose for your children can affect their **prospects** in life?

a .... (*v*) to mean, or to be a sign of something
b .... (*adj*) very old
c .... (*n*) the possibility of being successful
d .... (*n*) a quality that forms part of your character or personality

3 Work in pairs. Ask and answer questions 1–4.

TASK 2 Understanding the main idea of a lecture

1 7.1 Watch Extract 1, the introduction to the lecture. Complete the student notes.

> **Subject of lecture:**
> Significance of [1] ....
> **Part one:**
> [2] ....
> **Part two:**
> Naming traditions in [3] .... and [4] ....
> **Final part:**
> How [5] ....
> **Main focus of lecture:**
> [6] ....

2 Check your answers against the transcript on page 172.

TASK 3 Understanding signposting in a lecture

1 The lecturer uses phrases to signpost the structure of the lecture. Complete sentences 1–6.

1 ...., we're going to look at the significance of personal names in different cultures.

2 ...., we need to define our terms.

3 ...., we'll look in detail at naming traditions in two specific cultures.

4 ...., we'll see how these two examples relate to the wider question of the significance of names in society.

5 The .... in this lecture will be given names.

6 But ...., just a brief word about surnames.

2 ▶7.1 Watch Extract 1 again and check your answers.

> **ACADEMIC LANGUAGE**
>
> **Signposting language**
>
> During talks or lectures, speakers often explain what the main content of the talk will be. This is done using signposting language. For example:
>
> **Explaining the content**
>
> *Today, I'd like to talk about ...*
> *We are going to look at ...*
> *The main focus in this lecture will be ...*
>
> **Describing the sequence**
>
> *First, we need to define our terms.*
> *Then, I want to focus on surnames and their historical role.*
> *Finally, we'll see how these two examples relate to ...*

TASK 4 Using notes to complete a summary

1 ▶7.2 Watch Extract 2. Complete the student notes about surnames.

> **Surnames**
>
> Show a person belongs to a group:
>
> 1 .... e.g. MacDonalds in Scotland
> 2 .... e.g. Portuguese Da Silva, Da Costa
> 3 .... e.g. Carpenter
> 4 .... e.g. Eriksson (son of Erik)
>
> - in modern society, imp. for admin reasons
> - not common until 19thc in some cultures, e.g. 5 ....

2 Complete the summary of Extract 2 using your notes from 1.

Surnames show a person belongs to 1 .... This could be a 2 .... group, a 3 .... group, or an occupational group.
Many cultures use 4 .... surnames, based on the 5 ....'s name. In modern society, surnames have 6 .... importance, but are quite 7 .... – in the Netherlands and 8 ...., surnames were not common before the 19th century.

TASK 5 Organizing notes into summaries

1 7.3 **Watch Extract 3. Note down key information on ideas a–c.**

a sociologists' interest in names

b reasons for studying Native American names

c features of Apache names

2 Complete the summary based on your notes.

Sociologists are interested in factors which influence parents' [1] ____________________, and how the choice of name influences [2] ____________________. Native American Indian names are often studied because within this culture names have [3] ____________________. However, names within such cultures often changed during a person's life due to [4] ____________________.

3 Evaluate the summary in 2. Ask yourself if the summary is:

1 Complete: Does it include all the main ideas?

2 Concise: Is it shorter than the original text?

3 Clear: Is it easy to understand?

4 7.4 **Watch Extract 4 and make notes for each point.**

- Naming Apache women
- Differences between Apache men's and women's names

5 Compare notes and then write a short summary using your notes in 4.

TASK 6 Understanding a short spoken summary

1 7.5 **Listen to Extract 5, part of a short student presentation. Note down 1–3.**

1 Types of names discussed: ____________________

2 Perspectives mentioned: ____________________

3 Student's conclusion: ____________________

2 7.5 **Listen again and complete the signposting phrases that the speaker uses.**

1 OK, today ____________________ names and their cultural importance.

2 ... ____________________ I want to focus on surnames and their historical role.

3 ... ____________________, I'll explain why nowadays the meaning of names is less culturally important.

TASK 7 Giving a short spoken summary

1 Work in pairs. You are going to give a short spoken summary. **Student A: turn to page 163. Student B: turn to page 165.** **Follow steps 1–4.**

1 Take notes on the main points of the text.

2 Note down any perspectives that are mentioned.

3 Decide which signposting language you will use to sequence your summary.

4 Present your summary to your partner.

TASK 8 Evaluating a spoken summary

1 Evaluate your partner's spoken summary. Did they:

- give a complete, concise, and clear summary?
- use signposting language correctly?

INDEPENDENT STUDY

Speakers use signposting language to help their audience follow the structure of a lecture or presentation.

▸ **Find an online talk related to your subject or a subject you are interested in. Listen to the introduction to the talk and note down examples of signposting language.**

7B Reading Textbooks (6)

This module covers:

- Identifying key features of a summary
- Understanding references in a text
- Summarizing information in a text

TASK 1 Previewing the topic of a text

1 You are going to read a summary of a chapter entitled 'Ways of Knowing' from the textbook *Theory of Knowledge*. Before you read, note down the different ways in which we get knowledge of the world via (a) language and (b) our senses.

TASK 2 Understanding the main idea in a text

1 Read Text 1 quickly. Select the statement 1–3 which contains the main idea of the text. Give reasons for your selection.

1 Language is an important tool for gaining knowledge, but it has some limitations.
2 Language is only useful as a tool for sharing knowledge with each other.
3 Language is the only tool that can help us to develop our personal knowledge.

TEXT 1

Language as a way of knowing

1 At the beginning of this chapter, we looked at the various roles of language in our lives: thinking, sharing information, persuading others, interacting socially, etc. When we look at all the ways we use language, we tend to focus on the many positive opportunities that language gives us.

2 However, as we have seen with sense perception, language also has its problems and limitations as a way of knowing.

- Language is not always precise.
- There are many languages in the world and meaning can be lost in translation.
- There are experiences which cannot be expressed using language.

3 In spite of these limitations, language is one of the most important ways of knowing. It is our main means of building a bridge between personal knowledge and shared knowledge. Because of language, we are not isolated in our own thoughts; we are able to connect with others both socially and culturally.

4 Indeed, it could be said that the same features of language that we have highlighted as problems can also be seen as the things which make language so wonderfully human and different.

- Lack of precision and misunderstanding can lead to deeper enquiry, as well as to humour.
- The existence of different languages helps us to discover new ways of interpreting experiences.
- Language can be used by poets and writers to communicate ideas and feelings that others find difficult to express.

5 Language is the tool with which we claim knowledge and often the tool with which we share knowledge. We can gain knowledge using this tool, but we need to be aware of its limitations. In particular, we must be aware of the influence that the language user's perspective has on the knowledge that is transmitted.

SOURCE: Dombrowski, E. (2013). p.132. *IB Theory of Knowledge: Course Companion.* Oxford: Oxford University Press.

GLOSSARY

lack *(n)* not having something

limitation *(n)* a restriction on what you can do with something

sense perception *(n)* noticing things using your sight, smell, taste, touch, or hearing

transmit *(v)* to pass something from one person to another

TASK 3 Identifying key facts in a chapter summary

1 Read Text 1 again. Identify which information a–c Paragraph 1 includes.

a a summary of the information given in the chapter

b a summary of the different functions of language

c a summary of the benefits of language

2 Summaries often use bullet points to draw attention to key facts. Select the function a–c of the bulleted statements in Paragraph 2.

a the limitations of language as a way of gaining knowledge

b the similarities between language and sense perception

c the problems that people have expressing themselves

3 Read Paragraph 3. Select the main idea a–c.

a the limitations of language as a way of knowing

b the connection between language and thought

c the importance of language as a means of communication

4 Match sentences 1–3 from Paragraph 5 with summaries a–c.

1 Language is the tool with which we claim knowledge and often the tool with which we share knowledge. ....

2 We gain knowledge using this tool, but we need to be aware of its limitations. ....

3 In particular, we must be aware of the influence that the language user's perspective has on the knowledge that is transmitted. ....

a Language has limitations.

b Language helps us to gain and share knowledge.

c Perpective is a key limitation of language.

TASK 4 Understanding cohesion within a text

1 In Text 1, the author refers to information earlier in the book. Complete sentences (a) and (b) with the missing verbs.

a At the beginning of this chapter, we .... at the various roles of language in our lives. (para 1)

b However, as we .... with sense perception, language also has its problems and limitations as a way of knowing. (para 2)

2 Read sentences (a) and (b) in 1. Which verb tense is used to refer to:

a a specific point in the book?

b an unspecified point?

ACADEMIC LANGUAGE

Cohesion Referring back in texts

In academic texts it is common to remind the reader of points that have already been explained. In this way the reader can see how new ideas relate to other ideas already presented. Here are some common ways of referring back.

Referring back to an unspecified point

We have already seen that *language is not always precise ...*

As we have seen*, language also has its problems as a way of knowing ...*

Referring back to a specific point

At the beginning of this *chapter, we* ***looked at*** *the various roles of language in our lives ...*

In Chapter 2, we saw *that sense perception is one way of gathering knowledge ...*

TASK 5 **Identifying key features of a summary**

1 Read Paragraph 1 below, a summary of Text 1 from a student's essay. Answer questions 1–3.

> **Paragraph 1**
>
> As Eileen Dombrowski (2013) states, language is an essential tool for gaining knowledge. It has many advantages and forms 'a bridge between personal knowledge and shared knowledge'. However, it also has certain limitations: a lack of precision, problems when translating from one language to another, and an inability to express certain experiences. These disadvantages could also be advantages, because they lead us to explore knowledge more deeply. Dombrowski says that the important thing to remember is that knowledge which is gained through language is not always objective, because each user of the language has a different point of view.

1 What is the topic sentence in this paragraph?
2 How does the concluding sentence develop the main idea in the topic sentence?
3 How does the writer show that these ideas are not his/her own?

2 Read the key features of a summary 1–5 and tick those used by the writer in Paragraph 1.

1 Give the name of the author and/or the title of the source material. ☐
2 Give only the main ideas in the text. Leave out the less important details. ☐
3 Use your own language, or quotation marks if you quote from the source. ☐
4 Be objective. Do not give your personal view or reactions. ☐
5 Refer to the author: use phrases like 'According to …' or 'As … notes …' ☐

3 Note down examples of the key features in Paragraph 1.
Example: *1 As Eileen Dombrowski (2013) states …*

TASK 6 Summarizing information in a text

1 Read Text 2. Note down:

1 the topic sentence
2 how the paragraph develops the main idea
3 how the author shows that these ideas are not her own.

TEXT 2

In recent years emotions have become the subject of study for scientists researching the brain and how we learn. Our ability to understand our own emotions and the emotions of others has been given the name 'emotional intelligence'. In his book *Frames of Mind* (1984), Howard Gardner put forward a theory of seven intelligences: linguistic intelligence, logical-mathematical intelligence, spatial intelligence, musical intelligence, bodily-kinesthetic intelligence, interpersonal intelligence, and intrapersonal intelligence. These last two kinds of intelligences are related. Interpersonal intelligence means understanding other people and being able to cooperate with others. All sorts of successful people from teachers to religious leaders and politicians probably display these skills to a high degree. Intrapersonal intelligence involves the same abilities applied to ourselves. In other words, being sensitive to our own feelings and being aware of our own strengths and weaknesses. Although Gardner himself did not use the term 'emotional intelligence', it is now widely used to refer to interpersonal and intrapersonal intelligences.

SOURCE: Dombrowski, E. (2013). p051. *IB Theory of Knowledge: Course Companion.* Oxford: Oxford University Press.

2 Write one sentence, in your own words, stating the main idea of Text 2.

3 Work in pairs. Compare your sentences. Do you agree on the main idea?

4 Decide which details in the paragraph:

a help to understand the main idea
b can be omitted from a summary (e.g. detailed examples).

TASK 7 Summarizing a reading text

1 Write a summary of Text 2 in a maximum of three sentences. Use guidelines 1–5 to plan your paragraph.

1 Name the author(s) and the title(s) of the source material.
2 Give only the main ideas in the text.
3 Use your own words, or quotation marks if you quote the author exactly.
4 Be objective.
5 Refer to the author using phrases like 'According to ...' or 'As ... notes ...'.

2 Work in pairs. Read your partner's summary. Did they:

- include the same information as you?
- write an objective summary, or give a personal opinion?
- refer to the source material?

TASK 8 Critical thinking – evaluating the content of a text

1 Work in groups. Read Text 1 again and summarize (a) the positive things, and (b) the negative things about 'language as a way of knowing'.

2 In the author's opinion, what is the most important thing to be aware of when using language to gain knowledge? Do you agree? Give reasons.

INDEPENDENT STUDY

Textbooks often use summaries at the end of a chapter as a way of going over the main points again. It is a useful exercise to compare these summaries with your own notes.

▸ Find a chapter in a textbook with a summary at the end. Read the chapter and note the main points. Then read the summary and compare it with your notes.

7C Writing (1) Paraphrasing

This module covers:

- Paraphrasing sentences
- Paraphrasing a paragraph

TASK 1 Previewing a writing task

1 Work in pairs. Discuss questions 1 and 2.

1 Which languages are the easiest and most difficult to learn? Why?

2 What do you know about Japanese? Is it easy or difficult to learn? Why?

2 Read Paragraph 1. Compare your ideas.

> **Paragraph 1**
>
> [1]Japanese is one of the most complex languages. [2]One major reason that makes Japanese so difficult to learn is that there are considerable differences between the written code and the spoken code. [3]In addition, Japanese has an extensive grammatical system affected by sociolinguistics - particularly the expression of politeness and formality. [4]Chinese had a considerable influence on the vocabulary and phonology of Old Japanese. [5]However, since 1945 Japanese has borrowed a large number of words from English, especially vocabulary relating to technology.

3 Read Paragraph 1 again. Make notes on (a) the reasons for complexity and (b) the influences on Japanese.

TASK 2 Noticing paraphrasing

1 Compare sentences 1–3 from Paragraph 1 with the summary below. Identify:

1 two examples of synonyms

2 changes to word form (e.g. noun to verb)

3 changes to sentence structure or word order.

> Japanese is one of the hardest languages to learn. This is primarily because the written and spoken codes are very different. Also, the language has a complex system of grammar for expressing politeness and formality.

2 Which words and phrases are the same in both texts? Why?

3 Compare sentences 4–5 in Paragraph 1 with the version below. Identify any changes.

> Both Chinese and English have greatly influenced the vocabulary of Japanese. More recently, many technology-related English words have entered the Japanese language.

ACADEMIC LANGUAGE

▸Language reference page 155

Paraphrasing

Paraphrasing mean's rewriting an author's idea in your own words. For example:

Using synonyms (words that have the same meaning)

*Japanese has borrowed **a large number of** words from English, **especially** ...*

→ *Japanese has borrowed **many** English words, **particularly** ...*

A change to word form

*Chinese **had a considerable influence on** the vocabulary and phonology of Old Japanese.*

→ *Chinese **greatly influenced** Japanese in terms of vocabulary and phonology.*

TASK 3 Paraphrasing sentences

1 Paraphrase sentences 1–3 using the words in brackets.

Example: Finnish is the hardest language to learn. *(most difficult, to master)*
Finnish is considered *the most difficult language to master* ....

1 The research looked at the way older siblings behave towards a baby brother or sister. (*behaviour of, brothers or sisters, when, interacted, a baby sibling*)
The study observed ....

2 Most children starting school are linguistically able enough to succeed. (*majority of, have, the linguistic ability, successful*)
When they start ....

3 The study looked at how well a second language speaking task was performed when it was planned. (*planning, affected, performance of*)
The study investigated ....

2 Identify the features of the paraphrase used in 1.

TASK 4 Paraphrasing a paragraph

1 Read Paragraph 3. Match notes a–d with sentences 1–4.

a Sumerian language / originated around 4000 BC / is thought / world's first written language
b still used / written form / a further 2000 years
c lasted as spoken language / until around 2000 BC
d used across / most of old Middle East / in particular Mesopotamia (now Iraq)

Paragraph 3

[1]Sumerian is a long-extinct language, and is believed to be the earliest known written language, dating back to at least the 4th millennium BC. [2]Sumerian is documented throughout the ancient Middle East, with its heartland in southern Mesopotamia, in what today is modern Iraq. [3]Spoken Sumerian stopped being used in about 2000 BC. [4]However, it continued to be used as a religious and ceremonial written language until the 1st century AD.

2 Use notes a–d to write a paraphrase of Paragraph 3.

3 Compare your paraphrase with Paragraph 3. Identify:

- any synonyms you used
- changes in sentence structure or word order
- any specialized words you repeated.

4 Write a paraphrase of Paragraph 4 in about 60 words. Use guidelines 1–3 to help you plan.

1 Include the main ideas.
2 Paraphrase using synonyms and changes to word order.
3 Include any specialist words with no changes.

Sample answer: page 160

Paragraph 4

Python, one of the most popular programming languages, was developed in the 1980s by Guido van Rossum. It is open source and free to use, even when used for commercial applications. This has ensured that the language has been widely adopted by first-time programmers and large software companies. Another reason for Python's popularity is that programmers can use it to create large amounts of easily readable and functional code in a short time. Many commentators also note that Python is a useful teaching language as it provides many of the basics required by other, more sophisticated programming languages.

7C Writing (2) Citation

This module covers:

- Recognizing citation

TASK 1 Analysing sources

1 Read the source reference. Match features a–e with items 1–5.

SOURCE: [1]Scovel, T. [2](1998). [3]p.27. [4]*Psycholinguistics: Oxford Introductions to Language Study.* [5]Oxford: Oxford University Press.

a the author ....
b title ....
c publisher ....
d year of publication ....
e page numbers ....

2 Read citations 1 and 2. Identify which features a–e are included.

1 According to Scovel (1998: 50), understanding and producing language seem so automatic that they 'may appear to be relatively straightforward'.

2 As Hudson (2007) notes, second-language learners use a range of vocabulary learning strategies when becoming accomplished readers.

TASK 2 Referring to sources

1 Read Text 1 and citations a–c. Note down:

1 which citation is a direct quotation
2 which two citations use a paraphrase.

TEXT 1

One of the most influential models for speech production views it as a progression of four successive stages: (1) **conceptualization**, (2) **formulation**, (3) **articulation**, and (4) **self-monitoring**.

SOURCE: Scovel, T. (1998). p.27. *Psycholinguistics: Oxford Introductions to Language Study.* Oxford: Oxford University Press.

a There are four stages of speech production (Scovel, 1998). These are the conceptualization stage, the language formulation stage, the articulation stage, and self-monitoring.

b Scovel (1998) argues that there are four stages of speech production: the conceptualization stage, the language formulation stage, the articulation stage, and self-monitoring.

c Scovel (1998) states the model of speech production with most influence is 'a progression of four successive stages: (1) conceptualization, (2) formulation, (3) articulation, and (4) self-monitoring.'

2 Identify the citations which use reporting verbs (e.g. *says, claims*).

ACADEMIC LANGUAGE

▸ Language reference page 155

Citation

When you refer to an author's work in your writing, you must acknowledge the source of the ideas you are expressing. This is called *citation*. There are two main ways of showing that you have used another writer's ideas:

Direct quotation

Scovel (1998) states the model of speech production with most influence is 'a progression of four successive stages: (1) conceptualization, (2) formulation, (3) articulation, and (4) self-monitoring.'

Note that quotation marks are used around the words, which must be quoted exactly as they are in the original.

Paraphrasing

One of the most influential models for speech production views it as a four-stage process (Scovel, 1998).

Scovel (1998) states the model of speech production with most influence is ...

Using reporting verbs

A range of reporting verbs can be used to quote or paraphrase. For example:

Scovel (1998) ***argues*** *that there are four stages of speech production.*

Brown (2013) ***claims*** *that a far more effective approach is ...*

TASK 3 Practising reporting verbs

1 Match the verbs in bold in sentences 1–6 with synonyms a–f.

1 Dearing **states** that over half Toronto's population was born outside Canada.
2 Harper **notes** languages are dynamic – in a constant process of change.
3 The author **considers** environment to be a key factor in research.
4 Mathau **claims** that true knowledge can only be gained through the senses.
5 Carey and Black **suggest** that this policy does not help local people.
6 Grunwald does not **mention** the smaller languages.

a argues
b gives the idea
c says
d observes
e speak about
f believes

TASK 4 Writing citations

1 Read extracts 1 and 2 below. Write two citations for each source:

a a paraphrase with a reporting verb
b a quotation with a reporting verb.

1 Our ability to understand our own emotions and the emotions of others has been given the name *emotional intelligence*.
Dombrowski, E. (2013). p051. *IB Theory of Knowledge: Course Companion*. Oxford: Oxford University Press.

2 One remarkable thing about first language acquisition is the high degree of similarity which we see in the early language of children all over the world.
Lightbown, P. & Spada, N. (2003). p.001. *How Languages are Learned*. Oxford: Oxford University Press.

Sample answer:
page 160

2 Work in pairs. Read your partner's citations. Check that they have:

- identified the main idea ☐
- paraphrased using their own words, OR ☐
- quoted using the exact words. ☐

INDEPENDENT STUDY

Summary writing helps us to think in a clear and organized way.

▸ Find a description of a complex idea that you would like to understand. Read it and then write a short summary of it.

7D Vocabulary

TASK 1 Collocations (3): More verb and noun collocations

1 Match verbs 1-4 to nouns a-d, and verbs 5-8 to nouns e-h, to form appropriate collocations.

1 interpret	....	a a skill
2 put forward	....	b an action
3 perform	....	c a theory
4 display	....	d data
5 express	....	e terms
6 define	....	f emotions
7 fall into	....	g a pattern
8 follow	....	h categories

2 Select the most appropriate verb from 1 to complete sentences 1–7.

1 Many doctors *put forward / expressed / defined* their concern about the ethics of genetic research.

2 Each engineering project *defines / performs / follows* a sequence of stages – beginning with planning and ending with testing.

3 The aim of the test is to discover which of the candidates *performs / displays / expresses* the qualities to be a leader.

4 Library materials *display / define / fall into* two main groups: printed and non-printed materials.

5 Connolly *performed / interpreted / put forward* a new model of government, in which trade unions had an important role in decision-making.

6 Subject A was able to *perform / put forward / express* the task twice as fast as Subject B.

7 Before we begin, we need to *define / interpret / fall into* our concept of 'culture'.

3 Write three sentences of your own using three of the collocations from 1 or 2.

TASK 2 Using synonyms in paraphrasing

1 Synonyms are words with similar meanings. Select the phrase a–f that can replace each of the phrases in bold in sentences 1–6.

a certain characteristics
b significant differences
c complicated question
d new trend
e various roles
f a fast decrease

1 Even though they are related, there are **considerable variations** between the two languages. ....

2 Women had **several different functions** in Apache society. ....

3 There has been **a rapid decline** in the use of traditional textbooks in primary education. ....

4 The researchers found that children from poor backgrounds had **particular traits** in common. ....

5 Finding out where these names originated is a **complex issue**. ....

6 Using surnames for administrative purposes is a fairly **recent phenomenon**. ....

2 Work in pairs. Think of a suitable synonym for the phrases in bold.

1 First names in their culture have no **particular significance**.

2 There is a **definite link** between a person's name and where they come from.

3 Determining the precise meaning of each symbol was **not an easy task**.

7E Academic Language Check

TASK 1 Signposting language

1 Match sentence halves 1–4 with a–d, and 5–8 with e–h.

1 Today, we're going to look ....
2 I'd like to talk to you today ....
3 In this lecture we will focus ....
4 This lecture is an introduction ....

a on the use of colour in architectural design.
b at US politics from 1945.
c to the life and works of Pablo Picasso.
d about second language acquisition.

5 First I will give ....
6 Then, we'll look ....
7 Finally, we'll see ....
8 So, first, let's look ....

e how animal cells interact with each other.
f at the structure of a typical cell.
g in detail at the function of the nucleus.
h a brief introduction to the key features of animal cells.

TASK 2 Referring back in a text

1 Put the words in the correct order to complete sentences 1–5. The sentences refer back to something previously mentioned in a text.

1 .... the economy grew between 2000 and 2015.
that / seen / we / already / have

2 ...., deforestation has increased steadily in the last ten years.
have / as / seen / we

3 .... English is primarily a Germanic language.
that / you / recall / will

4 .... the universe is expanding at an increasing rate.
that / Chapter 2 / saw / we / in

5 .... at genetic engineering.
we / beginning / the / at / of / this / looked / chapter

TASK 3 Paraphrasing

1 Complete the paraphrase of the text. Use the words in the list.

economies such as changing from industrial knowledge
service-based same time moving low-wage countries

Economies such as the United States are changing from ...

....

....

The United States, along with a number of other manufacturing and industry-based nations, including Japan and Germany, is being transformed to a knowledge and service economy. There is a simultaneous shift in manufacturing to countries where wages are low.

TASK 4 Citation

1 Each citation 1–5 contains one mistake. Correct the mistakes.

1 Foster has shown that learners who plan tasks generally attempt more complex language (1996).
2 Mitchell concludes (2009) that 'over 50 species in the region are at risk of extinction.'
3 Dictionaries which contain grammatical information are generally more popular with learners of English than dictionaries with no grammar content (2008, Jones).
4 Gerrard (Gerrard, 2014) points out that the internet is a useful research tool.
5 Sangarun argues that 'the economy needs to return to innovation and production' (Sangarun, 2014).

UNIT 8 Formation

ACADEMIC FOCUS: DESCRIBING SEQUENCE AND PROCESS

LEARNING OBJECTIVES

This unit covers:

Listening and Speaking
- Noting down key events in a past narrative
- Identifying the sequence of events in a narrative
- Describing a past narrative

Reading
- Understanding a description of a process
- Identifying key language in a process

Writing
- Using the passive voice to describe a process
- Describing steps in a process using the passive voice
- Writing a paragraph describing a process

Vocabulary
- Prepositions of place
- Using verbs to describe a process
- Word formation: Describing dimensions

Academic Language Check
- Past narrative tenses
- The passive voice
- The passive voice and narrative sequencing words

Discussion

1 Work in pairs. Read the definition of *process* and put steps a–f in the correct order.

> **process** (*n*) a series of things that are done one after the other to achieve a particular result

The process of applying for university

a submit an application form ....
b receive an invitation for interview at the university ....
c select the university that you wish to apply for ....
d take the exams necessary for entrance ....
e receive a conditional offer from the university based on getting certain exam grades ....
f pass the exams with the right grades ....

2 Work in groups. Describe how you applied for a course in the past.

Example: *I applied to study biochemistry at King Saud University. First, I had to fill in an application form and then I was invited for an interview …*

3 Work in pairs. Answer questions 1 and 2.

1 What are the steps you take in the process of writing an essay?
2 Why do you think this is the best order?

Example: *I always plan the structure of my essay first by writing down the main points. Then I …*

4 Work with another pair. Compare answers and discuss any differences. Give reasons.

8A Listening & Speaking Presentations (3)

This module covers:

- Noting down key events in a past narrative
- Identifying the sequence of events in a narrative
- Describing a past narrative

TASK 1 Predicting the content of a presentation

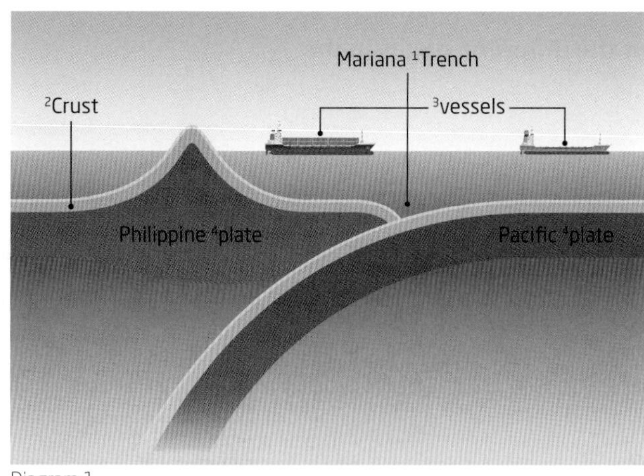

Diagram 1

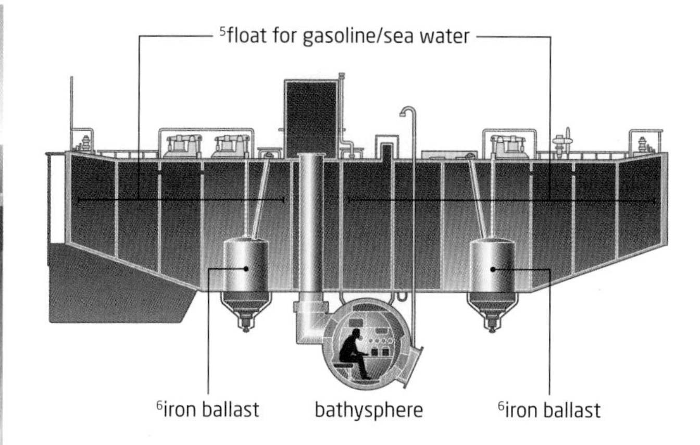

Diagram 2

1 Look at Diagrams 1 and 2. Match words 1–6 with the definitions.

a .... (*n*) a long deep hole in the ground
b .... (*n*) a hard layer on the surface of something
c .... (*n*) large pieces of rock that form the surface of the Earth
d .... (*n*) ships or boats
e .... (*n*) material placed in a ship to make it heavier and keep it steady
f .... (*n*) a light object that allows something to stay on the surface of water

2 Work in pairs. You are going to watch a student presentation on geographical exploration. Use the diagrams to predict the content.

TASK 2 Noting down key facts

1 8.1 Watch Extract 1 and compare your ideas from Task 1.2. What other details can you remember?

2 8.1 Watch Extract 1 again. Complete the table with the statistics mentioned by the presenter.

Mariana Trench: key facts and figures

Length	1 ....
Depth	2 ....
Location	3 .... Ocean, near island of Guam
Number of similar trenches	4 ....
Formation	5 .... meet and one is forced under the other
Reasons for exploration	Medical science; understanding earthquakes; new forms of life?
First time measured	Date: 6 .... – measured depth with 7 ....
Second time measured	Date: 8 .... – measured depth with echo sounder

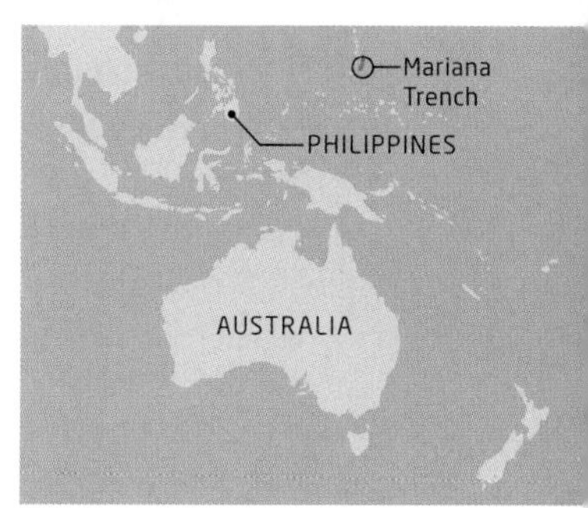

Slide 1

Slide 2

3 Complete the summary of Extract 1 using the information in the table.

The Mariana Trench lies [1] .... It was formed when [2] .... Scientists are keen to explore the trench as it may contain micro-organisms beneficial to medical research. Studying deep under water could also assist in learning about how [3] .... and provide an opportunity to discover [4] .... Scientists first measured [5] .... in the 19th century.

TASK 3 Identifying the sequence of events in a narrative

1 ▶8.2 Watch Extract 2. Complete the student notes on the different stages in the first expedition to the Mariana Trench.

1st expedition: 1960 in bathyscaphe
Descending: Uses float filled with [1] ....; this replaced with heavier [2] ....
Rising: Iron ballast dropped to [3] ....
Journey time = [4] ....
Time spent at bottom = [5] ....
Findings: [6] ....

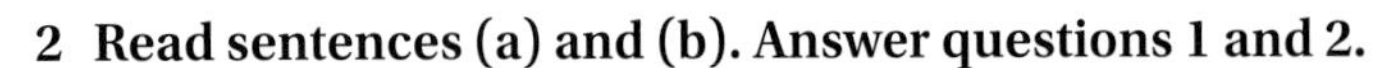

2 Read sentences (a) and (b). Answer questions 1 and 2.

a The first expedition to the trench was made in a US navy bathyscaphe in 1960. Up to then, most deep sea diving vessels had been bathyspheres.

b While they were exploring the trench, the crew noted that the seabed was soft and featureless.

1 Which sentence describes:
  i two events occurring at the same time?
  ii one event occurring before the other?

2 Which sequencing words and verb tenses indicate the sequence of events?

ACADEMIC LANGUAGE

▸ Language reference page 156

Past tenses

Use the **past simple** to talk about the main events.

*The oceanographer Jacques Piccard and US Navy Lieutenant Don Walsh **made** the first expedition to the bottom of the trench in 1960. They **used** a US navy bathyscaphe.*

Use the **past progressive** to describe something in progress at the time of the main event.

***While** they **were exploring** the trench, the crew **noted** that the sea bed was soft and featureless.*

Use the **past perfect** to describe an event that occurred before one of the main events or before the whole event began.

***When** the Trieste finally reached the bottom of the trench, the crew **had used** almost half their air supply.*

***Up to then**, most deep-sea diving vessels **had been** bathyspheres.*

TASK 4 Using past narrative tenses

1 Complete the text using the correct alternative from the words in italics.

The Trieste bathyscaphe [1]*reached / was reaching* the Mariana Trench five hours [2]*while / after* it [3]*was beginning / had begun* its descent from the surface. However, [4]*while / then* it [5]*was descending / had descended*, one of the windows in the vessel [6]*cracked / was cracking* under the intense pressure. The two crew members [7]*were concerned / had been concerned* about this and so they [8]*reduced / had reduced* the time that they [9]*originally planned / had originally planned* to spend on the bottom. [10]*While / When* they [11]*were completing / had completed* a quick observation of the environment, they [12]*returned / had returned* to the surface.

2 8.3 Watch Extract 3 and check your answers.

TASK 5 Describing past events

1 8.4 Watch Extract 4, in which another student describes an exploration of the Mariana Trench. Note down:

1 the purpose of the expedition
2 the length of the expedition
3 any findings of the expedition.

2 Read a summary of Extract 4. Put the verbs into the correct past tense form.

The next expedition [1] *took place* (take place) in 2012. Film director James Cameron, who fifteen years earlier [2] .... (make) the film *Titanic*, [3] .... (pilot) a new type of deep sea vessel that used special foam for flotation and had motors to power it. He also [4] .... (take) with him more scientific equipment. Once Cameron [5] .... (reach) the bottom, he [6] .... (be able) to explore the sea bed. While he [7] .... (drive) around on the seabed, he also [8] .... (observe) that the terrain was soft and flat, but unlike the previous expedition he [9] .... (see) no fish – only small shrimp-like creatures.

TASK 6 Explaining past events

1 Work in pairs. Describe an example of geographical exploration. Student A: look at the notes on page 163. Student B: look at the notes on page 165.

2 Work in pairs. Describe an important past event or discovery in your own area of study, or a subject you are interested in. Remember to:

- give a clear explanation of the events or process ☐
- use the correct verb tenses ☐
- using sequencing words to make the order of events clear. ☐

3 Evaluate your partner's description using the checklist in 2.

INDEPENDENT STUDY

Encyclopaedias often provide clear, well-sequenced descriptions of processes.

▸ Use an encyclopaedia, or online resource, to look up a discovery or geographical phenomenon that you would like to know more about. Note down the sequence of events and then explain these to another student.

8B Reading Textbooks (7)

This module covers:

- Understanding a description of a process
- Identifying key language in a process

TASK 1 Predicting the content of a text

1 Work in pairs. Discuss questions 1–3.

1 What stars or types of stars do you know the names of?

2 What are stars made of?

3 What do you know about how stars are formed? Can you describe any stages of the process?

2 Read the text. Find answers to the questions in 1.

Stellar evolution: how stars are formed

1 The observable universe is made up of more than 10^{20} stars at distances of up to 10^{27} miles away from the Earth. Our sun is a typical star. The only reason it appears to be bigger and brighter than other stars is that we are much closer to it.

2 Stars are essentially like large nuclear fusion reactors, where nuclei of lighter elements (hydrogen, helium, etc.) are converted into heavier nuclei (carbon, iron, etc.). The process releases a great deal of energy, in the form of thermal energy and electromagnetic radiation. The nuclear fusion which takes place in stars can only happen at very high temperatures and when material in the star is very dense. How did the stars become hot enough and dense enough for nuclear fusion reactions to start?

3 A star begins its life as a large cloud of gas. Atoms in the gas are attracted to each other by the force of gravity and the cloud then begins to collapse. As the material accelerates the gravitational energy is converted into kinetic energy and the temperature of the gas cloud increases. Once the gas cloud has reached a certain temperature, it is hot enough for nuclear fusion to take place. That means that the centre or nuclei of the atoms fuse together. This in turn releases more energy and causes the star to heat up. The heat which is generated inside the star is then radiated away from its centre, first to the surface of the star and then out into space. The heat and light that we experience from our own sun is this radiated energy. The Earth is also subject to the Sun's gravitational pull, but it is sufficiently far enough away not to be pulled into it.

4 Many stars radiate energy while remaining stable for billions of years and from this we can infer that the processes taking place inside the star must be balanced. A stable star then is one where there is a balance between the gravitational energy causing the nuclear reactions and the energy which is radiated away from the surface. A star can continue in this 'stable' state as long as there is enough hydrogen gas to fuel the reaction. When too much hydrogen has been burnt, the core of the star collapses under the force of gravity and the star changes state.

SOURCE: Kirk, T. & Hodgson, N. (2007). p.302. *IB Physics Course Companion*. Oxford: Oxford University Press.

GLOSSARY

core *(n)* the centre or heart of an object

dense *(adj)* thick, containing a lot of matter in a small space

gravity *(n)* the force in space that pulls objects towards each other

kinetic *(adj)* produced by movement

nucleus *(pl. nuclei) (n)* the centre and main part of an atom

thermal *(adj)* relating to heat

TASK 2 Understanding key information in a text

1 Work in pairs. Read the text again and complete the student summary.

There are a huge number of stars in the universe, many like our own sun. The sun is different only because [1] .... Stars are like [2] .... Nuclear fusion takes place when [3] .... and [4] .... [5] .... are attracted to each other and fuse together. This creates a lot of heat which is [6] .... This energy is balanced by [7] .... and so the star remains stable. The star only changes state when [8] ....

TASK 3 Understanding a description of a process

1 Work in pairs. Identify which paragraph in the text:

1 describes how a star is formed
2 describes the composition of a star
3 introduces the next stage in the life of a star.

2 Read Paragraphs 3 and 4 again. Complete the notes on the process of stellar evolution.

Stage 1: Cloud of [1] ....
Stage 2: Cloud [2] .... under force of [3] ....
Stage 3: Gravitational energy converted [4] .... and temperature [5] ....
Stage 4: [6] .... takes place, i.e. atoms [7] ....
Stage 5: Star [8] .... and [9] .... energy in the form of [10] .... and [11] ....
Stage 6: Star remains in [12] .... state – [13] .... vs radiated energy
Stage 7: When not enough [14] ...., [15] .... collapses and star [16] .... state

3 Read Paragraph 3 again and identify:

1 the main verbs used in the text to describe the process of stellar evolution
2 the tense the main verbs are in
3 other language used to signal steps in a sequence.

ACADEMIC LANGUAGE

▸ Language reference page 156

Describing a process (1) Sequencing in a process

Use the **present simple** to describe each stage of a process:
Atoms in the gas ***are attracted*** *to each other by the force of gravity.*
Use the **present perfect simple** to indicate that one thing happened before another:
Once the gas cloud ***has reached*** *a certain temperature, it is hot enough ...*
Use **time adverbials** to put the steps in sequence:
As *the material accelerates, the gravitational energy is converted ...*
Once *the gas cloud has reached a certain temperature, it is hot enough ...*
This ***in turn*** *releases more energy and causes ...*
The heat which is generated inside the star is ***then*** *radiated away from its centre,* ***first*** *to the surface of the star and* ***then*** *out into space.*
When *too much hydrogen has been burnt, the core of the star collapses.*

TASK 4 **Identifying key language for sequencing steps**

1 Read sentences 1–5 below and tick the best option for the sequence of A and B. Use Paragraph 3 of the text to help you.

Sentence	A happens first	B happens first	A and B happen at approximately the same time
1	☐	☐	☐
2	☐	☐	☐
3	☐	☐	☐
4	☐	☐	☐
5	☐	☐	☐

1 Atoms in the gas are attracted to each other by the force of gravity and the cloud then begins to collapse.
A = atoms in the gas are attracted to each other
B = the cloud begins to collapse

2 As the material accelerates, the gravitational energy is converted into kinetic energy.
A = the material accelerates
B = the gravitational energy is converted into kinetic energy

3 Once the gas cloud has reached a certain temperature, it is hot enough for nuclear fusion to take place.
A = nuclear fusion takes place
B = the gas cloud reaches a certain temperature

4 The centre or nuclei of the atoms fuse together. This in turn releases more energy and causes the star to heat up.
A = the nuclei of the atoms fuse together
B = more energy is released and the star heats up

5 The heat which is generated inside the star is then radiated away from its centre, first to the surface of the star and then out into space.
A = the heat generated by the star is radiated away to the surface of the star
B = the heat is radiated out into space

2 Work in pairs. Complete stages 1–5 with an appropriate word or phrase from the list.

once then as in turn when

1 .... the atoms are attracted to each other, the cloud begins to collapse.
2 .... the gas cloud has become hot enough, nuclear fusion takes place.
3 The atoms fuse together, ... more energy is released.
4 .... the heat has reached the surface of the star, it is radiated out into space.
5 Heat is radiated away from the sun and this heat .... is felt here on earth.

TASK 5 Putting stages in a process in sequence

1 Work in pairs. Complete the description of the next steps in the life of a star using notes 1–10 and appropriate sequencing language.

1 Hydrogen atoms in star fuse together → produce helium.
2 Amount of hydrogen in star reduces / amount of helium increases.
3 Helium atoms sink to centre of star + hydrogen atoms remain in shell around it.
4 Temperature in core of star rises.
5 Core reaches a certain temperature → helium atoms fuse together.
6 Energy radiated by helium burning causes star to expand.
7 Star changes colour from yellow to red.
8 This phase lasts a few million years: star called a 'red giant'.
9 All the hydrogen is used up → core of star collapses.
10 Star becomes a 'white dwarf'.

When hydrogen atoms fuse together, they produce helium.

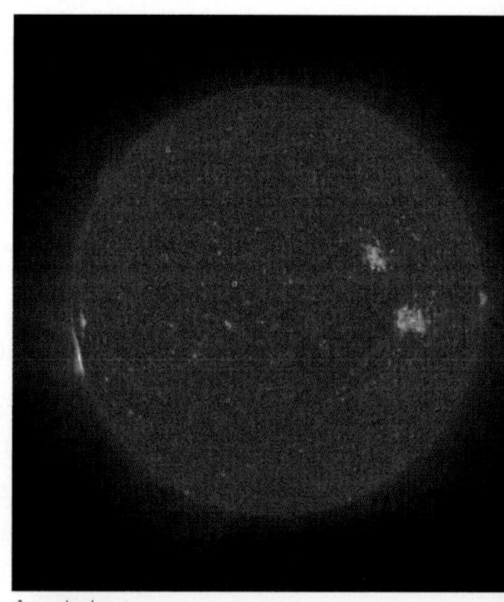

A red giant

A white dwarf

2 Work with another pair and compare answers.

TASK 6 Critical thinking – analysing a text

1 Work in groups. Tick which techniques the authors of the text on page 110 use to help the reader understand the process of stellar evolution.

Short sentences ☐
Diagrams ☐
Comparisons with other processes ☐
Sequencing words ☐
The passive voice ☐

2 Discuss which technique was most useful for you in helping to understand the process.

INDEPENDENT STUDY

Sequencing words, e.g. *then, next, once,* can help you to understand how the process works in a description of a process.

▶ **Find short descriptions of different processes and make a note of the sequencing words and phrases that they use.**

8C Writing (1) Sentences using passives

This module covers:

- Using the passive voice to describe a process
- Describing steps in a process using the passive voice

TASK 1 Previewing a writing task

1 Complete the definition of a black hole using the words in the list.

gravity light space

> **black hole** (*n*) [C] (ASTRONOMY) an area in [1] .... that nothing, not even [2] ...., can escape from, because [3] .... is so strong there.

2 Read Paragraph 1, describing how a black hole is formed. Complete the notes.

Paragraph 1

The term 'black hole' was first used in 1964. Black holes are formed by dying stars. In the normal life of a star there is a balance between gravity pulling in and pressure pushing out and so the stability of the star is maintained. This outward pressure is produced by nuclear reactions in the core of the star. However, when a star runs out of nuclear fuel, gravity becomes the stronger force and the material in the core is compressed. Eventually, the star collapses completely and forms a black hole.

GLOSSARY

core *(n)* the centre or heart of an object

outward *(adj)* away from the centre of something

Black holes

- Formed by [1] ....
- Normally, balance between [2] .... and pressure maintains stability
- Outward pressure produced by [3] ....
- When fuel runs out, gravity [4] .... and star eventually [5] ....
- Term 'black hole' first used [6] ....

ACADEMIC LANGUAGE ▸ Language reference page 157

Describing a process (2) The passive voice

The passive voice expresses what happens to something, rather than what someone or something does. The passive is formed with *be* + past participle.

The passive is used without an agent (the person or thing that carries out or causes the action) or when the agent is obvious, unimportant, or unknown.

*... the stability of the star **is maintained**.*

*The term 'black hole' **was** first **used** in 1964.*

The passive can be used with an agent. This is usually when providing new information about an existing topic. Use *by* to introduce the agent.

*Black holes **are formed by** dying stars.*

*This outward pressure **is produced by** nuclear reactions in the core of the star.*

The active voice is used to express what someone or something does.

*However, when a star **runs out** of nuclear fuel, gravity **becomes** the stronger force ...*

*Eventually, the star **collapses** completely and **forms** a black hole.*

TASK 2 Recognizing the passive voice

1 Identify the verbs in Paragraph 1 which are in the passive voice.

Example: *Black holes are formed by dying stars.*

2 Identify two examples of the passive voice in Paragraph 1 which have an agent. Why is this?

TASK 3 Using the passive voice

1 Complete paragraphs 1 and 2 with the correct passive or active form of the verbs in brackets.

1 The main body of a comet [1] *is made* (make) mainly of ice and its tail [2] .... (form) by dust and gases that [3] .... (release) as the comet [4] .... (travel) through space. It [5] .... (think) that comets [6] .... (make) from the gas, dust, ice, and rocks that initially [7] .... (form) the solar system about 4.6 billion years ago.

2 Carbonated water [8] .... (first / produce) in 1767. It [9] .... (invent) by an English chemist called Joseph Priestley. Today, carbonated water [10] .... (make) by passing pressurized carbon dioxide through water. The pressure [11] .... (allow) more carbon dioxide to dissolve than is possible under standard atmospheric pressure. When the bottle [12] .... (open), the pressure [13] .... (release), which [14] .... (allow) the gas to come out of the solution, forming the characteristic bubbles.

2 Rewrite sentences 1–5 in the passive voice. Include an agent if necessary.

Example: The Chinese invented paper over 2,000 years ago.
Paper was invented over 2,000 years ago by the Chinese.

1 The Chinese originally made paper from a mixture of plant materials.

....

2 Today, manufacturers make most paper from wood.

....

3 Worldwide, the paper industry produces about 300 million tonnes of paper each year.

....

4 They manufacture a third of this from recycled paper.

....

5 The manufacturing process requires around 70% less energy to recycle paper compared with making it from raw materials.

....

3 Work in pairs. Which voice, active or passive, do you think is most appropriate in sentences 1–5? Give reasons.

8C Writing (2) Describing a process

This module covers:

- Writing a paragraph describing a process

TASK 1 Analysing a written process

1 Read Paragraph 2, a student's description of a process. Identify whether the writer has (a) selected a suitable topic and (b) answered the essay title.

TITLE: *Describe a process which has changed the surrounding environment. Clearly outline the stages in the process.*

Paragraph 2

In the multi-stage method of desalination, heat is used to convert salt water into fresh water. First, salt water enters the heating chamber. It is then rapidly heated and at the same time is subjected to high pressure. This causes the water to boil quickly. Once the water has boiled, the vapour which has been produced is collected. This water vapour is fresh water. Not all the salt is removed from the water during the first heating, so the process is repeated multiple times. After all the salt has been removed, only water vapour remains. Finally, the water vapour is cooled to form liquid water. Chemicals or water softening agents are not usually used during the process, so the fresh water produced is very pure. Although energy use in multi-stage desalination is high, the final product has no risk for the environment.

2 Read Paragraph 2 again. Complete the steps in the process.

Step 1: *salt water enters the heating chamber*

Step 2: ……

Step 3: ……

Step 4: ……

Step 5: ……

3 Work in pairs. Discuss questions 1 and 2.

1 Do you think that the process described in Paragraph 2 is important?

2 Which areas of the world could most benefit from the process?

ACADEMIC LANGUAGE ▸ Language reference page 157

Describing a process (3) The passive voice, tenses, sequencing words

In academic writing it is sometimes necessary to describe a man-made or naturally occurring process. Some of the key features of describing a process are:

Use of the passive

Not all the salt ***is removed*** *from the water during the first heating, so the process* ***is repeated*** *multiple times.*

Use of tenses

The present simple describes the key stages of the process.

First, salt water ***enters*** *the heating chamber.*

The present perfect indicates that one thing happened before another.

Once *the water* ***has boiled****, the vapour which* ***has been produced*** *is collected.*

Use of sequencing words

First*, salt water enters the heating chamber. It is* ***then*** *rapidly heated and* ***at the same time*** *is subjected to high pressure.*

TASK 2 Recognizing features of a process description

1 Read Paragraph 2 again. Identify examples of the features outlined in Academic Language.

2 Complete the text about the process of fracking using the words / phrases in the list.

finally first once then causes uses this causes is removed is collected next

Fracking is the name used to describe the process of extracting natural gas from shale rock. Fracking [1] .... water pumped at very high pressure to remove gas from beneath the Earth's surface. [2] ...., holes are drilled about 2.5 km deep into the ground. [3] ...., electrical currents are sent into the rock. This [4] .... small cracks to open in the rock which contains the gas supplies. [5] ...., fracturing fluid, a mixture of sand, water, and chemical additives, is pumped into the hole. [6] .... the cracks to enlarge. The fluid [7] .... and the sand which remains in the rock keeps the cracks open. [8] .... the gas begins to flow from the cracks, it [9] .... by a gas well. [10] .... the extracted gas is piped from the well-site.

3 Identify examples of the features from Academic Language in the text in 2.

TASK 3 Writing a description of a process

1 Look at the diagram. Then expand notes 1–7 into sentences about the production of glass bottles.

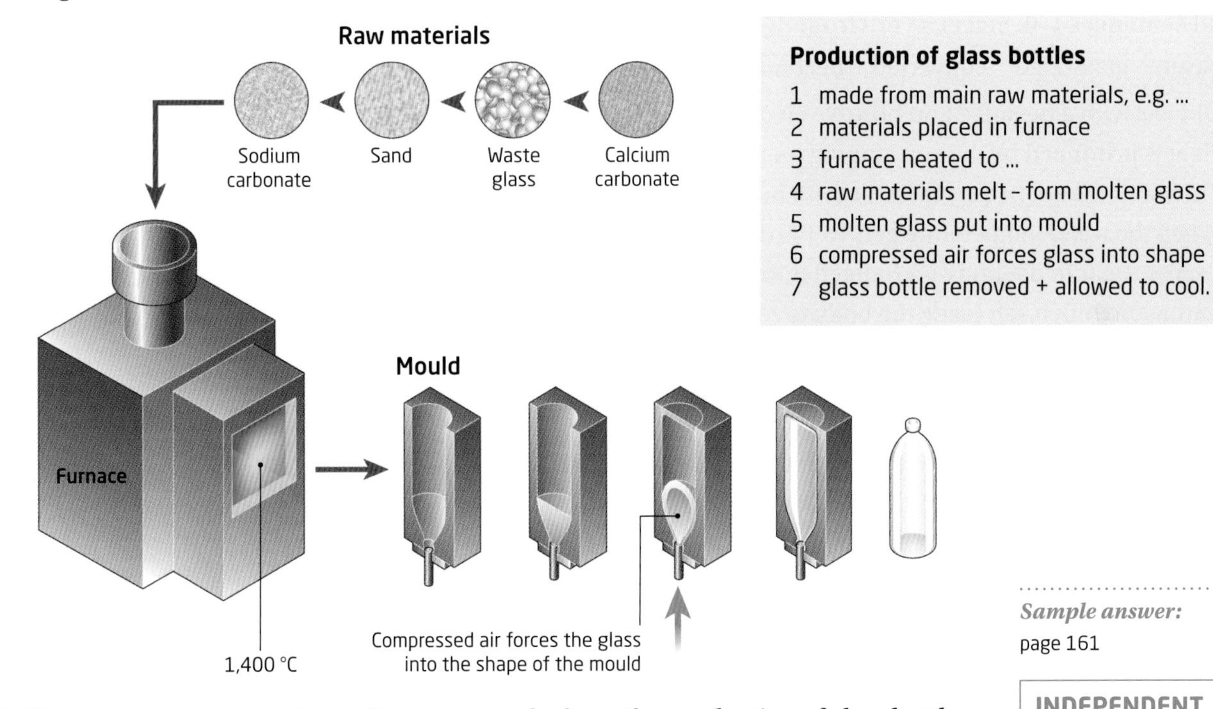

Production of glass bottles

1 made from main raw materials, e.g. ...
2 materials placed in furnace
3 furnace heated to ...
4 raw materials melt – form molten glass
5 molten glass put into mould
6 compressed air forces glass into shape
7 glass bottle removed + allowed to cool.

Sample answer: page 161

2 Use your sentences in 1 to write a paragraph about the production of glass bottles. Remember to mark each stage using an appropriate sequencing word / phrase.

TASK 4 Evaluating your writing

1 Read your paragraph. Check that the description contains:

- appropriate verb forms / tenses ☐
- appropriate examples of the passive voice ☐
- appropriate sequencing words. ☐

2 Work in pairs. Evaluate your partner's description using the checklist in 1.

INDEPENDENT STUDY

Descriptions of processes are often supported by diagrams that show the sequence of steps.

▶ **Find a process on the internet that is described using diagrams or pictures. Write a description of the process using the correct sequencing words.**

8D Vocabulary

TASK 1 Prepositions of place

1 Select the correct preposition to complete sentences 1–8.

1 At its deepest point, the trench is 11 kilometres *below* / *in* the sea's surface.
2 In the past, bathyspheres were lowered *onto* / *into* the sea bed with a cable.
3 Although we have sent men *on* / *to* the moon, we have not explored our oceans.
4 The heat is radiated *outside* / *away from* the sun and *towards* / *into* the Earth.
5 The Palm Jumeirah is an artificial island *on* / *onto* the coast of Dubai.
6 With this vessel, Cameron was able to drive *along* / *around* the sea bed.
7 In a stable star, the processes taking place *into* / *inside* the star are balanced.
8 The sun appears bigger because we are close *to* / *from* it.

2 Work in pairs. Complete sentences 1–6 using prepositions from 1.

1 Over the last ten years I have built ....
2 The rooms on this side of the building face away ....
3 The university is close ....
4 We don't know what lies beneath ....
5 People like to drive ....
6 Students who do well at school are sent ....

TASK 2 Using verbs to describe a process

1 Read sentences 1–6. Select a verb from the list to replace each verb in bold.

released generated converted becomes causes stored reaches attracted

1 Objects with a negative and positive electric charge are **drawn** to each other.
2 Heat is **produced** by the sun shining on the building.
3 The water is **kept** in the reservoir until needed, then **let out** to produce electricity.
4 When the water temperature **gets to** 100 degrees, the water **turns into** water vapour.
5 Excess sugar in the body is **changed** into fat.
6 Eating too much salt **leads** the body to retain too much water.

TASK 3 Word formation: Describing dimensions

1 Work in pairs. Complete the table with the words in the list.

big length weight depth high width

Adjective	Noun	Adjective	Noun
deep		wide	
long		heavy	
	height		size

2 Complete sentences 1–4 with the correct word from the table.

1 The vessel descended to a .... of 10,000 metres.
2 Mount Everest is 8,848 metres .... and is the tallest mountain on Earth.
3 The average .... of a baby African elephant at birth is 90 kg.
4 There is no fixed .... for a football pitch. It can be between 90m and 120m long and between 45m and 90m ....

8E Academic Language Check

TASK 1 Past narrative tenses

1 Put the verb in brackets into the correct narrative tense: past simple, past continuous, or past perfect.

1 Alexander Fleming [1] .... (discover) penicillin when he [2] .... (grow) some bacteria and [3] .... (notice) a strange mould that [4] .... (appear) to be killing it. The bacteria [5] .... (become) contaminated because someone [6] .... (forget) to replace the petri-dish lid.

2 The invention of the wheel may seem an obvious idea, but people [7] .... (develop) boats, weapons, lamps and even writing before they [8] .... (invent) the wheel. In actual fact, the wheel [9] .... (be) in existence long before people [10] .... (realize) how useful it could be for transport. The potter's wheel [11] .... (be used) by the people of Mesopotamia (now southern Iraq) since about 3500 BC. But it [12] .... (be) three centuries later, in 3200 BC, that the same circular shape [13] .... (first / be turned) on its side and [14] .... (be used) to create a means of transport.

TASK 2 The passive voice

1 Complete sentences 1–6 using the present simple passive or past simple passive form and the verbs in the list.

emit discover grow develop manufacture ~~produce~~

1 The first carbonated water *was produced* in 1767.
2 Over 65 million cars .... every year.
3 Infrared, visible, and ultraviolet light .... by the sun.
4 The first dinosaur bones .... in the early 1800s.
5 Coffee .... in more than 50 countries.
6 Graphene .... by Andre Geim and his colleagues in 2004.

TASK 3 The passive voice and narrative sequencing words

1 Complete the text using the correct alternative from the words in italics.

The production of petrol

The process of petrol production [1]*begins / is begun* in the oil field. [2]*First / Then*, the crude oil is extracted from underground. [3]*When / Next* the oil [4]*has extracted / has been extracted*, it is pumped via pipelines to an oil refinery plant. [5]*After / Next*, the oil is refined to produce different products such as petrol, diesel, and aviation fuel. Each of these products [6]*requires / is required* a different treatment. During the refining process, sulphur and water [7]*remove / are removed* and sometimes other chemicals [8]*add / are added* to improve the quality of the end product. [9]*Next / After* the petrol [10]*has refined / has been refined*, it is transported to storage facilities and it is [11]*then / after* shipped to its destination countries. [12]*While / Finally*, the petrol [13]*transports / is transported* by road to petrol stations.

UNIT 9 Health

ACADEMIC FOCUS: CAUSE AND EFFECT

LEARNING OBJECTIVES

This unit covers:

Listening and Speaking
- Understanding cause and effect
- Recognizing and noting down key cause and effect relations
- Using indirect questions to respond to lecture content
- Giving a brief explanation of causes and effects

Reading
- Understanding cause and effect relationships in a text
- Using verbs to describe cause and effect

Writing
- Using noun expressions to express cause and effect
- Expressing cause and effect using verbs and nouns
- Writing a paragraph expressing cause and effect

Vocabulary
- Collocations (4): Adjective + noun
- Recognizing the meaning of homonyms

Academic Language Check
- Cause and effect language

Discussion

1 Work in pairs. Discuss questions 1–4 and note down your answers.

1 What are the major health problems (a) globally and (b) in your country?
2 How has human health and its treatment changed over the centuries?
3 What are the most important medical advances in the last 100 years?
4 What negative effects, if any, are caused by improved medical care?

2 The factors below can all contribute to good health. Rank them from (1) the most important to (5) the least important.

a healthy diet regular exercise a positive attitude strong genes luck

3 Work in groups. Discuss your answers to 1 and 2. Give reasons for each answer.

4 Work as a whole class. Discuss the statement below. Give reasons and examples.

Medical science has a good understanding of the causes of illnesses, but treatment alone won't necessarily solve our healthcare problems.

9A Listening & Speaking Lectures (6)

This module covers:

- Understanding cause and effect
- Recognizing and noting down key cause and effect relations
- Using indirect questions to respond to lecture content
- Giving a brief explanation of causes and effects

TASK 1 Preparing for a lecture

1 Work in pairs. Complete the list of the five senses.

1 hearing   2 sight   3 ....   4 touch   5 ....

2 A *sensory stimulus* is information which affects one of your senses. Note down at least one sensory stimulus for each of the five senses.

3 Think of examples of when you have used each of the senses in the past day. Discuss (a) which sense you used the most, and (b) which sense was particularly important.

TASK 2 Understanding key ideas

1 9.1 You are going to listen to part of a lecture about a condition called synaesthesia. Watch Extract 1 and complete the student notes.

Synaesthesia = condition where senses seem [1] ....

Main effects

Synaesthetes experience [2] .... to sensory stimulus.

e.g. - hear a musical note and [3] ....

- hear a word, e.g. [4] ...., and [5] ...., e.g. chocolate
- see a number and [6] ....

2 Work in pairs and help each other to complete the information.

3 Decide whether statements 1 and 2 are true or false. Note down any supporting evidence given by the lecturer.

1 Scientists think understanding the causes of synaesthesia could benefit everyone.

2 People who have synaesthesia find it unpleasant.

4 9.1 Watch Extract 1 again and check your answers.

TASK 3 Recognizing key cause and effect relations

1 9.2 Watch Extract 2 and complete the student notes.

Possible causes of synaesthesia

A a .... difference in ....

B .... factors

2 9.2 Watch Extract 2 again and complete the cause and effect relations.

1 Psychologists think synaesthesia develops in childhood because the associations that synaesthetes make are ....

2 Some scientists think synaesthesia is due to a physical difference in the brain because scans have shown ....

3 Work in pairs. Compare answers and complete any missing information.

TASK 4 Critical thinking – evaluating evidence

1 Work in pairs and discuss questions 1–3.

1 What evidence was given to support each possible cause of synaesthesia?

2 Was any evidence given against each possible cause?

3 Which of the two explanations for synaesthesia do you find more convincing? Why?

TASK 5 Understanding cause and effect relationships

1 9.3 Listen to Extract 3. Complete sentences 1–5 with appropriate cause and effect language.

1 Synaesthesia attracts a lot of interest .... scientists believe that understanding why it occurs could help us to understand how our brains process sensory stimuli.

2 Most synaesthetes find these associations pleasant rather than unpleasant. ...., synaesthesia is not considered to be an illness.

3 Is synaesthesia .... a physical difference? Or do people become synaesthetic .... environmental factors?

4 However, there are others who believe synaesthetes make these unusual associations .... a physical difference in their brain structure.

5 The suggestion is that their brains are cross-wired .... when they receive a signal, more than one part of the brain is activated.

2 Work in pairs. Discuss whether the words or phrases in each sentence in 1 introduce a cause or an effect.

ACADEMIC LANGUAGE

Cause and effect (1) Relationships

Cause and effect relationships can be expressed in a number of different ways.

Subordinators

Synaesthesia attracts interest, ***because*** *scientists believe it could help us to understand how our brains process sensory stimuli.*

Their brains are cross-wired ***so that*** *when they receive a signal, more than one part of the brain is activated.*

Prepositions

Is synaesthesia ***due to*** *a physical difference?*

Do people become synaesthetic ***because of*** *environmental factors?*

Synaesthetes make these unusual associations ***owing to*** *a physical difference in their brain.*

TASK 6 Using cause and effect language

1 Select an appropriate word / phrase to complete sentences 1–5.

because due to owing to so that (x2)

1 The study was significant .... nobody had ever interviewed so many patients before.

2 The results were examined closely .... any irregular data could be removed.

3 It is difficult to know the frequency of synaesthesia .... the large numbers of people that need to be tested.

4 Many scientists now think that the associations that synaesthetes make are .... strong childhood impressions.

5 Researchers at Oxford University have created a series of tests .... more accurate data can be gathered on synaesthesia and brain activity.

2 Work in pairs. Compare answers and give reasons for your choice.

TASK 7 Using questions to respond to lecture content

1 9.4 **Listen to Extract 4, students asking questions in a follow-up seminar. Tick the three items they ask about.**

positive / negative effects of synaesthesia ☐
the percentage of people with synaesthesia ☐
the number of senses that can be mixed ☐
possible cures for synaesthesia ☐
the most common types of synaesthesia ☐

2 9.4 **Listen again. Complete questions 1–4.**

1 I'm .... why people think that.
2 I .... if people can have more than one type of synaesthesia.
3 .... us what the most common types are?
4 .... why that's more common than other types?

ACADEMIC LANGUAGE ▸ Language reference page 157

Questions (2) Indirect questions

After lectures or talks, and in discussions, you will often need to ask questions to get further information. Indirect questions (e.g. ***Can you explain*** *how people get synaesthesia?*) are generally more tentative than direct questions (e.g. *How do people get synaesthesia?*). You can use a number of common question types. For example:

Can you explain *how people get synaesthesia?*
I didn't understand *why it affects some people and not others.*
Can you tell us *what the most common types are?*
Does anyone know *if there is a cure for synaesthesia?*
I'm not sure why *people say it is a pleasant condition.*

TASK 8 Asking questions about a presentation topic

1 9.5 **Listen to Extract 5, a presentation about another condition. Note down:**

1 a brief definition of narcolepsy
2 how many people are affected
3 possible effects of narcolepsy.

2 **Work in pairs. Note down questions you could ask to get further information about the points in 1.**

Example: *'Narcolepsy is a condition which affects the brain's ability to control the normal sleep-wake cycle.'*
Could you define what a normal sleep-wake cycle is?

3 9.6 **Listen to Extract 6. Ask your questions during the pauses.**

4 **Work in pairs. Take turns describing a cause / effect relationship from your own area of study, or a subject you are interested in. Remember to:**

- give a clear explanation of the main idea
- clearly define any new terms
- draw attention to probable causes
- draw attention to possible effects.

5 **After each explanation, ask and answer questions to get further information.**

INDEPENDENT STUDY

Reports on accidents, disasters, or changing situations often use a range of cause and effect language.

▸ **Find a report on a recent incident and note down the causes and effects given. Then describe these to another student in the class.**

9B Reading Textbooks (8)

This module covers:

- Understanding cause and effect relationships in a text
- Using verbs to describe cause and effect

TASK 1 Previewing the theme of a text

allergy (*n*) a medical condition that causes you to react badly or feel ill when you eat, breathe, or touch a particular substance

1 Work in pairs. Read the definition, then discuss questions 1–3.

1 What do you know about common allergies, e.g. hay fever, nut allergies? Give information on each of the following points:
   - causes
   - symptoms

2 Do you think more people have allergies now than in the past? Why?

3 Why do you think that there has been an increase in the number of patients reporting allergies?

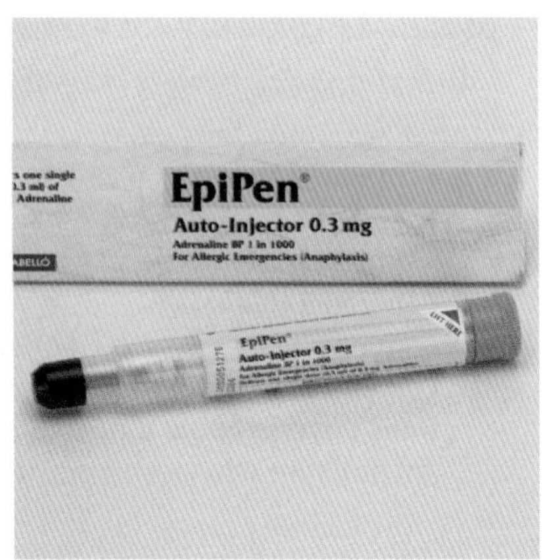

2 Read Text 1 and check your answers in 1.

TEXT 1

Allergies

An allergy is a negative physical response to something in the environment: pollen or certain foods, for example. Symptoms include skin irritation and breathing difficulties. In recent years there has been an increase in the number of patients reporting allergies of one kind or another. Between 30 and 35% of the world's population report allergic reactions at some time in their lives. No one knows the real reasons for this increase, although several causes have been suggested: additives in food, more pollutants in the atmosphere which affect breathing, or cleaner home environments that make us less able to resist bacteria.

GLOSSARY

pollen *(n)* a fine, usually yellow powder, which is formed in flowers and carried to other flowers by the wind or by insects

skin irritation *(n)* when part of the skin is dry, sore, or painful

TASK 2 Understanding the structure of a text

1 You are going to read a text about the causes of a medical condition. Predict the order for items a–e.

a an overview of recent research into causes ....
b a description of the condition ....
c an overview of possible causes ....
d reference to a specific cause ....
e research findings ....

2 Read Text 2 quickly. Match items a–e to Paragraphs 1–5.

The causes of asthma

TEXT 2

1 Asthma is a chronic lung condition where the air passages in the lungs become inflamed. The **lining of the airway is swollen**, the **muscles become tight**, and **mucus** builds up. This results in breathing problems for the patient. Asthma typically causes wheezing, coughing and shortness of breath. The symptoms are often worse during the night, when the patient is lying down, or after physical exercise.

2 It is not known exactly what causes asthma, but we do know that certain conditions make a person more likely to develop it. For example, living in an industrial area, where people are more exposed to air pollution, leads to an increased risk of developing asthma. Similarly, a family history of asthma or other allergies, such as hay fever, can mean that your chances of getting asthma are greater. Studies have also shown that being exposed to tobacco smoke when young results in increased risks.

3 As well as examining the deeper causes, an important area of research for medical scientists is finding out what can trigger an asthma attack. Asthma attacks vary according to the time of year and are sometimes caused by sudden changes in the weather. Autumn, for example, is known to be a bad time for sufferers, as are heatwaves in the summer.

4 One particular focus of study has been the relationship between the pollen count and asthma. A study was carried out in New York to determine if an increase in the amount of pollen in the air caused an increase in the number of asthma attacks. Over a period of 270 days, the number of people admitted to New York hospitals with asthma attacks was recorded.

5 The findings show clearly that the increase in the number of hospital admissions of asthma cases, which reached a peak in October, were not a result of the increase in the pollen count, which reached a peak a month earlier. Although there are many patients who say their asthma attacks are caused or made worse by pollen in the air, the evidence shows that this is not the case for the majority. Instead, it seems more likely that asthma attacks occur more frequently in October because it is the season when people catch colds and flu most often.

SOURCE: Allot, A. (2012). p.351. *IB Biology: Course Companion*. Oxford: Oxford University Press.

GLOSSARY

admitted *(v)* taken to hospital to receive special care

lungs *(n)* the organs inside the chest that are used for breathing

pollen count *(n)* the amount of pollen in the air

trigger *(v)* to make sth happen suddenly

wheezing *(n)* breathing noisily, for example if you have a chest illness

TASK 3 Understanding cause and effect within a longer text

1 Read Paragraph 1 of Text 2 again. Use the words in bold to complete Diagram 2.

Diagram 1 Normal air passages

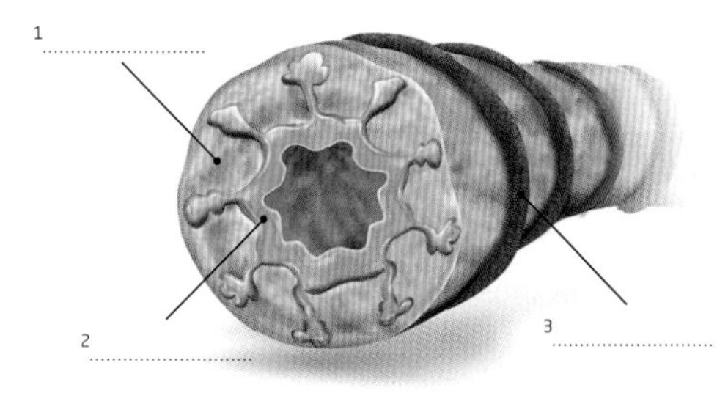

Diagram 2 Air passage in asthmatic patient

2 Read the whole text again and complete the table.

Asthma	a condition where .... become inflamed
Main symptoms (effects)	breathing problems: ...., ..., ...
Possible causes of asthma attacks	1 .... 2 .... 3 ....
Known causes of asthma attacks	....
Connection between asthma and pollen count according to research	....

3 Use the notes in the table to complete the summary of Text 2.

Asthma is a condition where [1] .... and breathing is affected. Sufferers feel the effects of asthma more strongly at night and after exercise. The main symptoms are breathing problems such as coughing or [2] .... The precise cause of asthma is not known, but we know what makes people more likely to develop it. Scientists are investigating possible causes, which include [3] .... Current research indicates that [4] .... can cause asthma attacks. However, it has been concluded that there is [5] .... causal link between pollen count and asthma outbreaks.

4 Read Text 2 again and check your answers.

TASK 4 Identifying cause and effect relationships in a text

1 Use the information in Paragraphs 1–4 of Text 2 to match each cause 1–4 to its effect a–d.

1 the lungs become inflamed	....	a an asthma attack
2 living in an industrial area	....	b breathing problems for the patient
3 sudden changes in the weather	....	c an increased risk of developing asthma
4 an increase in pollen count	....	d no increase in hospital admissions for asthma

2 Identify the verbs used to link the causes and effects in 1.

Example: *... the lungs become inflamed. This* <u>*results in*</u> *breathing problems for ...*

3 Read Paragraph 5 again and the pairs of sentences 1–3. For each pair, decide which sentence is the *cause* and which is the *effect*.

1 Hospital admissions for asthma increased in October. The number of asthma attacks rose.

2 People think there is more pollen in the air. People link the amount of pollen to their asthma attacks.

3 Asthma attacks occur in greater numbers during October. Autumn is the season when people catch colds and flu.

4 Rewrite the pairs of sentences in 3 using the words / phrases in the list.

because   as a result   due to this

ACADEMIC LANGUAGE

▸Language reference page 157

Cause and effect (2) Verbs

Academic texts often include explanations of cause and effect relationships. In some cases the effect is described before the cause. In other cases the cause is given first, followed by the effect it produces. For example:

Cause → Effect

Asthma typically ***causes*** *wheezing, coughing, and shortness of breath.*
Living in an industrial area ***leads to*** *an increased risk of developing asthma.*
A family history of asthma can ***mean*** *that your chances of getting asthma are greater.*
Being exposed to tobacco smoke when young ***results in*** *increased risks.*

Effect → Cause

Asthma attacks ***are*** *sometimes* ***caused by*** *sudden changes in the weather.*
The increase in hospital admissions ***were*** *not* ***caused by*** *the increase in the pollen count.*

Note that the passive form of the verb is often used to express effect → cause relationships.

TASK 5 Using verbs to express cause and effect

1 Complete sentences 1–4 with the words in the list.

mean caused results causes leads

1 Asthma .... the lungs to become inflamed and this .... in coughing and shortness of breath.
2 Being exposed to air pollution .... to an increased risk of developing asthma.
3 A family history of asthma or other allergies can .... that you have a greater chance of getting asthma.
4 Asthma attacks are sometimes .... by a heatwave.

2 Use the prompts in 1–5 to write sentences describing cause and effect.

1 One in five car accidents / cause / drivers not paying attention

....

....

2 A serious mistake in their calculations / result / some surprising statistics

....

....

3 Ice melting in the mountains / lead / the large amount of water in the rivers

....

....

4 Increased internet access / mean / more and more people are searching for the causes of illnesses online

....

....

5 Exercising gently / not / cause / stress to the muscles and joints

....

....

3 Select from topics 1–3. Write at least two sentences using cause and effect verbs.

Example: *Lightning is caused by a positive and negative electrical charge in a thundercloud. When the charge is large enough, it results in a giant spark occurring in the cloud.*

1 something that is bad for your health
2 a natural phenomenon (e.g. a rainbow, an eclipse)
3 something people do that is bad for the environment

TASK 6 Critical thinking – examining the ideas in a text

1 Work in groups. Discuss questions 1 and 2 about Text 2 and note down your ideas.

1 Which facts caused researchers to explore the link between pollen count and asthma in New York?
2 What do the results of the study in Text 2 tell us about the importance of medical research?

2 Briefly present your group's ideas from 1 to the whole class. Use the following phrases to help you.

We discussed ...

Our group feel that ...

It's our opinion that ...

INDEPENDENT STUDY

The long-term effects of certain behaviours and practices are not always clearly known.

▸ **Think about what the long-term effects of one or more of the following things are: smoking, living in space, marathon running, using a computer all day. Then look them up on the internet and compare your answers.**

9C Writing (1) Cause and effect connections

This module covers:

- Using noun expressions to express cause and effect
- Expressing cause and effect using verbs and nouns

TASK 1 Analysing cause and effect in a paragraph

1 Work in pairs. Discuss questions 1 and 2.

1 How would you feel (physically and emotionally) in the situations in photographs 1–3?

2 What do you know about adrenaline? When, how, and why is it produced in the body?

1

2

3

2 Read Paragraph 1 from a student's essay. Complete the diagram.

Paragraph 1

The release of adrenaline in the body is usually a result of a sudden feeling of fear or danger. The reason for this is to create the state of readiness that is needed to deal with the situation. The hypothalamus, which is the part of the brain that is responsible for maintaining the balance between stress and relaxation in your body, sends out a chemical signal to the adrenal glands. This in turn releases the hormone adrenaline into the body. As a consequence, some changes happen. The heart rate increases, breathing gets faster, eyes get wider, and muscles tighten. As a result, the mind and body are now more alert and ready to react.

GLOSSARY

alert *(adj)* aware of sth, especially a problem or danger

confront *(v)* to deal with a problem or difficult situation

gland *(n)* a small organ inside the body that produces a chemical for the body to use

TASK 2 Recognizing cause and effect

1 Note down which event (a) or (b) from Paragraph 1 is a cause and which is an effect.

Example: *a the release of adrenaline in the body*
b sudden feeling of fear or danger

1 a the release of adrenaline
b the state of readiness that is needed to deal with a situation

2 a the hypothalamus sends out a chemical signal to your adrenal glands
b the adrenal glands release the hormone adrenaline

3 a the hormone adrenaline is released
b raised heart rate, faster breathing, and tightening of muscles

4 a the body is now more ready to physically react
b faster breathing, widening of eyes, and tightening of muscles

2 Identify the phrases in Paragraph 1 which indicate cause and effect.

Example: *The release of adrenaline in the body* *is usually a result of* *a sudden feeling of fear or danger.*

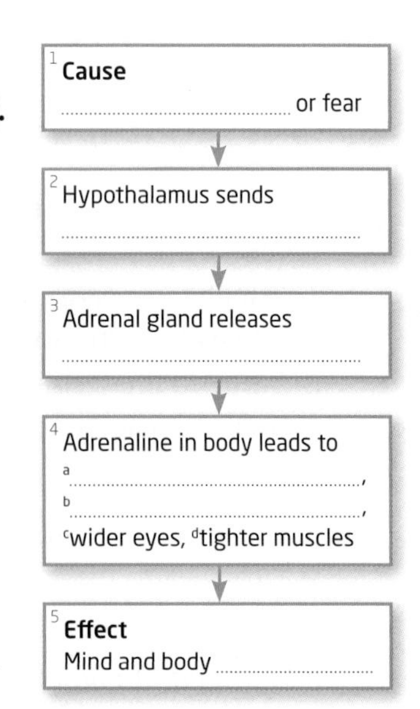

3 Write sentences about the cause and effect relationships in Paragraph 1. Use your own words and the diagram to help plan your ideas.

Example: *An unexpected feeling of fear or danger often causes adrenaline to be released in the body.*

ACADEMIC LANGUAGE ▸Language reference page 158

Cause and effect (3) Noun expressions

Cause and effect relationships can be expressed using certain expressions that include nouns.

Cause → effect

The heart rate increases, breathing gets faster, eyes get wider, and muscles tighten. ***As a result****, the mind and body are now more alert and ready to act.*

This in turn releases the hormone adrenaline into the body. ***As a consequence****, some changes happen.*

The reason for *this is to create the state of readiness that is needed to deal with the situation.*

A lack of Vitamin B1 is often ***the cause of*** *a loss of appetite.*

Effect → cause

The release of adrenaline in the body is usually ***a result of*** *a sudden feeling of fear or danger.*

Malnutrition is ***a consequence of*** *disease and a poor diet.*

Shivering is ***an effect of*** *the body's need to produce heat.*

TASK 3 Varying cause and effect language

1 Read Paragraph 2 from a student essay. Replace the cause and effect language in italics with a word / phrase from the list.

a result of consequence consequences for effect reason for

Paragraph 2

For many people life is becoming more stressful because of increasing economic and social pressures. As a [1]*result*, more people are suffering from stress-related problems which have negative [2]*effects on* their health and well-being. Many young people report an increase in social pressures; this is partly [3]*due to* living more public lives through online media. One [4]*impact* of this lifestyle shift is that teenagers who use social media often feel that they have to project an identity that is difficult to maintain. This can have many negative consequences, and is often the [5]*cause of* increased anxiety and a fear of failure.

2 Write sentences from prompts 1–5 expressing cause and effect relationships. Begin with the words given and use the word in brackets.

Example: life more stressful than ever / more people suffering from stress-related problems (consequence)
Life is more stressful than ever and, as a consequence, more people are suffering from stress-related problems.

1 increased global temperatures / global warming (result)
Increased global temperatures ....

2 low life expectancy / high levels of childhood poverty (effect)
Low life expectancy is ....

3 a drop in blood sugar / there are reactions in the nervous system (result)
There are reactions in the nervous system ....

4 a lot of healthcare is now delivered outside the hospital / hospital stays are shorter (result)
A lot of healthcare ....

5 people have high protein intakes / energy levels are reduced (consequence)
Reduced energy levels ....

9C Writing (2) Cause and effect paragraphs

This module covers:

- Writing a paragraph expressing cause and effect

TASK 1 Analysing a cause and effect paragraph

1 **Work in pairs. Discuss which items a–c cause the most health problems. Give reasons.**

a poor diet
b smoking
c lack of exercise

2 **Note down any specific health conditions that can be caused by items a–c.**

3 **Read Paragraph 3, part of a student's answer to the following essay title. Match functions a–e to sentences 1–5.**

TITLE: *Describe a health condition which has impacted on society. Outline causes and effects.*

Paragraph 3

[1]Diabetes is a lifelong medical condition which causes a person's blood sugar level to become too high. [2]The condition is caused by the body not making enough of the hormone insulin or as a result of the body not being able to use insulin effectively. [3]This results in glucose building up in the blood, which in turn leads to diabetes. [4]Over time, high blood glucose damages nerves and blood vessels and can eventually cause complications such as heart disease, kidney disease, and blindness. [5]It is not certain what starts the processes that cause diabetes, but scientists believe that it is due to a combination of genetic and environmental factors.

a description of effects ....
b topic sentence – providing a definition ....
c description of further causes and effects ....
d overview of causes ....
e conclusion with some evaluation ....

TASK 2 Recognizing cause and effect language in a paragraph

1 **Identify the cause and effect language in Paragraph 3.**

Example: *The condition* <u>*is caused by*</u> *the body not making ...*

2 **Rewrite sentences 1–5 about the cause and effect relationships in Paragraph 3. Use the word in brackets.**

1 Diabetes causes blood sugar levels to rise. (result)

....

2 Glucose builds up because insulin is not used effectively. (reason)

....

3 High blood glucose leads to nerve damage. (cause)

....

4 Damaged nerves can lead to blindness. (consequence)

....

5 Scientists believe diabetes is due to genetic and environmental factors. (result)

....

TASK 3 Using cause and effect language in a paragraph

1 Select the most appropriate cause and effect language to complete the next paragraphs in the student's essay.

as a result   a consequence   cause   caused by   due to   results in

The most common form of diabetes, Type 2, affects 90% of diabetics globally. It is [1] .... of a combination of factors, including a condition in which the body's muscle, fat, and liver cells do not use insulin effectively. [2] .... the body is not able to produce enough insulin to compensate for its inefficient use. A healthy diet, regular physical activity, and maintaining a normal body weight can prevent or delay the condition.

Type 1 diabetes is an autoimmune disease. The symptoms of Type 1 diabetes are [3] .... a lack of insulin [4] .... the destruction of insulin-producing cells in the pancreas. This [5] .... the body's immune system attacking and destroying its own cells, including the cells which produce insulin. Currently there is no known [6] .... of the condition, although if you have a close relative with Type 1 diabetes, you have a 6% chance of also developing the condition, as opposed to 0.5% for those without family links.

TASK 4 Writing a paragraph including cause and effect language

1 Read the student paragraph plan. Note down the key cause and effect of malaria.

Sentence 1: a definition of malaria
Malaria: a mosquito-borne infectious disease → thousands of deaths each year. (lead to)

Sentence 2: causes of malaria
Malaria ← the Plasmodium parasite / humans contract parasite ← being bitten by an infected female mosquito. (caused by / as a result of)

Sentence 3 - effect / result:
the parasite enters bloodstream and travels to liver → an infection in the liver (results in)

Sentence 4 - further causes and effects:
the parasite re-enters the bloodstream and grows in red blood cells → blood cells burst → the body becomes more infected (causes / as a consequence)

Sentence 5 - conclusion:
the WHO (World Health Organization) see malaria as a serious global health risk → it publishes a World Malaria Report every year. (as a result)

2 Write five sentences based on the notes in 1. Use the words / phrases in brackets.

Example: *Malaria is a mosquito-borne infectious disease which leads to thousands of deaths each year.*

3 Write a paragraph of around 120 words about a cause and effect relationship connected to your field of study, or a topic you are interested in (e.g. how earthquakes happen, how exchange rates fluctuate). Use stages 1–6 to plan.

1 Note down key stages in the process and the cause and effect relationships.
2 Plan a topic sentence defining the process.
3 Plan a sentence giving an overview of causes.
4 Plan a sentence describing effects.
5 Plan a sentence describing further causes and effects.
6 Plan a conclusion offering evaluation.

4 Work in pairs. Evaluate your partner's paragraph. Use stages 1–6 in 3 as guidelines.

INDEPENDENT STUDY

Descriptions of medical conditions are good sources for cause and effect information; in most explanations of illnesses online you will find a list of the symptoms and causes.

▸ Think of a common medical condition (e.g. common cold, tiredness, headaches). Work with another student and note down what you think the causes and symptoms of it are. Then check online and compare your answers.

Sample answer: page 161

9D Vocabulary

TASK 1 Collocations (4): Adjective + noun

1 Cross out the adjective that does NOT collocate with each noun in sentences 1–7.

1 The experiments gave *inconclusive* / *deep* / *surprising* results.
2 For people who smoke, there is a(n) *higher* / *increased* / *harder* risk of developing the illness.
3 The researchers wanted to find the *serious* / *deeper* / *real* causes of the condition.
4 One explanation is that the illness is caused by *dramatic* / *sudden* / *strong* changes in the weather.
5 In the Far East the colour white often has *strong* / *negative* / *high* associations with death.
6 The medicine was withdrawn because of its *physical* / *certain* / *negative* effects on patients.
7 The question of the cost of the treatment is a(n) *certain* / *unrelated* / *separate* issue.

2 Select three collocations from 1 and write new sentences.

3 Work in pairs. Read your sentences to each other.

TASK 2 Recognizing the meaning of homonyms

Homonyms

Homonyms are words with more than one meaning. For example: the adjective *right* means *correct* and is also the opposite of *left.*

Homonyms can be different parts of speech, e.g.
You're right. (adjective)
You have a right to know. (noun)

1 Select the correct meaning (a) or (b) of each homonym in sentences 1–8.

1 Adrenaline puts the body in a **state** of readiness to face danger.
a emotional or physical condition b say something
2 Asthma is a **condition** which affects the lungs.
a the state of something b an illness or medical state
3 The scientists wanted to prove that this was the **case**.
a a bag or container b the true situation
4 At night time, moths are attracted to the **light**.
a not heavy b energy (e.g. from the sun) that makes it possible to see things
5 It is important to **note** that synaesthesia affects only one in 2000 people.
a observe b a single sound in music
6 Environmental factors play a **key** role in how the illness develops.
a a piece of metal that opens or closes a lock b important or significant
7 The patient associates each different letter with a **certain** colour.
a particular b sure
8 The doctor must **match** the patient's symptoms to the correct illness or condition.
a a game or contest b find something connected

2 Work in pairs. Note down five more homonyms in English.

INDEPENDENT STUDY

When you look up words in a dictionary, you will find that some are homonyms (have more than one meaning). Check very carefully which meaning fits the context you are looking at.

9E Academic Language Check

TASK 1 Cause and effect language

1 Complete texts 1–4 with the cause and effect language in the lists.

lead means result

1 Research has shown that physical exercise can [1] .... to lasting positive effects on patients' lives during recovery from illness. Exercise can [2] .... in improvements in both physical health as well as psychological health. This [3] .... that lifestyle behaviour is also generally improved.

due cause caused

2 A number of factors [4] .... unemployment levels to fluctuate. Unemployment that is [5] .... by changes in the requirements of the labour market is called *frictional unemployment*. Unemployment that is [6] .... to structural changes in the economy is called *structural unemployment*.

result because due

3 One of the most high-profile sporting drug cheats of all time is Canadian sprinter Ben Johnson. In 1988, he won the Olympic 100m gold medal, but a failed drug test showed that his world record time of 9.79 seconds was not [7] .... to human effort, but [8] .... he had been taking the anabolic steroid drug stanozolol. As a [9] ...., Johnson was stripped of his title and was subsequently banned from the sport.

result because due lead result

4 Physical exercise may be chemically addictive. One theory is that this addiction is [10] .... to the 'feel-good' chemicals, endorphins, and dopamine, which are produced in the brain when exercising. As a [11] ...., some people become addicted to the psychological effects of physical exercise and fitness. This may in turn [12] .... to over-exercise and can [13] .... in the condition of 'overtraining.' Overtraining is when the intensity of an individual's exercise is greater than their ability to recover from the exercise. [14] .... of this, an athlete may begin to lose strength and fitness. Overtraining is particularly common in weight training, but it can also be experienced by runners and other athletes.

2 Write sentences to express the cause and effect relationship. Use different cause and effect language for each sentence.

Example: *Greenhouse gas emissions → global warming*
Greenhouse gas emissions may lead to global warming.

1 shale gas extraction → possible chemical and radiological pollution

....

2 excessive and prolonged overeating → obesity

....

3 a successful advertising campaign → sales rose by over 200%

....

4 increased public awareness → there are fewer cases of sun-related medical conditions

....

5 damage in the brain → dementia

....

UNIT 10 Location

ACADEMIC FOCUS: ARGUMENT

LEARNING OBJECTIVES

This unit covers:

Listening and Speaking

- Identifying main argument and supporting evidence
- Identifying structure of a well-reasoned argument
- Presenting arguments *for* and *against*

Reading

- Understanding a short argument text
- Identifying arguments
- Evaluating the strength of arguments

Writing

- Identifying arguments and supporting ideas
- Writing main body paragraphs
- Planning opening and concluding paragraphs
- Writing an argument essay

Vocabulary

- Formal and informal vocabulary
- Using common prefixes

Academic Language Check

- Linking words (1): Addition
- Linking words (2): Contrast

Discussion

1 Work in pairs. Discuss statements 1–3. Note down one argument *for* and *against* each statement.

1 People should try to take more holidays in their own country.

2 Companies should locate their businesses in their own country, not in other countries.

3 It is better to locate factories close to where employees live.

2 Work with another pair. Select one side of the argument in each case and discuss the statements.

- *I think that companies should ... because ...*
- *People should travel abroad because it ...*

3 Discuss which arguments you found the most convincing. Give reasons.

10A Listening & Speaking Lectures (7)

This module covers:

- Identifying main argument and supporting evidence
- Identifying structure of a well-reasoned argument
- Presenting arguments *for* and *against*

TASK 1 Previewing the topic of a lecture

New trends in travel and tourism
Thursday 4 March
11.30 – 13.00
Lecture Hall 14
Dr Paula Elbisser

1 Work in pairs. Read the lecture title and discuss questions 1–3.

1 Do you think fewer or more people in the world are travelling abroad for holidays than twenty years ago? What are the reasons for the change?
2 Are people more or less concerned about the environmental impact of tourism?
3 The lecturer speaks about *responsible tourism*. How would you define this?

2 10.1 Watch Extract 1 and compare your definition to the lecturer's.

3 10.1 Watch Extract 1 again and complete the notes.

Three main aims of responsible tourism:
1 reduce ....
2 protect ....
3 limit ....

TASK 2 Identifying main arguments and supporting evidence

1 10.2 Watch Extract 2 and complete the notes.

Key arguments in support of responsible tourism. Tourists should ...
1 understand ....
2 support ....
3 be aware of ....

2 Match examples a–c with key arguments 1–3.

a Stay in a hotel run by local people. ....
b Use a company that does not waste resources. ....
c Read a guidebook before you visit a country. ....

3 Note down two other examples which could match the key arguments in 1.

4 10.2 Watch Extract 2 again. Identify which argument the lecturer feels is the most important in support of responsible tourism. Do you agree? Give reasons.

TASK 3 Summarizing main arguments and supporting evidence

1 10.3 Watch Extract 3. Note down the two main arguments about tourism and respect.

1 Benefits host and traveller:
host .... ; traveller ....
2 Creates conditions where ....

2 10.3 Watch Extract 3 again or look at the transcript on page 174. Note down the supporting evidence the lecturer gives for arguments 1 and 2.

3 Work in pairs. Use your notes to take turns summarizing arguments 1 and 2.

TASK 4 Identifying structure in an argument

1 Look at the typical stages of an argument 1–5. Match them with the stages a–e in the lecture.

Structure of an argument
[1]Give the background / context → [2]Define key terms → [3]Ask the main question(s) → [4]Give the answer → [5]Give evidence to support the answer

a Explaining what responsible tourism is ....
b Stating that responsible tourism could be an answer ....
c Explaining the context of tourism today *1*
d Giving arguments in favour of responsible tourism with supporting evidence ....
e Highlighting the issues that the present situation raises ....

2 Read the transcript of Extracts 1–3 on page 174. Identify and number the beginning of each of the stages outlined in 1.

Example: *The first thing I want to discuss is the growing trend for responsible tourism. [1]As air travel becomes …*

TASK 5 Identifying language for developing an argument

1 Complete sentences 1–4 with the most appropriate words / phrases.

1 Responsible tourism has several key principles. *First of all / In addition / Also*, a responsible tourist should understand the place they are visiting – its culture, its economy, and its politics – and show respect for these things.
2 Responsible tourism *also / first of all* means supporting the local economy.
3 *Furthermore / In addition / Also*, responsible tourism means being aware of your impact on the environment.
4 The traveller benefits from knowing they are making a positive contribution. They get that 'feel good' effect. *Furthermore / In addition / Also*, by showing respect, the traveller creates the conditions where he or she can get closer to the culture of a particular place.

2 10.4 Watch Extract 4 and check your answers.

ACADEMIC LANGUAGE ▸Language reference page 158

Linking words (1) Addition

Often in academic argument, speakers give a number of points to support their stance. For example:

*It **also** means supporting the local economy.*
***As well as** providing income, tourism **also** encourages local businesses to start up.*
***In addition**, responsible tourism means being aware of your impact on the environment.*
***Furthermore**, the traveller can get closer to the culture of a particular place.*

TASK 6 Critical thinking – examining arguments

1 Work in pairs. Discuss questions 1 and 2.

1 Do you think the lecturer's arguments in favour of responsible tourism are convincing? Why / Why not?
2 Note down two points for and against responsible tourism.

TASK 7 Making concessions within arguments

1 🔊 10.5 Listen to Extract 5, a seminar discussion. Complete the table.

	Speaker's view on travelling	Tutor's response
Elena		Agree / Disagree
Carsten		Agree / Disagree

2 Work in pairs. Discuss which arguments presented in Extract 5 you (a) agree or (b) disagree with. Give reasons.

3 Each speaker conceded that there was some truth in the other's arguments. Listen again and note down which phrases in Academic Language are used by:

Elena ....

Carsten ....

Tutor ....

ACADEMIC LANGUAGE

Linking words (2) Conceding

Often in discussions you will agree in part with other people. In these cases you can admit, or concede, to the other person that they have made a good point. There are a number of verbs which show concession. For example:

*I **understand** why you say that.*
*Well, I **realize** that it might look like that.*
*OK. Yes, I **see** what you're saying.*

When you want to show that the other person's argument is strong, but you still disagree, you can use countering expressions. For example:

*I understand why you say that, **but actually** I don't agree.*
*OK. Yes, I see what you're saying. **Although** I'm not convinced.*

TASK 8 Presenting arguments *for* and *against*

1 Work in small groups. Read the discussion topic and prepare your ideas. Use steps 1–4.

Is tourism a good thing or a bad thing?

1 Decide what your position is.
2 Form small groups so there are students with opposing positions.
3 Prepare your case, noting down arguments *for* and *against*.
4 Note down supporting evidence and examples.

2 Work in small groups. Discuss the topic. Use Academic Language to help you make concessions.

INDEPENDENT STUDY

Find an online debate related to your area of study or a subject you are interested in.

▸ Listen and note how the different speakers (a) structure their arguments and (b) concede points to the other debaters.

TASK 9 Evaluating an argument

1 Evaluate your partners' contribution in the debate. Did they:

- state their stance clearly?
- build on their argument with supporting evidence?
- offer supporting examples?
- concede the points against their argument?

10B Reading Textbooks (9)

This module covers:

- Understanding a short argument text
- Identifying arguments
- Evaluating the strength of arguments

TASK 1 Previewing the topic of a text

1 Work in pairs. Discuss questions 1 and 2.

1 Match the most important location factors 1–3 to the companies a–c.

1 close to a cheap labour force ....
2 close to their customers ....
3 good telephone and internet connections ....

a a restaurant   b a shoe factory   c a call centre

2 Is location more important for some of these businesses than others? Give reasons.

2 Complete the definition with the words below.

operations   country   company

> **offshoring** (*n*) [U] (BUSINESS) the practice of locating or relocating a [1].................... or some of its [2].................... in a different [3]....................

3 Work in pairs. Discuss questions 1 and 2.

1 Why do some companies practise offshoring?
2 What are possible positives and negatives of offshoring?

TASK 2 Understanding an argument text

1 Read Text 1. Note down which of the ideas that you discussed in Task 1.3 are mentioned in the text. Which other factors, if any, are mentioned?

2 Identify the parts of the text that:

1 state whether the author is for or against companies offshoring
2 give the author's conclusion about offshoring.

TEXT 1

Offshoring - whether to locate domestically or internationally

1 We have looked at the various factors that companies consider in their choice of location - the cost of rent, competition, transport infrastructure, closeness to the customer or suppliers, availability of labour, and taxes. The next section examines whether a business should locate domestically or internationally.

2 With globalization, there has been a trend in the last 25 years for companies in the west to relocate their operations to developing countries, where conditions may help them to grow and to be more competitive. This is known as 'offshoring'. Critics of offshoring say that it damages the economy of the company's home country.

3 The main criticism is the loss of domestic jobs. However, there is evidence to suggest that this is not the case. Although some jobs are lost when companies relocate to a foreign country, studies have shown that the numbers are not great. Offshoring accounts for only 0.1% of annual job losses in the services sector in the USA. In the manufacturing sector, where companies move their factories to countries with lower labour costs, job losses have been greater.

4 However, this is offset by two factors. First, the type of jobs which are done abroad tend to be low-skilled. This leaves more opportunity for high-skilled jobs to grow domestically. In other words, if the company is successful and sales grow, jobs will be created in the home country in areas of the business like sales, marketing, and research and development. In addition, offshoring promotes economic growth in developing countries, raising people's incomes and demand for the company's products there.

5 Critics of offshoring worry that it is a trend that will increase in the future, resulting in further job losses. But this concern ignores a basic principle of economics. As developing countries become richer, workers in these countries demand higher salaries. So, over time, the labour costs of companies operating in these countries increases. At a certain point, the wages will become unaffordable and the advantage of offshoring will be lost. The company will then relocate (or 're-shore') to its home country.

6 So, in summary, despite having a short-term negative impact on the domestic economy, in the medium and long-term, the benefits of offshoring are generally greater than its disadvantages.

SOURCE: Clark, P. et al. (2012). p.258. *IB Business and Management: Course Companion.* Oxford: Oxford University Press.

GLOSSARY

demand *(n)* the desire or need of customers for a particular product or service

income *(n)* the money people receive as payment for their work

manufacturing sector *(n)* part of the economy which comprises companies which make products, often in factories

offset *(v)* to use one cost or situation in order to reduce or cancel the effects of another

services sector *(n)* part of the economy which comprises businesses whose work involves doing sth for customers but not producing goods

TASK 3 Identifying arguments in a text

1 The author presents a number of criticisms of the arguments against offshoring. Identify where he does this in the text.

2 Work in pairs. Discuss your selection in 1. Give reasons why the author has chosen to present an argument in this way.

3 Read Text 1 again. Complete the table.

Subject	Criticism	Author's response
Effect on jobs		
Trend for offshoring		

TASK 4 Critical thinking – evaluating arguments

1 Work in pairs. Discuss which arguments for and against offshoring in Text 1 you think are strongest. Give reasons.

2 Add at least one more argument for or against offshoring. Think of examples to support your ideas.

TASK 5 Identifying connected arguments in a text

1 Read the summaries of contrasting arguments 1–4 from Text 1. Note down which word is used to link the arguments and to show contrast.

Example: The main criticism is the loss of domestic jobs. / There is evidence to suggest that this is not the case.
The main criticism is the loss of domestic jobs. However, there is evidence to suggest that this is not the case.

1. Some jobs are lost when companies relocate to a foreign country. / Studies have shown that the numbers are not great.
2. In the manufacturing sector, where companies move their factories to countries with lower labour costs, job losses have been greater. / This is offset by two factors.
3. Critics of offshoring worry that it is a trend that will increase in the future, resulting in further job losses. / This concern ignores a basic principle of economics.
4. Offshoring has a short-term negative impact on the domestic economy. / In the medium and long term, the benefits of offshoring are generally greater than its disadvantages.

ACADEMIC LANGUAGE

▸ Language reference page 158

Linking words (3) Contrast and concession

It is often necessary to present and contrast two sides to an argument. This is often done using linking words. Many linking words introduce a contrast between two situations.

Contrast

The main criticism is the loss of domestic jobs. ***However****, there is evidence to suggest that this is not the case.*

On the one hand*, offshoring offers much-needed employment opportunities.* ***On the other hand****, it can sometimes be seen as exploiting the local workforce.*

Concession

Although / Even though *unemployment rates dropped, there was no measurable benefit to the local economy.*

Despite *selling over five million units, the product made very little profit.*

Note that *even though*, *although*, and *despite* are generally used to express that something is surprising or unexpected, or to express concession.

TASK 6 Using linking words

1 Complete the paragraph using the most appropriate words/phrases in italics.

Tourist trips to villages in countries such as Thailand and Vietnam have been popular for a number of years, [1]*even though / however* some tourists feel a little uncomfortable about the idea. [2]*Despite / On the one hand*, tourists want to experience authentic, remote, traditional villages, but on the other, they do not want to change these places. [3]*Although / But* the visitors sometimes feel uncomfortable, the people who live there are often happy with the money tourists bring. They are especially happy when tourists make them gifts of money, [4]*however / even though* this is discouraged by the tour companies. [5]*Although / Despite* being aware of the negative impacts on local communities, tour companies continue to offer these tours.

2 Write six sentences that link the two contrasting arguments. Use the word or phrase in brackets.

Example: The area is relatively poor. It has abundant natural resources. (despite)
Despite having abundant natural resources, the area is relatively poor.

1 Unemployment levels decreased. They were still greater than twelve months previously. (although)
2 Air travel is becoming more frequent. It is at the same time also becoming more expensive. (however)
3 Vaccines have many common and serious side effects. They have many benefits. (despite)
4 Nuclear energy is very clean. There is always the risk of some form of environmental contamination. (on the other hand)
5 There is a consistent decline in oil production globally. Production of oil in some regions is booming. (even though)
6 Tourism worldwide is having a positive economic impact. It is at the same time putting greater stress on local environments. (however)

TASK 7 Evaluating arguments and their evidence

1 Read an extract from a student's essay about offshoring. Identify arguments (a) *for* and (b) *against* offshoring.

Text 2

Offshoring has become an increasingly attractive way of doing business for many large multinational companies. Reasons for this include more efficient transport systems and cheaper communication brought about by the internet. According to research by Duke University in the USA, in 2011 80% of large companies were offshoring. This approach has financial benefits - for example, labour costs can be kept low. In 2012, the average hourly wage in the US was $23.32, while in China it was $1.36.

However, offshoring isn't always a success story. In 2010, the consulting firm Grant Thornton reported that 44% of companies it had talked to felt that they did not benefit from offshoring. On the one hand, goods can be produced more cheaply; but on the other hand, there is a perceived reduction in the quality of products made overseas. Often, factories which are chosen by multinational companies take on too much work. This means that smaller clients are often sent products later than agreed, or receive products which have been made quickly, and badly. A further problem with offshoring is protecting designs. Even though companies try to protect their designs, products which are made overseas are sometimes copied by the local producers, or one of their suppliers. This often means that fake goods enter the market, and this affects both profits and reputation.

2 Identify the linking words used to contrast different sides of an argument.

3 Read the extract again. Note down which arguments (a) have evidence to support them and (b) you think are the strongest.

4 Work in pairs. Give reasons for your selection in 3.

TASK 8 Critical thinking - responding to ideas in a text

1 Work in groups. Read two of the author's conclusions from Text 1. Discuss whether you agree. Give reasons and examples.

1 When low-skilled jobs go abroad, there is more opportunity for people to get higher-skilled employment in their own country.
2 Most companies eventually 're-shore'.

2 Discuss whether you think individuals should relocate for work to improve their own quality of life, or stay in their own country to help its economy develop.

INDEPENDENT STUDY

Online articles are often followed by comments that respond to the arguments in them.

▶ **Find an article with comments on a subject that interests you and identify the main argument. Then look at the comments and see what the responses are to this argument and what other arguments people put forward.**

10C Writing (1) Main body paragraphs

This module covers:

- Identifying arguments and supporting ideas
- Writing main body paragraphs

TASK 1 Previewing a writing task

1 Work in pairs. Read the essay title and discuss arguments *for* and *against* the statement.

TITLE: *'When companies set up manufacturing operations in a foreign country where costs are lower, it often has more negative than positive impacts.' Argue for or against this statement.*

2 Consider the essay title from the following perspectives. Make notes.

economic environmental ethical political

3 Compare your notes, and evaluate which perspectives are most useful.

4 Note down:

a whether the essay requires you to give both sides of the argument or just one side

b your own stance.

TASK 2 Identifying arguments and supporting ideas

1 Read Essay 1, which responds to the essay title in Task 1. Note down:

a the writer's stance

b the perspectives mentioned in the essay.

Essay 1

1 While setting up factories and other manufacturing operations in a foreign country (known as 'offshoring') may have some benefits, this essay will argue that this often has a negative impact on the local population and environment.

2 First of all, one negative aspect of offshoring is that many overseas businesses employ local people under unfair or even illegal working conditions. This may include low pay and long working hours. In addition, in some cases the workforce often includes child labour.

3 Furthermore, health and safety standards are sometimes ignored. This is often in part because local laws and regulations are not as strict as in the business's home country. There have recently been a number of instances where buildings have collapsed, injuring and killing many people.

4 There is also often a lack of concern for the local environment and there can be mismanagement of natural resources, such as pollution and the destruction of forests, which can result in long-term ecological damage.

5 As well as the negative impact at a local level, there are wider issues. Even though there are economic benefits for the host country, these may not be distributed evenly. Landowners and local business people certainly often profit from foreign investment. However, while they become richer, the local workforce is often being exploited and the poor get poorer.

6 To conclude, while the companies that set up their operations may well benefit themselves in terms of income and profit, there is a great deal of negative local impact on both the people and the environment.

2 **Complete the notes outlining the writer's key arguments and supporting evidence.**

Argument	Supporting evidence/example
People often employed under	....
Businesses ignore	....
Natural resources can be	....
The economic benefits are not	....

3 **Work in pairs. Compare the writer's stance and arguments with your own stance and arguments in Task 1.**

TASK 3 Identifying essay structure

1 **Read Essay 1 again. Note down the main function of paragraphs 1–6.**

Paragraph	Part of essay	Function
1	Introduction	Introduces the topic and ...
2	Main body	....
3	Main body	....
4	Main body	....
5	Main body	....
6	Conclusion	....

2 **Identify the linking words that connect the points the writer makes.**

Additive linking words (e.g. *also*)	**Contrastive linking words** (e.g. *while*)
In addition	

TASK 4 Writing main body paragraphs

1 Work in pairs. Read the essay title below. Discuss reasons *for* and *against* preserving dying languages.

TITLE: *'Language extinction is a natural consequence of a more globalized world, and effort should not be made trying to preserve dying languages.' Argue for or against this statement.*

2 Read a student's notes for each main body paragraph of the essay in 1. Note down any similarities and any differences between the notes and your own ideas.

Language important part of a culture / key to preserving different cultures, e.g. last speaker of Alaskan language Eyak recently died / Eyak culture now lost

Tells us about history / movement of people / people travelled to other countries / integrate their languages and cultures with others

Fewer languages = easier global communication, but fewer languages = fewer cultural perspectives

Language is depository of knowledge and information / when language dies, information (scientific, anthropological, historical) lost forever, e.g. a lot of Australian aboriginal vocabulary describes local ecology

....

....

....

....

3 Write four main body paragraphs for the essay in 1. Follow stages 1–5.

1 Expand the student notes and / or use your own ideas.
2 Focus on the main points. Give each point one paragraph.
3 For each paragraph, write a topic sentence.
4 Write one or two sentences to summarize your main points. These can be used later as a conclusion.
5 Use appropriate additive and contrastive linking words to introduce each new argument and to express any contrast or concession.

4 Work in pairs. Evaluate your partner's main body paragraphs using criteria 1–4.

1 Are the arguments clearly expressed with examples and supporting evidence?
2 Does each body paragraph express one point?
3 If the paragraph has a concluding sentence, does this summarize or evaluate the main idea?
4 Have linking words been used correctly?

Marie Smith-Jones, last speaker of the Eyak language

10C Writing (2) Openings and conclusions

This module covers:

- Planning opening and concluding paragraphs
- Writing an argument essay

TASK 1 Previewing a writing task

globalization *noun* [U] (ECONOMICS) the idea that different cultures around the world are becoming more similar because of the influence of large multinational companies and improved communication.

1 Read the definition of *globalization*. Note down:

1 examples of large multinational companies

2 aspects of improved communication.

2 Read the essay title. Note down any positive and negative consequences of globalization you can think of.

TITLE *'As globalization increases, it is having more of a negative impact on the world than a positive one.' Argue for or against this statement.*

3 Work in pairs. Discuss whether you think globalization is mainly a positive or negative phenomenon.

4 Read Essay 2. Compare the writer's ideas with your own.

Essay 2

1 There is a growing debate over whether globalization is a good thing and it can be argued that it is in fact having more of a negative impact than a positive one. While there are some negative aspects to globalization, this essay will argue the positive consequences of globalization.

2 First of all, globalization brings wealth and economic growth to poorer countries due to investment by foreign companies. An example of this is a number of South-East Asian countries, which in recent years have experienced substantial economic growth due to foreign investment and international trade.

3 In addition, globalization increases competition and therefore keeps prices for the consumer low and quality high. For example, cheaper clothing manufactured in East Asia is now much more commonplace in the west.

4 Furthermore, globalization can foster more cultural awareness and acceptance. Even though it is sometimes argued that globalization could lead to a homogenization of the world's cultures, a positive consequence of countries and cultures becoming more interconnected is greater incentive to respect each other's cultures and to maintain cooperative and stable relationships.

5 In conclusion, even though there are perhaps some negative consequences, globalization is primarily having a positive impact on the world. Globalization has great economic benefits as well as bringing people together and bringing stability to the world. And as communication and travel become more efficient and more immediate, globalization is likely to increase even more.

5 Complete the table. Note down the writer's argument and supporting evidence on issues 1–3.

	Argument	Supporting evidence/example
1Wealth	Foreign investment brings wealth and economic growth to poorer countries	
2Competition		
3Cultures		

TASK 2 Analysing opening paragraphs

1 Read the opening paragraph of Essay 2, which states the aim and purpose of the essay. Number features a–c in the correct order.

a a statement of the writer's viewpoint / stance ....
b concession to the opposing viewpoint ....
c a summary of the main idea of the question ....

2 Note down the word or phrase that introduces features (a) and (b).

ACADEMIC LANGUAGE

Essay-writing (1) Stating aim and purpose

Stating aim and purpose

A statement of purpose can be written in both a personal (*I will argue (that) ...*) or impersonal (*This essay will argue (that) ...*) style. It is generally more usual to use an impersonal style.

*... **this essay will argue** the positive consequences of globalization.*
*... **this essay will argue that** dying languages should be preserved.*

Expressing a concession

It is common to acknowledge and show that you have considered the opposing view in the opening paragraph.

***While** there are some negative aspects to globalization, this essay will argue ...*
***Although** there may be an argument that language extinction is natural, this essay will argue ...*

TASK 3 Writing an opening paragraph

1 Work in pairs. Read essay titles 3 and 4. For each title, discuss:

a the arguments for and against
b your viewpoint / stance.

3 *'The ever-increasing quantity of information available online is having both a positive and negative impact on the world.' Argue one of these viewpoints.*

4 *'One aspect of globalization is that societies are becoming more and more alike. Some people fear that globalization will inevitably lead to the total loss of cultural identity.' Argue for or against this statement.*

2 Write the opening paragraph for each essay. Include the following features:

- a summary of the main idea of the question
- a concession to the opposing view
- a statement of your stance.

TASK 4 Analysing a concluding paragraph

1 Read the concluding paragraph of Essay 2. Number features a-c in the correct order.

a a brief summary of the main arguments ....
b the writer's concluding viewpoint / stance ....
c acknowledgement of, and concession to, the opposing viewpoint ....

2 Read the concluding paragraph of Essay 1 on page 142. Note down which features it shares with the concluding paragraph in Essay 2.

3 Note down which phrases are generally used to begin the concluding paragraph.

ACADEMIC LANGUAGE

Essay-writing (2) Concluding paragraphs

Begin the concluding paragraph with ***In conclusion, ...*** or ***To conclude, ...***

__In conclusion,__ even though there are perhaps some negative consequences, globalization is ...

__To conclude,__ while language extinction may be inevitable, as much as possible should be done to preserve dying languages.

TASK 5 Writing a concluding paragraph

1 Write the concluding paragraph for each of the essays in Task 3. Make sure you:

- acknowledge the opposing view
- briefly summarize the main arguments
- state your stance.

TASK 6 Writing an argument essay

1 Work in pairs. Read the essay title and discuss the advantages and disadvantages for the host countries.

TITLE: *'Increased freedom of movement has meant that more people are now living in foreign countries than previously. There are both advantages and disadvantages of this for the host countries.' Argue one of these viewpoints.*

2 Read the notes for the essay title in 1. Add any different ideas that you discussed and any further supporting evidence or examples you can think of.

Advantages: people do jobs others will not do, e.g. manual labour such as fruit-picking / often cheaper / economic benefits / brings new expertise / more cultural diversity / increases cross-cultural awareness and respect.

Disadvantages: cheaper labour force = higher native worker unemployment / money often sent back to home country, i.e. taken out of host country economy / extra pressure on resources, e.g. schools and healthcare / possible cultural clashes or dilution

3 Choose to write about EITHER the advantages OR disadvantages. Expand the relevant notes to write the main body paragraphs of an argument essay.

4 Write an opening and concluding paragraph for the main body paragraphs you wrote in 3, to produce a full essay of approximately 250 words.

Sample answer: page 161

TASK 7 Evaluating your writing

1 Read your essay and check that:

- you have used the correct essay structure ☐
- the sentences fit together to make paragraphs ☐
- the paragraphs fit together to make a complete essay ☐
- you have used appropriate additive and contrastive conjunctions ☐
- you have spelled everything correctly ☐
- you have used capital letters and punctuation correctly. ☐

INDEPENDENT STUDY

Find an argument article or essay online. Read the opening paragraph and note down which features it contains: a summary of the main arguments, a concession to counter-arguments, and a statement of the author's stance.

▸ Think about your own stance on this topic and then write your own version of this opening paragraph.

10D Vocabulary

TASK 1 Formal and informal vocabulary

1 Select the more formal academic word to replace the informal words in bold.

briefly various negative concern address wider

1 There have been some **bad** consequences.
2 We should also examine the **bigger** issues.
3 Responsible tourism tries to **deal with** these questions.
4 This essay will **in a few words** outline both the positive and negative consequences of globalization.
5 We have examined **a few different** factors that companies consider in choosing a location.
6 There is a **worry** that offshoring will result in large-scale job losses.

2 Replace the words in italics using the words in brackets. You will need to add other words.

1 There have been *some* cases where buildings have collapsed. (number)
2 Globalization *will probably* increase even more. (likely)
3 By showing respect, both the traveller and the host can *be helped by* tourism. (benefit)
4 *People who criticize* offshoring say that it damages the economy of the company's native country. (critics)
5 So, *to sum up*, the benefits of offshoring are generally greater than its disadvantages. (summary)

TASK 2 Using common prefixes

1 Match each prefix in bold in sentences 1–5 to its meaning a–f.

a again b too much c not enough d wrong e between f many

1 The decision to **re**locate manufacturing to another country is usually a financial one. ....
2 **Multi**-national companies have more than one base for their operations around the world. ....
3 **Mis**management of the forest caused many of the native trees and plants to disappear. ....
4 The two electrical systems are **inter**connected by a high voltage cable that runs under the sea. ....
5 Many of the employees feel they are **over**worked and **under**paid. ....

2 Complete sentences 1–6 with the correct prefix from 1.

1 The product was ....*priced* and as a result sales were very low.
2 Many parts of the city are ....*populated* and there is not enough housing for everyone.
3 The job prospects for a ....*-skilled* engineer are better than for an engineer who concentrates on only one area, like mechanical engineering.
4 In the experiment, the researchers ....*created* the conditions of the desert in the laboratory.
5 The two branches of geography – physical and cultural – are closely ....*related*.
6 The word *satellite* is often ....*spelled* by many native speakers of English.

3 Work in pairs. Find two other words with each prefix *re-*, *multi-*, *mis-*, *inter-*, *over-*, and *under-*. Use a dictionary if necessary.

INDEPENDENT STUDY

Make a note of any useful words that begin with a prefix as you come across them in your academic reading.

10E Academic Language Check

TASK 1 Linking words (1): Addition

1 Select the correct word or phrase from each pair to complete essay extracts a–c.

a The study used a small sample [1]*and / also* was criticized for this reason. [2]*Another example / Furthermore*, the gender bias in the study was considered questionable.

b There are a number of arguments in favour of sustainable tourism. [3]*In addition / First of all*, sustainable tourism does not exhaust the resource base on which it is constructed. [4]*Also / As well as*, it does not negatively impact on local social and cultural aspects of the host community.

c There are a number of reasons for relocating a retail business. [5]*First of all / In addition*, relocation is a sensible choice if it puts the business closer to its customers. The customers will be more likely to travel to the business to purchase products. [6]*As well as / In addition*, if the relocation is close to other successful businesses, the company will be more visible [7]*also / and* therefore more likely to attract new customers. Research suggests that visibility is the best form of free advertising. [8]*Furthermore / As well as* proximity to customers, cost is [9]*also / in addition* a key consideration. Moving to cheaper premises is a common reason for relocating. However, even if the cost is higher than the current location, it may be worth relocating if the new location will generate more business. [10]*Another example / Furthermore*, a more expensive and more prestigious business premises will reflect positively on the image of the company.

TASK 2 Linking words (2): Contrast

1 Complete the essay extracts with the contrastive conjunctions in the lists.

even though but on the one hand on the other hand

The global demand for international higher education is growing. [1] .... students choose to study abroad for various reasons. [2] ...., this may be because a student's preferred course of study is not available locally. [3] ...., it may be because an overseas course is better than a local one. Whatever the reason or motivation, the benefits of an international education are clear. And [4] .... learning and obtaining a qualification are the main reasons for overseas study, the global perspective gained and international contacts made will be invaluable for any future career.

despite even if even though however

[5] ...., an international education is very expensive and the choice of where to study has to be the right one. There are a number of questions that should be carefully addressed before the selection of a final study destination. [6] .... the course itself may be attractive, does the institution have a reputation for quality education? Will the qualification gained be recognized and accepted in your home country and in other countries? And [7] .... it is internationally recognized, is it held in high regard? And one final key question is that [8] .... all the academic considerations, will the social and cultural experience also be beneficial in terms of future employability in today's globalized world?

Language reference

Unit 1

1.1 Questions (1): Asking for further information

One use of questions is to get further information after a talk or lecture. It is important that the questions are accurate and concise. Common and useful questions include:

Is / Are there …

Is there *internet access in all rooms?*

How / Where do / can …

How do *we log on to ATHENS?*
How can *we get an extension on our assignments?*
Where do *you get a form M1 from?*

Can you / we …

Can you *re-submit assignments?*
Can we *miss lectures?*

Do you / we have to …

Do you have to *sign up for evening lectures in advance?*

What happens if …

What happens if *you miss an exam, say, because you are ill?*

Note that in these questions, *you* and *we* refer to people in general.

1.2 Factual information: Present and past simple and progressive

The **present simple** is used to express:

- facts and situations which are generally true
  Each year over a thousand people ***apply*** *for just 50 places on the course.*
  The study ***shows*** *that survival rates* ***are*** *50% better than ten years ago.*
- regularly repeated events, such as habits and routines
  Lectures ***start*** *at 9 o'clock. The last one* ***is*** *usually at five.*
  The comet ***passes*** *the earth every 76 years.*

The **present progressive** is used to express:

- something in progress now
  We're ***studying*** *cytogenetics this term.*
  The study ***is investigating*** *sleep patterns.*
- a changing situation
  University entrance requirements ***are getting*** *stricter.*
  The global population ***is increasing*** *by about 1.2% per year.*

The **past simple** is used to talk about completed events or situations in the past.

Initially, the university ***taught*** *only a few different subjects.*
I ***applied*** *to three different universities.*
The study ***was*** *very detailed.*

The **past progressive** is used to talk about something in progress and not yet completed at a time in the past.

I ***was teaching*** *at Winchester University in 2012.*
Around this time, animals ***were starting*** *to colonize the land.*

The progressive aspect can also be used to emphasize process or activity, rather than stating something as a simple fact. Compare the following pairs of sentences:

Website spelling mistakes ***are costing*** *companies millions of pounds each year.*
Website spelling mistakes ***cost*** *companies millions of pounds each year.*

The study ***was looking into*** *ageing in primates.*
The study ***looked into*** *ageing in primates.*

1.3 Sentences (1)

Simple sentences can be:

- subject + verb
  Student numbers are increasing.
  The lecture has started.
- subject + verb + object
  Most universities have a residential campus.
  I studied economics.
- subject + verb + complement
  The department is very big.
  The problem seems quite serious.
  Professor Jones is in charge.

A complement is a word or phrase that gives more information about the subject of the sentence. The subject and the complement refer to the same thing. A complement can be:

- an adjective or adjective phrase
  The university is ***very modern****.*
- a noun or noun phrase
  The event was ***a great success****.*
- a prepositional phrase
  The economy seemed ***in good shape****.*

Verbs which are commonly followed by a complement include *appear, be, become, feel, seem.*

1.4 Sentences (2)

Simple sentences often have one or more adverbials. Adverbials are used with or without an object or complement.

I went to university in 2008.
The university rejects over 20,000 student applications every year.
The department is possibly one of the best in the world.

An adverbial typically gives information about:

- when (e.g. *in 2008, before he became a lawyer*)
- where (e.g. *to university, at Harvard, in Saudi Arabia*)
- how (e.g. *slowly, regularly, soon after*)
- why (e.g. *to develop his skills*)

1.5 Sentences (3) and (4)

A compound sentence consists of two simple sentences clauses which are joined together with a coordinator. The most common coordinators are:

- *and* for addition
  I studied biology for my first degree ***and*** *I have a Master's degree in Education.*

- *but* for contrast
  The study produced some interesting results, ***but*** *the findings have not been replicated.*
- *or* for alternatives
  In the UK, all 16-year-olds continue their education in the sixth form ***or*** *they do some kind of vocational training.*

The two clauses in a compound sentence are usually closely related simple sentences that can stand alone.

Course applications are increasing year on year. The number of available places is not increasing at the same rate.

However, joining two ideas together in compound sentences shows that the ideas are closely related and can make writing seem more fluent.

Course applications are increasing year on year, ***but*** *the number of available places is not increasing at the same rate.*

Note that *but* is often preceded by a comma (,). *And* and *or* are generally not preceded by a comma in compound sentences if the subject does not change.

Unit 2

2.1 Definitions and explanations

In both speaking and writing, it is often necessary to define or explain what an item, idea, or concept is. There are a number of typical words and phrases for giving definitions.

An antonym ***is*** *a word with the opposite meaning to another word.*
Photolysis ***is when*** *a plant absorbs light energy.*
Binary ***means*** *composed of two parts.*
Obesity ***is / can be defined as*** *a BMI above the 95th percentile.*

Is a ... of can be used with a number of words (e.g. *branch, species, sub-division, component*).

Amoxicillin ***is a type of*** *penicillin.*
Topology ***is a branch of*** *mathematics.*
A comma ***is a species of*** *butterfly.*

To ask for a definition or explanation, we can use:

What is *an angiosperm?*
What does *'mitosis'* ***mean?***
Can you define / explain what *random sampling* ***is?***

It is sometimes necessary to explain an item, idea, or concept rather than to define it. Typical phrases for doing so include:

Some cell membranes are selectively permeable. ***This means that*** *they allow only certain substances to pass through.*
The plants became chlorotic. ***In other words,*** *they weren't producing enough chlorophyll.*

2.2 Definitions using relative clauses and prepositional phrases

We can define an item, idea, or concept by giving a general word (e.g. a symbol, a device, an instrument, a system, a process, a person) for the term we are defining and then adding specific defining detail using a relative clause or a prepositional phrase.

Note that for countable nouns, we use the indefinite article *a / an* before the item we are defining.

Relative clauses

For things and ideas, use the relative pronouns *which* or *that*.

A hashtag is a symbol ***which*** *is placed in front of a key topic within a tweet.*
A barometer is a device ***which*** *measures air pressure.*
An isoneph is a line on a map ***that*** *joins places with the same cloud density.*

For people, use *who* or *that*.

A polyglot is someone ***who*** *speaks several languages.*

For places, use the relative adverb *where*.

Tundra is a habitat ***where*** *tree growth is hindered by low temperatures and short growing seasons.*

For times, use the relative adverb *when*. Note that we often do not include a general word when defining a time.

The summer solstice ***is when*** *the sun is directly above the Tropic of Cancer.*

Prepositional phrases

A prepositional phrase begins with a preposition.

Taxonomy is a system ***of*** *classifying living things.*
An acid is a substance ***with*** *a pH of less than 7.*
A spectrometer is an instrument ***for*** *measuring wavelengths of light.*

Definitions using prepositional phrases and relative clauses

Definitions can include more than one relative clause (RC) or prepositional phrase (PP) or a combination of the two.

A smartphone is a mobile phone that is able to perform many of the functions of a computer and which can run general-purpose applications. (RC +RC)
Communism is a system of social organization with property ownership shared by the community. (PP +PP)
The nervous system is a network of nerve cells and fibres which transmits nerve impulses between parts of the body. (PP +RC)

Unit 3

3.1 Using adjectives and nouns to modify nouns

You can add description or detail to a noun (called the head noun) by combining it with other words to make a noun phrase. One common way of doing this is to pre-modify the noun using:

- **adjective + noun**
  There are several ***important considerations.***
  It was a ***serious problem.***
  It is ***international law.***
- **participle + noun**
  It was a ***fascinating study.***
  Study the ***following examples.***
  They worked in ***converted sheds.***

Note that participles used in this way are sometimes considered as adjectives.

- **noun + noun**
  It is ***company policy****.*
  There was no ***business plan****.*
  He had been a ***science teacher****.*
  The law does not allow ***cigarette advertising****.*

Note that nouns used in this way are sometimes known as defining nouns.

A head noun can have a combination of adjectives, participles, and/or defining nouns. When there are two or more pre-modifiers, the order is generally:

evaluation / opinion → description → classification / definition + head noun

It was not based on ***reliable research data****.*
What are the ***main political considerations****?*
A number of ***large Western multinational*** *companies use* ***cheap local labour****.*

3.2 Articles

There are a number of rules regarding the use of articles. One key use of articles is when talking more in general about something non-specific or about something specific.

To talk more generally about something indefinite or non-specific, when it is one of many, use:

- *a* or *an* (indefinite article) for singular nouns.
  Research generally starts off with ***a hypothesis****.*
  The city doesn't have ***a university****.*
  The law in most countries allows research that uses animals, but only when there isn't ***an alternative research technique****.*
- no article (zero article) for nouns which are plural or uncountable.
  Research *generally starts off with a hypothesis.*
  The law in most countries allows ***research*** *that uses* ***animals****, but only when there isn't an alternative research technique.*
- *the* (definite article) is used to talk about something definite or specific. This is usually when something is unique, clear in context, or has been mentioned before.
  Over 60 participants took part in ***the study****.*
  The law *in most countries allows research that uses animals, but only when there isn't an alternative research technique.*

Note that we use *a* before a consonant sound and *an* before a vowel sound.

a university   a unit   a euro
an unfair decision   an hour   an auditorium

3.3 Determiners

Determiners (*the, this, their,* etc.) are used before a noun or at the beginning of a noun phrase. They specify something about the noun, such as whether it is known or not known. Nearly 10% of all words in academic texts are determiners.

- Determiners used with something specific, definite, or known:

Definite article (*the*)

The *results of* ***the*** *study were first published in 2012. Smith's findings had a significant influence on subsequent research in* ***the*** *field.*

Demonstratives (*this, that, these, those*)

All research has to follow ***these*** *standards. There was a new definition of what a planet is.* ***This*** *reclassification led to Pluto becoming a dwarf-planet.*

Note that demonstratives can be used without a noun.

Any student caught cheating in an exam may be expelled from their university. ***This*** *is automatic in a number of universities.*

Possessive adjectives (*my, your,* etc.) and nouns (*Smith's,* etc.)

The participants had ***their*** *IQs tested at the beginning of the study.*
Any student caught cheating in an exam may be expelled from ***their*** *university. This ...*
Smith's *findings had significant influence on subsequent research in the field.*

- Determiners used with something non-specific, indefinite, or unknown:

Indefinite article (*a / an*)

Any student caught cheating in ***an*** *exam may be expelled from their university.*
There was ***a*** *new definition of what* ***a*** *planet is. This reclassification led to Pluto becoming* ***a*** *dwarf-planet.*

Quantifiers (*some, any, much, a few, a number of,* etc.)

Any *student caught cheating in an exam may be expelled from their university. This is automatic in* ***a number of*** *universities.* ***Some*** *universities, however, are more tolerant of plagiarism.*

3.4 Using determiners, adjectives, and nouns

A combination of determiners, adjectives, and nouns is often used to add descriptive detail to a head noun.

Most of the initial participants *in* ***Jones's preliminary studies*** *were* ***European undergraduate university students****.*
Wikileaks is ***an international non-profit media organization****. In 2010, they released* ***a number of leaked classified US diplomatic communications****.*

Unit 4

4.1 Comparison and contrast (1): Adjectives

Comparative adjectives are often used to compare and contrast.

Form

- We generally form the comparative of one-syllable adjectives by adding *-er*:
  slow → slower
  large → larger
  hot → hotter

- We generally form the comparative of multi-syllable adjectives with *more*:
  frequent → more frequent
  developed → more developed
  complicated → more complicated
- The comparative of two-syllable adjectives ending in *-y*, *-er* and *-le* are generally formed by adding *-er*. However, they can also be formed with *more*.
  sunny → sunnier / more sunny
  clever → cleverer / more clever
  simple → simpler / more simple
- We can use *less* to express a smaller amount or degree of something.
  frequent → less frequent
  developed → less developed
- Note the irregular comparative forms:
  good → better
  bad → worse
  far → further

Structures

- We use *than* to make a direct comparison with something else.
  *Canada is **bigger than** the USA.*
  *Football is **more popular than** rugby in most countries.*
  *Sales were **slower than** predicted.*
  *Immigration was **more widespread than** in the past.*
- We use *not as … as* with similar meaning to *less*.
  *The USA is **not as big as** Canada.*
  *The process was **not as complex as** expected.*
- We use quantifiers such as *a little, slightly, much, significantly, three times, 20%, 3°* to express degree of difference.
  *Canada is **slightly bigger than** the USA.*
  *It is a **much simpler** process.*
  *Unemployment was **5% higher than** the previous year.*

4.2 Comparison and contrast (2): Using different word classes

Similarities and differences can be expressed using a number of forms. Forms used in academic contexts include:

like / unlike

*Chinese, **like** many Asian languages, is a tonal language.*
*In individual sports, **unlike** in team sports, success or failure is solely down to the individual.*

similar to / different from

*Influenza is **similar to** the common cold, but its symptoms are more severe.*
*GNP (Gross National Product) is **different from** GDP (Gross Domestic Product).*

We can use quantifiers such as *very* and *quite* to express degree of difference.

*Laser light is **very different from** normal light.*
*Portuguese is **quite similar to** Spanish in a number of ways.*

(not) the same / different

*Cabbage, broccoli, and cauliflower **are the same** species.*
*GNP (Gross National Product) and GDP (Gross Domestic Product) are **not the same / different.***

We use *(not) the same as* and *different from* to make a direct comparison with something else.

*GNP (Gross National Product) is **not the same as / different from** GDP (Gross Domestic Product).*

differ

*Attitudes to competition **differ** around the world.*
*Human and cow's milk **differ** in composition.*

We use *differ(s) from* to make a direct comparison with something else.

*Cabbage, broccoli, and cauliflower **differ from** each other because they are cultivars.*

We can use quantifiers such as *slightly, greatly, considerably*, and *significantly* to express degree of difference.

*Most identical twins **differ slightly** in appearance.*
*Saturn's moons **differ considerably** from the moons of Jupiter.*

4.3 Comparison and contrast (3): Showing similarities and differences

Similarities and differences can be expressed using a range of linking adverbials. Some of the most common in academic contexts include:

To express similarities:

- *Also* most commonly goes before the main verb or after *be*.
  *Aristarchus **also** proposed that the Earth moved around the sun.*
  *French, Spanish, Portuguese, and Italian are the most spoken neo-Latin languages. Romanian is **also** a neo-Latin language.*
- *Similarly* generally goes at the beginning of a second sentence or clause.
  *The blue whale was hunted almost to extinction. **Similarly**, the humpback whale population has fallen to 1% of its pre-commercial whaling population.*
  *If you understand Russian, you can partly understand Ukrainian and, **similarly**, the other way around.*

To express differences:

- *By / In comparison* and *by / in contrast* generally go at the beginning of a second sentence or clause.
  *Cricket soon became India's national sport. **In contrast**, football in India remained a minority sport.*
  *Chinese has almost 1,700 different sounds. **By comparison**, English has nearer 1,000.*

You can sometimes put *by / in comparison* and *by / in contrast* in other positions in the second sentence or clause. It is quite common to put it after the subject.

*Chinese has almost 1,700 different sounds. English, **by comparison**, has nearer 1,000.*

- *However* generally goes at the beginning of a second sentence, but it can also go in the middle or at the end.
  Sydney is the biggest city in Australia. ***However,*** *it isn't the capital.*
  Sydney is the biggest city in Australia. It isn't the capital, ***however.***
  Sydney is the biggest city in Australia. It isn't, ***however,*** *the capital.*

4.4 Approximation

It is often appropriate or necessary to approximate quantitative information or data. Common words and phrases for approximation in academic contexts include:

around *approximately* *in the region of*
almost *just under* *just over*

The global population in 1900 was ***around*** *two billion.*
By 2000, it had risen to ***just over*** *six billion.*
A newborn human has ***in the region of*** *a trillion cells.*
Mandarin speakers account for ***almost*** *15% of the world's population.*

Unit 5

5.1 Stance (1): Referring to someone else's views

It is often necessary to report the stance, viewpoint, or position of other people. Common ways of doing this include:

- using adverbial phrases
  In *Harrison's (2009)* ***view,*** *desertification will continue in the area for some time.*
  In the opinion of *Richards (2012), the find is not of major significance.*
  According to *several studies, smoking in some social sectors is in decline.*
- using verbs such as *note / comment / observe / report* (+ *that*) + subject clause
  Smith (2012) ***notes that*** *the species is declining in some areas.*
  A number of studies ***have reported that*** *health awareness is increasing.*
  James (2014) ***commented that*** *the study sample size was insufficient.*
- to show stance from a particular perspective, we can use ***a / the ... view is / was that ...*** + subject clause:
  A *minority* ***view was that*** *the UN should not have become involved.*
  The *anthropological* ***view is that*** *religion developed from animalism.*

5.2 Stance (2): Giving an opinion, agreeing, and disagreeing

- In some academic contexts, for example in seminars and tutorials, you may be required to express your personal stance, viewpoint, or position. Expressions for doing this include:
  I think / believe / would argue / would say + that + subject clause:
  I think / believe that *there will be further instability in the region.*
  I would argue / say that *unemployment in the area will decline.*

To express our stance less strongly, we can also use *It seems (to me) that* + subject clause.

It seems to me that *further research is needed.*
It seems that *habitat destruction is the prime cause of species extinction.*

- In more formal academic writing, there is a tendency to avoid using the subject pronoun 'I' when expressing stance. Adverbials such as *clearly, no doubt,* and *without doubt* can be used to show that your stance is being expressed.
  Attempts to regenerate the area have ***clearly*** *been ineffective.*
  There is ***no doubt*** *that a preliminary study would have highlighted the problems.*
- When you express your personal stance, viewpoint, or position, it is often important to provide supporting information or evidence. Expressions for introducing supporting evidence include:
  An example of this is *shale gas.*
  For example, *the rural population in some regions is actually increasing.*
  Take *the Olympics* ***for example / instance,*** *which can generate billions of dollars.*

5.3 Hedging (1) and (2)

It is often necessary to use hedging language to avoid expressing stance and degree of certainty too strongly. This is especially important when making claims rather than stating proven facts. In both spoken and written academic contexts, there are a number of ways of doing this. These include:

- *It is probable / possible / likely / unlikely (that) +* subject clause
  It is possible that *the area was once inhabited.*
  It is unlikely that *disease was the cause of the decline in population.*
- Verbs such as *think, believe, indicate, suggest, point to* are used in a number of patterns:
  - *is / are thought to*
    The ruins ***are thought to*** *be of a 12th-century fortress.*
  - *It is thought / believed that ...*
    It is thought / believed that *sunglasses were invented in China about 1000 years ago.*
  - *suggest / indicate (+ that) +* subject clause
    The discovery ***suggests that*** *the port was a major international gateway.*
    The design on the ring ***indicates that*** *it belonged to a member of the royal family.*
  - *point to* + noun
    The findings ***point to*** *a previously unknown species of fox.*
- *Appear* and *seem* are used in two ways:
  - *It appears / seems that*
    It appears that *the last use of the site was in about 1850.*
    It seems that *the land tax triggered the uprising.*
  - *appear / seem to*
    The artefacts ***appear to*** *be of Greek origin.*
    The asteroid ***seems to*** *be increasing in size.*

- The modal verbs *may*, *could*, and *can*:
  *There **may** be several further unknown species living in the caves.*
  *The discovery **could** result in a change in the way the disease is treated.*

Unit 6

6.1 Perspective (1) and (2)

It is important to recognize and to be able to express the perspective from which something is being discussed or described. The main ways of expressing perspective are:

- adverbs (*politically*, *historically*, *ecologically*, *financially*, *theoretically*, etc.)
  ***Historically**, the main industries in the area were farming and lead mining.*
  ***Politically** and **economically**, the country went through enormous change.*
  *The proposed development would have been **ecologically** damaging.*

We can also use *speaking:*

  ***Scientifically speaking**, black is the absence of all colour.*
  ***Medically speaking**, the common cold is an upper respiratory infection.*

- *From a ... perspective / standpoint / point of view*
  ***From a** business **perspective**, membership of the European Union has pros and cons.*
  ***From an** economic **point of view**, human migration has a number of benefits.*
  *We shall now look at forestry **from a** commercial **standpoint**.*
- *As far as ... is concerned*
  ***As far as** sport **is concerned**, a number of countries enjoy huge success compared to their population size.*
- *In ... terms, In terms of ...*
  ***In** health **terms**, there is evidence that urban living can impact in a negative way.*
  *Low-cost air fares may be very costly **in terms of** climate change.*

Unit 7

7.1 Paraphrasing

Paraphrasing is a crucial aspect of academic writing. It allows you to rewrite an author's idea or other published material in your own words. Paraphrasing can be complex and it can take time to develop a full understanding of when and how to use it. However, most basic paraphrasing includes a combination of the following:

- A change in word form or part of speech (e.g. *invaded → invasion of*, *is relevant → has relevance*; *succeed → be successful*)
  *The Romans first **invaded** Britain in 43AD. → The first Roman **invasion of** Britain took place in 43AD.*
  *Most children when starting school **are linguistically able** enough to **succeed**. → When they start school, the majority of children **have the linguistic ability** to **be successful**.*
- Synonyms (e.g. *most → the majority of*, *have the right → be entitled*, *indicate → suggest*)
  ***Most** children when starting school ... → When they start school, **the majority of** children ...*
  *The **automatic provision** of primary school education for every child in England and Wales **was established** in the 1870 Education Act. → In England and Wales, all primary-aged children **were given the right** to an education in 1870.*
- A change in sentence structure or word order
  The right to secondary education at age eleven had to wait until the implementation of the 1944 Education Act. → It wasn't until the 1944 Education Act that secondary school-aged children were entitled to an education.
  Following the 1944 Education Act, there was such a rapid increase in educational provision, in the USA and many countries of Western and Eastern Europe as well as in Britain, that some writers refer to the 'educational explosion' of the 1950s and 1960s. → Once the 1944 Education Act was implemented, secondary education in the UK and in many other countries across the world expanded rapidly during the 1950s and 1960s in the so-called 'educational explosion.'
- Note that it is generally acceptable to repeat key specialized words.
  *A number of studies have indicated that **pre-task planning** can impact positively on language performance in terms of **fluency** and **complexity**. → It has been shown that **pre-task planning** of speaking tasks can result in increased **fluency** and **complexity**.*

7.2 Citation

When you refer to, summarize, or paraphrase an author's work in your writing, you must acknowledge the source of the ideas you are expressing. You do this by including the author's name and the date of publication. This is called citation.

- When using a reporting verb (e.g. *states*, *suggests*), you include the name of the author with the date of publication in parentheses.
  ***Howarth (2001) suggests** that planning plays a key role in interlanguage development.*
  ***Jones (2013) states** that university entrance requirements vary greatly.*
  ***Sangarun (2005) claims** the results are inconclusive.*
- When not using a reporting verb, you include both the author's name and the date (separated by a comma) in parentheses
  *Planning is believed to play a key role in interlanguage development **(Howarth, 2001)**.*

When there is more than one author, you separate them with a semi-colon:

  *Research has shown that learners who plan tasks generally attempt more complex language **(Skehan, 1999; Wigglesworth, 2001; Yuan & Ellis, 2003)**.*

- The sources are then included in more detail in the list of references or bibliography at the end of the essay.

There are three main ways of showing that you have used another writer's ideas:

Direct quotation

The author's exact words are used. Quotation marks are used around the words, which must be quoted exactly as they are in the original.

Smith (2002) states 'the three stages of labour are early labour, active labour, and transition into delivery.'

Paraphrasing

There are three stages of labour (Smith, 2002). These are the early labour stage, the active labour stage, and the transition into delivery stage. → *Smith (2002) states that there are three stages of labour: the early labour stage, the active labour stage, and the transition into delivery stage.*

Using reporting verbs

Reporting verbs that can be used for direct quotation or for paraphrasing include *argue, believe, claim, indicate, note, state, suggest.*

Harrison (2014) ***argues*** *that food plays a much greater role than the purely nutritional.*
Sangarun (2011) ***claims*** *that further research will show ...*
Leech (2001) ***notes*** *that 'habitat destruction will lead to ...'*

Unit 8

8.1 Past tenses

A narrative is a description of a past event. A narrative may require a variety of tenses, but the main tenses that are generally used are the past simple, the past continuous, and the past perfect.

Even though early forms of bicycle ***had existed*** *for a few hundred years, it* ***wasn't*** *until the 1830s that a bicycle with pedals* ***was invented.*** *The inventor was Scottish blacksmith Kirkpatrick McMillan and the idea* ***came*** *to him while he* ***was watching*** *some children riding a hobbyhorse. He* ***had*** *the idea of making a version which could be propelled without the rider's feet touching the ground. Once McMillan* ***had introduced*** *his invention to the public, other inventors and engineers* ***started*** *to develop their own version of the bicycle. By the end of the century, the bicycle* ***was*** *almost the same as the bicycle of today.*

- The **past simple** is used to describe the main events, which are usually told in chronological order.
  ... the idea ***came*** *to him one day while he was watching some children riding a hobbyhorse. He* ***had*** *the idea of making a version which ...*
  ... other inventors and engineers ***started*** *to develop their own version of the bicycle. By the end of the century, the bicycle* ***was*** *almost the same as the bicycle of today.*
- The **past progressive** is used in contrast with the past simple to describe events or situations that were in progress at the time of one or more of the main events.
  ... the idea came to him while he ***was watching*** *some children riding a hobbyhorse.*
- The **past perfect** describes an event that occurred before the whole event began or before one of the main events.
  Even though early forms of bicycle ***had existed*** *for a few hundred years, it wasn't until the 1830s ...*
  Once McMillan ***had introduced*** *his invention to the public, other inventors and engineers ...*

8.2 Sequencing in a process

Key features when describing sequence in a process are the use of the present simple and present perfect tenses and the use of sequencing words and phrases which indicate the order the events occur in. The passive voice is also sometimes a feature.

Tenses

- The **present simple** is used to describe each stage of a process.
  A star ***begins*** *its life as a large cloud of gas. Atoms in the gas* ***are attracted*** *to each other by the force of gravity and the cloud* ***begins*** *to collapse. As the material* ***accelerates,*** *the gravitational energy is* ***converted*** *into kinetic energy and the temperature of the gas cloud* ***increases.***
  Light energy ***is absorbed*** *by the green chemical chlorophyll. This energy* ***allows*** *the reaction between carbon dioxide and water, which* ***produces*** *glucose.*
- The **present perfect simple** is used to indicate that one thing happened before another.
  Once the gas cloud ***has reached*** *a certain temperature, it is hot enough for nuclear fusion to take place.*
  When too much hydrogen ***has been burned,*** *the core of the star collapses under the force of gravity and the star changes state.*

Sequencing words and phrases

- Linking adverbials (e.g. *first, then, next, after that, in turn, finally*) are used to show the sequence of events.
  First, *crude oil is pumped into a separator, which separates the oil from the gas and water. The oil is* ***then*** *pumped to the onshore terminal. The oil is 'cleaned' again and* ***after that*** *it is sent to a storage tank.* ***Finally,*** *the crude oil is exported to the refinery either by pipeline or tanker.*
- Subordinators (e.g. *when, after, as, once, as soon as*) are also used to show sequence and how events relate to each other.
  Tectonic plates sometimes get stuck. ***Once*** *this happens, pressure inside the earth's crust starts to build up.* ***As*** *the pressure increases, it begins to force its way through the gaps between the tectonic plates.* ***When*** *this pressure is eventually released, an earthquake tends to occur.* ***After*** *the initial earthquake, there may be a series of after-shocks as the tectonic plates adjust to the effects of the main shock.*

Note that linking adverbials and sequence subordinators can go in a number of positions in the sentence, but they tend most frequently to go at the beginning of a sentence or clause. In this position a linking adverbial is followed by a comma (,).

8.3 The passive voice

Form

The passive is formed with *be* + past participle.

Ethanol ***is produced*** *from ethene and water.*
When the component parts ***have been combined****, the mixture* ***is heated*** *to 100°C.*
Glass ***was first produced*** *around 3500 BC.*

Use

The passive voice is very frequent in academic texts and is used for a number of reasons. One common use is when describing a man-made or naturally occurring process. This is because the passive voice puts the focus on what happens to something, rather than what someone or something does.

The passive can be used with or without an agent (the person or thing that carries out or causes the action). In academic texts it is most commonly used without an agent.

- The passive is used without an agent when the agent is obvious, unimportant, or unknown.
  The heat which ***is generated*** *inside the star is then radiated away from its centre ...*
  Gold ***is purified*** *through a process of heating or through chemical exposure.*
  Chemicals, called neurotransmitters, ***are released*** *at the nerve terminal.*
  After all the salt ***has been removed****, only water vapour remains.*
- The passive is used with an agent usually when we are providing new information about an existing topic. We use *by* to introduce the agent.
  These chemicals ***are released by*** *the pituitary gland, which is located in the base of the brain.*
  Waste such as carbon dioxide, water, ammonia, and salts ***is removed*** *from the body* ***by*** *the urinary system.*

Unit 9

9.1 Questions (2): Indirect questions

Indirect questions (e.g. *Could you explain how a virus replicates?)* are generally more tentative than direct questions (e.g. *How does a virus replicate?*).

- Indirect questions begin with a question phrase. Common question phrases include:
  Could / Can you explain ...?
  Could / Can you tell me/us ...?
  Do you / Does anyone know ...?
  Have you any idea ...?
  I'm / We're not sure ...
  I / We don't / didn't understand ...
  Could you tell us *when the study was carried out?*
  Does anyone know *if there's a connection between the two diseases?*
  I don't understand *how transfer RNA works.*
- The question phrase is followed by a question word or *if*. We use *if* for a question that requires a 'yes' or 'no' answer.
  Could you tell us ***when*** *the study was carried out?*
  Does anyone know ***if*** *there's a connection between the two diseases?*
  I don't understand ***how*** *transfer RNA works.*

Note that we can also sometimes use *whether* instead of *if*.

- The word order after the question word / *if* is the same as in a statement. We do not put the verb before the subject and we do not use the auxiliary verb *do*.
  Could you tell us when ***the study was carried out****?*
  NOT ~~Could you tell us when was the study carried out?~~
  I don't understand how ***transfer RNA works****.*
  NOT ~~I don't understand how does transfer RNA work.~~
- We can also sometimes use **question phrase** + **noun phrase**.
  Do you know the date of the research?
  Could you explain the selection process?
  I didn't understand the last stage of the procedure.

9.2 Cause and effect

Cause and effect connections are frequent in academic contexts. There are a number of ways of showing cause and effect relationships. Some of the most common include:

Verbs

We can use **verbs** such as *cause, lead to, result in,* and *mean.*

- These mention cause before effect:
  Hydrocephalus ***causes*** *the brain to swell.*
  Smoking ***leads to*** *premature skin ageing.*
  Kidney damage often ***results in*** *high blood pressure.*
- Use the passive of *cause* to mention effect before cause:
  Frostbite ***is*** *usually* ***caused*** *by prolonged exposure to cold temperatures.*

Linking words

We can use a number of linking words. These include the subordinators *because* and *so (that)* and the complex prepositions *because of, due to,* and *owing to.*

- These mention effect before cause:
  One theory is that we dream ***because*** *the brain needs to process all the day's information.*
  Many people suffer ill health ***because of*** *the work that they do.*
  Usually, tiredness is ***due to*** *a combination of causes.*
  There is risk of ill health ***owing to*** *air pollution.*
- Use *so (that)* to mention cause or condition before effect:
  The inner layer of blood vessels is very smooth ***so (that)*** *the blood can flow easily.*

Nouns

We can use a number of expressions using nouns such as *cause, effect, consequence,* and *result*:

- These mention cause before effect:
  Vitamin B1 deficiency is often ***the cause of*** *a loss of appetite.*
  The diaphragm constricts and ***as a consequence****, the volume of the lungs increases.*
  The programme ran for 6 months. ***As a result****, participants lowered their average cholesterol count from 219 to 205.*
  Too much time spent online can have ***consequences for*** *a person's health and well-being.*
  Too much protein in the diet can have a number of negative ***effects****, such as nausea and diarrhoea.*
- These mention effect before cause:
  A person's health is ***a result of*** *internal and external factors.*
  Malnutrition is ***a consequence of*** *disease and inadequate dietary intake.*

Note that we can use hedging words such as *can, may, possibly, probably,* and *perhaps* and adverbs such as *often, usually, sometimes* and *occasionally* with some of the cause and effect language.

There are many diseases that ***can cause*** *obesity.*
Prolonged use of some medication ***may lead to*** *vitamin B12 deficiency.*
Premature skin ageing is ***possibly due to*** *a combination of factors.*

Unit 10

10.1 Linking words: Addition, contrast and concession

Addition

Often in academic argument, it is necessary to present a number of points to support an argument, stance, or point of view. To do this, we can use linking additive adverbials.

- *First (of all), furthermore, in addition,* and *moreover* generally go at the beginning of the sentence that contains the additional point.
  First of all*, globalization can refer to the creation of a 'world society.'*
  In addition*, globalization also refers to the increasing global mobility of people.*
  Furthermore*, global contraction may lead to social relationships becoming 'disembedded,' i.e. they may no longer depend on sharing the same geographical space.*
- *As well as* goes before the first point or before the additional point. It is followed by a noun phrase or a gerund (*-ing*) clause.
  As well as *the increased speed and range of travel, the impact of electronic media also makes the world seem a smaller place.*
  or
  The increased speed and range of travel ***as well as*** *the impact of electronic media make the world seem a smaller place.*
  As well as *becoming more flexible, the workforce is becoming less standardized.*
- *Also* most commonly goes before the additional point. It goes before the main verb or after *be*.
  Globalization can ***also*** *refer to 'global contraction,' i.e. the way the world appears to be shrinking.*
  As well as the increased speed and range of travel, the impact of electronic media ***also*** *makes the world seem a smaller place.*

Contrast and concession

It is often necessary to present and contrast two sides to an argument. To do this, we can use contrastive linking words.

- *On the one hand* most commonly goes at the beginning of the first point. *On the other hand* generally goes at the beginning of a second sentence and/or after a coordinator such as *but*.
  On the one hand*, globalization unifies the world. But* ***on the other hand****, it excludes a large proportion of the global population.*
- *But* is the most common way of showing contrast. It goes between the ideas it is contrasting. It can continue the sentence, usually after a comma, or it can start a second sentence.
  Product demand remained high in Europe. ***But*** *it declined in the Far East.*
- *However* goes at the beginning, in the middle, or at the end of a second sentence. We can use *nevertheless* in a similar way.
  The brand image was modernized. ***However****, sales remained static.*
  The brand image was modernized. Sales, ***however****, remained static.*
  The brand image was modernized. Sales, remained static, ***however****.*
- ***Yet*** goes between the ideas it is contrasting.
  The company experienced huge losses in the early 2000s, ***yet*** *it continued to expand its operations.*
- *Although* and *even though* can generally go at the beginning of the sentence or between the ideas they are contrasting. They are followed by a subject clause.
  Although *air travel is statistically safer than travelling by car, many people are afraid to fly.*
  Many people are afraid to fly ***even though*** *air travel is statistically safer than travelling by car.*
- *Despite* and *in spite of* go at the beginning of the sentence or between the ideas they are contrasting. They are followed by a noun phrase, a gerund (*-ing*) clause, or *the fact that* + subject clause.
  Despite *a number of concerns, the product launch went ahead.*
  RBC's profits increased by over 20% ***in spite of*** *losing over 100,000 customers.*
  Despite *the fact that it occurred well over a century ago, this particular financial crisis is still being felt today.*

Note that *yet, although / even though, despite / in spite of* are generally used to show or to emphasize that something is unexpected or surprising. In doing so, they can often present an element of concession.

Writing Sample answers

Unit 2C Writing (2) Task 5 (page 033)

Economic geography

Geography is the scientific study of the earth's surface, physical features, and populations.[1] Economic geography is a branch of geography which focuses on people's economic activity around the world.[2] It looks at the relationship between economic activity and the environment.[3] It also examines industries in different countries and the way that these industries are organized. In a globalized world, economic geography is becoming an increasingly important subject.[4]

▸ Key features in Academic writing

[1] A clear definition of a key term, 'geography'.
[2] A relative clause providing a definition.
[3] Prepositional phrases which extend the definition.
[4] An evaluative sentence concluding the paragraph.

Unit 3C Writing (2) Task 3 (page 047)

Good preparation for lectures is important, as students who are familiar with the topic of a lecture are able to follow it more easily. Therefore, it is always a good idea for students to do some background reading before a lecture. This gives students the opportunity to think about the main ideas surrounding the topic, consider supporting details, and note down any questions which they have.[1] It also helps students to think about their response to the content of the lecture.

▸ Key Features in Academic Writing

[1] A clear use of a determiner to show cohesion.

Unit 4C Writing (2) Task 4 (page 061)

Figure 3 compares the amount of sugar in eight different foods, measured in teaspoons per serving.[1] The amount of sugar varies greatly from one food to another, from as little as 0.5 teaspoons in a serving of cornflakes to 9 teaspoons in ice cream.[2] The amount of sugar in products such as a chocolate bar or a can of cola is very similar – 6 and 7 teaspoons respectively.[3] Interestingly, the amount of sugar in savoury foods like baked beans is similar to sweet foods like chocolate biscuits – 2 teaspoons per serving. However, in other products the difference is much greater. For example, ice cream has nearly[4] three times more sugar per serving than low-fat yoghurt – 9 teaspoons compared to 3.25.

▸ Key Features in Academic Writing

[1] A clear statement of what the visual is presenting.
[2] A clear statement of the overall trends.
[3] Use of language of comparison and contrast.
[4] Use of approximation.

Unit 5C Writing (2) Task 4 (page 075)

'Due to limited resources, and an environment that is changing for the worse, humans need to make bold technological decisions to survive.' Do you agree or disagree with the statement?

There are now over seven billion people on the planet and the population is growing. More importantly, economic development in countries like China and India is also increasing rapidly. This growth in population and economy leads to increased demands on natural resources. However, it seems that[1] the environment cannot cope with this rapid development.[2] In many Chinese cities, for example, air pollution is now at dangerous levels. Research conducted by the China Agricultural University of Beijing has shown that this pollution cuts light by about 50% and affects plant growth.[3] Perhaps the only answer is to find new technology that can control or reduce this pollution.[4]

▸ **Key Features in Academic Writing**

[1] Use of hedging language to moderate claims.
[2] A clear transition from broader background content to topic-specific material.
[3] Use of evidence to support the main idea.
[4] A concluding sentence that sums up the writer's stance and refers to the essay title.

Unit 6C Writing (2) Task 4 (page 089)

Studying abroad can give you valuable experience in your future life. Professionally, most people will come into contact with people from other cultures at some time in their lives.[1] For example, if you work for a multi-national company, you will probably have colleagues from different cultural backgrounds. In this way, experience of living and studying in another country can be very helpful, as it opens the mind to different cultural behaviours.[2]

▸ **Key Features in Academic Writing**

[1] Introduction of a perspective to support the main point.
[2] A concluding sentence that restates the main point and offers evaluation.

Unit 7C Writing (1) Task 4 (page 101)

Python is a free, open source programming language that was developed in the 1980s by Guido van Rossum. It is used both by first-time programmers and large software companies because it is easy and quick to use. It has also been noted that Python is good for teaching programming since it uses many of the same basic principles of more complicated[1] programming languages, like C++.[2]

▸ **Key Features in Academic Writing**

[1] Use of synonyms to show paraphrase.
[2] Own language used to capture the main ideas of the paragraph.

Unit 7C Writing (2) Task 4 (page 103)

A Lightbown and Spada (2003) note that in first language acquisition there is significant similarity in children's early language, wherever they are from in the world.

B Lightbown and Spada (2003) state that first language acquisition is remarkable for 'the high degree of similarity which we see in the early language of children all over the world.'

Unit 8C Writing (2) Task 3 (page 117)

Production of glass bottles

Glass bottles are made from[1] four main raw materials: calcium carbonate, sodium carbonate, waste glass, and sand. These materials are placed in a furnace and then heated to 1,400°C. At this temperature, the raw materials melt and molten glass is formed. A quantity of molten glass is then dropped into a mould. When it is in the mould, it is treated with compressed air, which forces the glass into the shape of the mould.[2] After it has been shaped into a bottle, the glass is removed from the mould and allowed to cool.

▶ **Key Features in Academic Writing**

[1] The passive voice is used to place the focus on process instead of people.
[2] Stages in the process are shown by the use of subordinators.

Unit 9C Writing (2) Task 4 (page 131)

Environmental science study

The aim of the study was to find out the causes of flooding in an urban area. Many homes had flooded and water had also caused damage to roads and public areas. As a result, people were forced to leave their homes, and local businesses and factories were also affected.

While the direct cause of the flooding – long periods of heavy rain in the area – was clear, our research group wanted to examine the indirect causes. The study found that a major reason for the flooding was intensive building in the area and the fact that there was too little grassland where the water could escape into the ground. This has important implications for the ways that towns are planned and built in the future.

Unit 10C Writing (2) Task 6 (page 147)

Increased freedom of movement has meant that more people are now living in foreign countries than previously. There are both advantages and disadvantages of this for the host countries. Argue one of these viewpoints.

In the past two decades, there has been an increase in the movement of workers from one country to another. The main reason for this has been the demand of international companies to make global business easier. However, there is a debate about whether this large-scale migration of people is a positive or a negative phenomenon. This essay will argue that increased freedom of movement has in fact had positive effects on the host countries, both economically and culturally.[1]

People migrate to work in other countries for several reasons: they cannot find work in their own country; the pay is better in another country; or they are recruited by companies in the host country which need their skills and expertise. In each of these cases, the new worker arrives in the host country in a highly motivated condition. In addition, he or she is very often able to do the same job more cheaply than a local worker and is sometimes willing to undertake jobs that local workers may not do.

Even though an increased number of workers may put extra pressure on the host country's resources, on balance there is an advantage from an economic point of view. Migrant workers often help to improve the infrastructure of a country – which can help create more jobs – and the taxes that these workers pay also help to improve services for the local people. Culturally, there are also benefits. If local people accept the new migrants, the whole country benefits from the increased cultural diversity and the new ideas these migrants bring. With more increased cultural understanding, a population is more likely to be successful in the global workplace.

In conclusion, freedom of movement of workers around the world is a way of helping countries to make economic and cultural progress, rather than remaining isolated from each other. Everyone benefits from the free movement of goods these days, and the movement of people, and their skills, is a natural part of this.

▶ **Key Features in Academic Writing**

[1] A clear statement of aims that outlines essay structure.

Additional material from units

Unit 1A Listening and Speaking TASK 7 (page 011)

1 **Read the information in the table below.**

2 **Form questions to ask Student B about subjects b, d, f, and h. Write your questions in column 2.**

3 **Ask Student B your questions. Note down the answers in column 3. Try to ask a follow-up question to get further information.**

4 **Answer Student B's questions about subjects a, c, e, and g. Use the information in column 3.**

	1 Subject	2 Question	3 Answer
a	Get advice about changing my course		You must see your course tutor if you want to change your course, but it may not be possible.
b	Get a list of books to buy	*Where ...?*	
c	If you are sick or unable to attend a lecture		You must email your tutor to tell them a minimum of two hours before the lecture.
d	Pay for my accommodation	*When ...?*	
e	Taking my laptop / tablet / mobile into lectures		You can take a laptop or tablet into a lecture but you can't use a phone.
f	Get a student card	*How ...?*	
g	Eat at lunchtime		There are restaurants and sandwich bars in the Student's Union building.
h	Use the university fitness centre	*Is ...?*	

Unit 2A Listening and Speaking TASK 6 (page 025)

1 **Explain the concept of *speed reading*. Use the notes.**

Speed reading = reading fast. Two main methods:
1 Skimming = read approximately 600 words per minute to get general idea of text
2 Meta guiding = use a pen or finger to guide you down the page

Unit 3A Listening and Speaking TASK 7 (page 039)

1 **Read information (a) and (b) to Student B and then answer his / her questions.**

a The body that controls the use of drugs in sport is called the World Anti-Doping Agency.
(*doping* means taking drugs to improve performance)

b The founder of the Olympics said the important thing in life is not conquering but fighting well.
(*conquering* means winning or overcoming others)

2 **Now listen to Student B's information and ask him / her questions for repetition or clarification.**

Unit 4A Listening and Speaking TASK 7 (page 053)

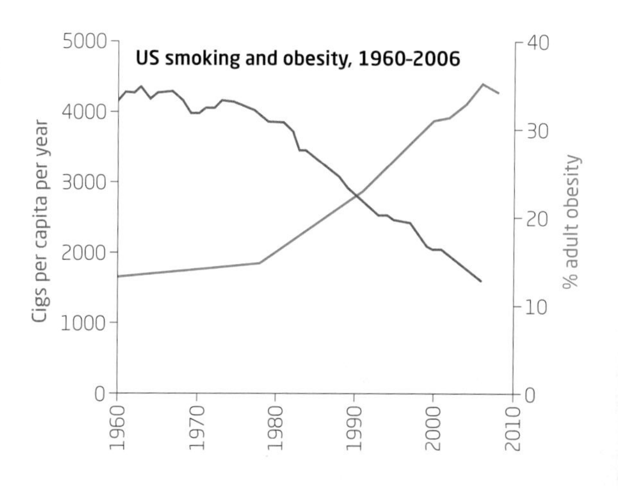

1 **Look at the two lines in this graph showing the number of cigarettes smoked in the US and the percentage of obese (very overweight) adults.**

2 **Compare the two trends. Use Academic Language and the sentences in Task 7 to help you.**
Make sure your presentation:
- introduces the topic
- describes what each line in the graph shows
- compares these two trends.

Unit 6A Listening and Speaking TASK 7 (page 081)

1 **Read the information and prepare a short presentation. Use Academic Language on perspectives and end your presentation with a conclusion.**

Sea salt production	
Industrial process	made from evaporating sea water
Chemical composition	natural product - nothing added
Nutritional benefits	+ contains beneficial minerals such as magnesium - potential pollution in sea water
Financial perspective	expensive to produce

Unit 7A Listening and Speaking TASK 7 (page 095)

TEXT 3

Toponymy

Toponymy is the study of place names. It is a subject that is useful to geographers, because it provides a reference system for mapping places in the world and understanding the changes that have taken place there. For example, a place may be named after a forest that no longer exists. It is also useful for sociologists and historians, because understanding place names can help us to follow patterns of migration among different peoples. A place may have a name in a language that is not the same as that of the current inhabitants, indicating that another people lived there at some point. By following the development of its place names, historians can also understand better the cultural development of a particular region. Place names could have religious significance, for example, or they could show that a place was a military base, as in the name *Fort William*.

Unit 8A Listening and Speaking TASK 6 (page 109)

1 **Read the notes and use them to give a spoken description of an Arctic expedition. Remember to use sequencing words and the correct tenses.**

North Pole in the Arctic Ocean in area covered with sea ice
First men to set foot on North Pole: Russian team in 1948
1870-1900 - many try and fail to reach North Pole
1920-1940 planes fly over North Pole, but unable to land
Russian team land there in a plane in 1948
They spend two days making scientific observations, then return

2 **Describe the events to your partner.**

Unit 1A Listening and Speaking TASK 7 (page 011)

1 **Read the information in the table below.**

2 **Form questions to ask Student A about subjects a, c, e, and g. Write your questions in column 2.**

3 **Answer Student A's questions about subjects b, d, f, and h. Use the information in column 3.**

4 **Ask Student A your questions. Note down the answers in column 3. Try to ask a follow-up question to get further information.**

	1 Subject	2 Question	3 Answer
a	Get advice about changing my course	*Where ...?*	
b	Get a list of books to buy		You can get a list of books from your department, but check if they are in the library before you buy them.
c	If you are sick or unable to attend a lecture	*What ...?*	
d	Pay for my accommodation		You must pay for your accommodation before the first day of term.
e	Taking my laptop / tablet / mobile into lectures	*Can ...?*	
f	Get a student card		You can get a student card from the Student's Union. You will need a passport photo. The card costs £10.
g	Eat at lunchtime	*Where ...?*	
h	Use the university fitness centre		There is a fitness centre on campus which is free to all students, but you need your student card.

Unit 2A Listening and Speaking TASK 6 (page 025)

1 **Explain the concept of *memorization*. Use the notes.**

Memorization = making sure something stays in your memory. Two main methods:
1 Loci method = connect each thing you want to remember to a particular place (e.g. the place on a page where you saw it)
2 Rote learning = say or write something many times until you have learned it

Unit 3A Listening and Speaking TASK 7 (page 039)

1 **Listen to Student A's information and ask him / her questions for repetition or clarification.**

2 **Read information (a) and (b) to Student A and then answer his / her questions.**

1 The use of new materials in sport can be a difficult ethical area. An example is polyurethane swimsuits that cover the whole body.
(*polyurethane* is a kind of thin plastic used in paints)

2 Sportspeople always face an ethical dilemma in deciding what steps they can take to win.
(a *dilemma* is a difficult choice)

Unit 4A Listening and Speaking TASK 7 (page 053)

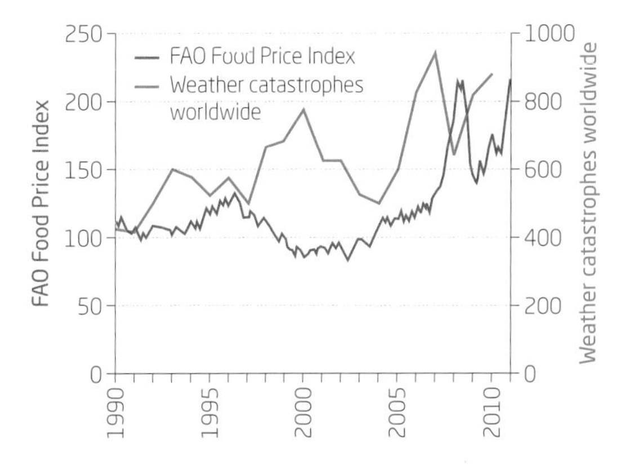

1 Look at this graph showing the world price of food and the number of extreme weather events in the world.

2 Compare the two trends. Use Academic Language and the sentences in Task 7 to help you.
Make sure your presentation:
- introduces the topic
- describes what each line in the graph shows
- compares these two trends.

Unit 6A Listening and Speaking TASK 7 (page 081)

1 Read the information and prepare a short presentation. Use Academic Language on perspectives and end your presentation with a conclusion.

Table salt production

Industrial process	intensive process - rock salt mined, then processed to remove impurities
Chemical composition	minerals, e.g. magnesium, removed
Nutritional benefits	+ iodine (essential for brain development) added
Financial perspective	cheap to produce

Unit 7A Listening and Speaking TASK 7 (page 095)

Diminutives

TEXT 4

A diminutive is a linguistic term for words which mean something small or something which is special to someone. They are generally formed by adding a particular ending to an existing word. For example, the French word for a truck or lorry is *camion*. The diminutive suffix is *-ette*, so a small lorry is a *camionette*. Diminutives are used in many languages also as a term of affection. In Portuguese these are very common in names: *Paulinho* is the diminutive of *Paulo*.

Some languages use diminutives much more than others. Spanish, for example, has a lot of diminutive forms, whereas English has relatively few. One is the suffix *-let*, as in *booklet* to mean *small book*. Another, used as a term of affection mainly, is the adding of the letter *-y*: *Johnny* instead of *John*, *doggy* instead of *dog*.

Unit 8A Listening and Speaking TASK 6 (page 109)

1 Read the notes and use them to give a spoken description of an Antarctic expedition. Remember to use sequencing words and the correct tenses.

Antarctica the last continent to be explored by geographers
First man to reach South Pole: Roald Amundsen in 1911
Antarctica first seen in 1820; after that, discovered little by little
Between 1930 and 1950 Antarctica mapped by plane and ship
South Pole station set up in 1956; now a permanent station for international scientific research

2 Describe the events to your partner.

Answer key

Unit 1

Vocabulary

1 1 proportion
2 trend
3 phenomenon
4 institutions
5 expand
6 fund
7 achieve
8 goal
9 available

2 Student's own answers

3 Student's own answers

1 1 A: verb; B: noun
2 A: verb; B: noun
3 A: noun; B: verb
4 A: verb; B: noun
5 A: verb; B: noun
6 A: noun; B: verb
7 A: noun; B: verb

2 Student's own answers

Academic Language Check

1 1 is
2 goes
3 was trying
4 didn't have
5 established
6 became
7 changed
8 is entering
9 are
10 is
11 attracts
12 is
13 received
14 are
15 is expanding

1 1 S = King Saud University
V = is
C = the premier university
A = in the Kingdom of Saudi Arabia
2 S = It
V = is
C = the oldest university
A = in Saudi Arabia
3 S = The university
V = has
O = about 40,000 students
4 S = It
V = has
O = students
A = from a number of different countries
5 S = Tuition
V = is
C = free
A = at the university

1 1 and
2 but
3 or
4 but
5 or
6 and
7 or
8 but

Unit 2

Vocabulary

1 1 distinguish between
2 increased
3 derive from
4 shown
5 determine
6 occur

2 Student's own answers

3 Student's own answers

1 1 follow
2 make
3 gave
4 set
5 carried out
6 reached
7 work out
8 used

2 Student's own answers

3 Student's own answers

Academic Language Check

1 1 means
2 which
3 term
4 type
5 when

2 1 **A** What is cryptography?
B It's the study of making and breaking codes.
2 **A** What does auditorium mean?
B It's the place where a theatre audience sits.
3 **A** Can you explain what a first draft is?
B It's the first version of something that you write, such as an essay.
4 **A** What's orca mean?
B It's another name for a killer whale.

1 1 b 2 d 3 c 4 a 5 f 6 c

2 1 Intelligence is defined as the ability to understand, learn, and think.
2 A metre is defined as the distance travelled by light in 0.000000003335 of a second.
3 A phoneme is a symbol that represents one of the sounds of a language.
4 Obesity is defined as having excessive body fat that may damage health.
5 Basic is one of the earliest computer languages.
6 Ageing can be defined as the process of physical deterioration of the body.

3 Student's own answers

Unit 3

Vocabulary

1 1 is concerned with covers
2 examines
3 consider
4 covers is concerned with
5 participate in
6 outlines
7 summarizes
8 state

2 1 summarize
2 consider
3 outline
4 participate in
5 consider
6 state
7 be concerned with

1 1 with
2 on
3 to
4 on
5 for
6 about
7 between
8 in

2 Student's own answers

Academic Language Check

1 1 WikiLeaks is an international, non-profit media organization which publishes secret information.
2 The WikiLeaks website was launched in 2006 by the Australian internet activist Julian Assange.
3 WikiLeaks publishes sensitive, publicly unavailable information from anonymous sources.
4 The organization has released a number of significant documents which have become front-page news items.
5 It always publishes original, unedited documents to support any new information it releases.

1 1 A
2 a
3 a
4 the
5 -
6 The
7 the
8 The
9 the
10 -
11 a
12 -
13 The
14 the
15 the
16 a
17 -
18 an
19 an
20 -
21 -
22 -
23 -

1 1 The
2 their
3 This
4 the
5 the other team's
6 their
7 These
8 The

2 The competitors
undergraduate students
their university
preliminary tournaments
the USA
the top 32 teams
the national finals
Each round
two teams
several questions
an ethical problem
Each team
the other team's answers
their responses
the winning team
the next round
These knock-out stages
an overall winner
The tournament
each year
the annual meeting
the Association
Practical and Professional Ethics

Unit 4

Vocabulary

1 1 significant
2 growth
3 varied
4 increase
5 rate
6 dramatic

2 Student's own answers

1 1 to
2 of; in
3 Over
4 At
5 of

2 1 uncompetitive; unproductive; uncreative; unpopular; uninterested; unsuccessful
2 inefficient; informal
3 different – same; high – low

3 1 unpopular
2 uninterested
3 unproductive; uncreative
4 informal
5 low
6 unsuccessful
7 same

6 Student's own answers

Academic Language Check

1 2 similarities / differences
3 differences / similarities
4 unlike
5 both
6 different
7 same
8 similar

1 1 more popular than; as popular as
2 more dangerous than
3 heavier than
4 more valuable than; as valuable as
5 as successful as
6 faster than; as fast as / faster than

Unit 5

Vocabulary

1 1 effects
2 existing
3 conduct
4 range
5 measure
6 factor
7 contributed
8 conditions

1 relocation
majority
agreement
activity
suggestion
statement

2 1 minority
2 contribution; education
3 improvement
4 ability
5 management

1 1 a noun; b verb
2 a verb; b noun
3 a noun; b verb

Academic Language Check

1 1 Greenpeace says that there may be just 10,000 blue whales worldwide.
2 Most experts' view is that deforestation must slow down.
3 Evans (2014) believes that many species may soon become extinct.
4 According to Peterson, humans must one day colonize another planet.
5 Smith (2012) notes that the research findings are inconsistent.
6 Harris and Jones claim that the survey findings are not reliable.
7 The most important research was perhaps that of Roberts and Hick.
8 A number of species clearly risk losing their habitats.

1 1 think
2 don't agree
3 seems
4 don't think
5 to me
6 think
7 right
8 but
9 agree
10 think
11 and

1 1 Average life expectancy could soon be over 100.
2 It seems that the number of different natural habitats is decreasing.
3 The results of the study appear to be inconclusive.
4 Many of the world's rainforests may one day disappear completely.
5 It appears that the physical workplace greatly affects a worker's performance.
6 Humans seem to be destroying much of the planet.
7 It is likely there will be a manned trip to Mars before 2050.
8 Global temperatures are thought to be rising faster than ever.

Unit 6

Vocabulary

1

Noun	Adjective	Adverb
commerce	commercial	commercially
emotion	emotional	emotionally
politics	political	politically
history	historical	historically
industry	industrial	industrially
psychology	psychological	psychologically
technology	technological	technologically
chemistry	chemical	chemically
machine	mechanical	mechanically

2 1 commercial
2 Psychologically
3 chemistry
4 political
5 industry
6 Historically
7 Technologically
8 mechanical

3 Student's own answers

4 1 find out
2 make up
3 looking into
4 break down
5 set up
6 looking at

Academic Language Check

1 Study at Heidelberg Uni on lucid dreaming, i.e. dreams which dreamer is aware of. Approx 300 participants questioned; used LD for diff reasons, e.g. solving problems, getting new ideas. Also LD v useful in sports training: learning new techniques, making sm improvements in performance.

1 1 From a physics perspective, 'light' is a series of particles moving through air.
2 *Pong* was the world's first commercially successful video game.
3 In terms of safety, *Finnair* is the number one airline.
4 Scientifically speaking, the experiment was a great success.
5 As far as cost is concerned, solar energy is the most economical method.

1 1 d 2 b 3 c 4 f 5 a 6 e

Unit 7

Vocabulary

1 1 d 2 c 3 b 4 a 5 f 6 e 7 h 8 g

2 1 expressed
2 follows
3 displays
4 fall into
5 put forward
6 perform
7 define

3 Student's own answers

1 1 b 2 e 3 f 4 a 5 c 6 d

2 Suggested answers:
1 special meaning
2 strong connection
3 a difficult job

Academic Language Check

1 1 b 2 d 3 a 4 c 5 h 6 g 7 e 8 f

1 1 We have already seen that the economy grew between 2000 and 2015.
2 As we have seen, deforestation has increased steadily in the last ten years.
3 You will recall that English is primarily a Germanic language.
4 We saw in Chapter 2 that the universe is expanding at an increasing rate.
5 At the beginning of this chapter we looked at genetic engineering.

1 Economies such as the United States are changing from industrial to knowledge and service-based economies. At the same time, manufacturing is moving to low-wage countries.

1 1 Foster (1996) has shown that learners who plan tasks generally attempt more complex language.
2 Mitchell (2009) concludes that 'over 50 species in the region are at risk of extinction.'
3 Dictionaries which contain grammatical information are generally more popular with learners of English than dictionaries with no grammar content (Jones, 2008).
4 Gerrard (2014) points out that the internet is a useful research tool.
5 Sangarun (2014) argues that 'the economy needs to return to innovation and production.'

Unit 8

Vocabulary

1 1 below
2 onto
3 to
4 away from; towards
5 on
6 around
7 inside
8 to

2 Student's own answers

1 1 attracted
2 generated
3 stored; released
4 reaches; becomes
5 converted
6 causes

1

Adjective	Noun
deep	depth
long	length
high	height
wide	width
heavy	weight
big	size

2 1 depth
2 high
3 weight
4 length; wide

Academic Language Check

1 1 discovered
2 was growing
3 noticed
4 appeared
5 had become
6 had forgotten
7 had developed
8 invented
9 had been
10 realized
11 had been used
12 was
13 was first turned
14 was used

1 1 was produced
2 are manufactured
3 are emitted
4 were discovered
5 is grown
6 was invented

1 1 begins
2 First
3 When
4 has been extracted
5 Next
6 requires
7 are removed
8 are added
9 After
10 has been refined
11 then
12 Finally
13 is transported

Unit 9

Vocabulary

1 1 deep
2 harder
3 serious
4 strong
5 high
6 certain
7 certain

2 Student's own answers

3 Student's own answers

1 1 a 2 b 3 b 4 b 5 a 6 b 7 a 8 b

2 Student's own answers

Academic Language Check

1 1 lead
2 result
3 means
4 cause
5 caused
6 due
7 due
8 because
9 result
10 due
11 result
12 lead
13 result
14 Because

2 1 Shale gas extraction leads to possible chemical and radiological pollution.
2 Excessive and prolonged overeating can result in obesity.
3 Sales rose by over 200% as a result of a successful advertising campaign.
4 There are fewer cases of sun-related medical conditions due to increased public awareness.
5 Dementia is caused by damage in the brain.

Unit 10

Vocabulary

1 1 negative
2 wider
3 address
4 briefly
5 various
6 concern

2 1 There have been a number of cases where buildings have collapsed.
2 Globalization is likely to increase even more.
3 By showing respect, both the traveller and the host can benefit from tourism.
4 Critics of offshoring say that it damages the economy of the company's native country.
5 So, in summary, the benefits of offshoring are generally greater than its disadvantages.

1 1 a 2 f 3 d 4 e 5 b; c

2 1 mispriced / overpriced
2 overpopulated
3 multi-skilled
4 recreated
5 interrelated
6 misspelled

3 Student's own answers

Academic Language Check

1 1 and
2 Furthermore
3 First of all
4 Also
5 First of all
6 In addition
7 and
8 As well as
9 also
10 Furthermore

1 1 But
2 One the one hand
3 On the other hand
4 even though
5 However
6 Even though
7 even if
8 despite

Unit 1

1.1 Extract 1

So good morning, everyone, and welcome to BCU, your new university. Welcome to the campus and welcome to your home for the next three years. My name is Clare Theakston, and I'm Head of Student Affairs. This is Sarah Wilkes, my deputy. Sarah has a few updates for your programme today, and she'll tell you about those in a moment. But first I just wanted to invite you to visit our offices at any time if you have any questions about university life. At Student Affairs we offer advice on all kinds of questions: academic, careers, accommodation, sports and social activities, and student welfare. My team is in the offices located on level 2 of this building and we're open from 8.30 to 5.30, Monday to Friday. So as I said, please don't hesitate to come and see us if you need information on anything to do with life here at BCU.

Now, just before Sarah speaks to you, I'm going to hand you over to Patrick O'Connor. Patrick is a second-year student, and he is going to give you a personal account of what it's like to be a student here at BCU.

1.2 Extract 2

Hi, everyone. I'm Patrick O'Connor and as Clare said, I'm a second-year undergraduate, and I'm studying for a degree in Business Administration.

So, in the next few days, you're going to get a lot of information in a short space of time. By the end of the week you will have more handouts than you'll ever need, you'll have sat through more talks than you can ever possibly want to hear .... but that's OK. You don't need to remember it all. The most important thing is that everything that happens this week will make your transition into university life easier.

Two years ago, I was sitting where you're sitting now. To be honest, I was pretty nervous and unsure of myself. I come from a small town, and my parents are not rich. I imagined that everyone else was from a big city and they had parents with really important professional jobs. I didn't know if the course I had chosen was the right one for me. I didn't know if I'd meet people with the same interests as me. But I did. And what's more, my interests developed as I studied new things and met new people. I took up singing ... Yeah. And I'm now part of a six-person singing group. Each of you has a different story to tell about why you're here at BCU. Some of you have a clear idea about what you want to achieve, others probably don't have such a clear idea. Maybe some of you dreamed of being here since you began to think of going to university; for others perhaps BCU wasn't your first choice. But we're glad you're here, anyway. BCU welcomes you all. Our goal is to help you find the path that's right for you, no matter who you are or where you want to go, in business or the arts, in science or sports. So don't be nervous, because you'll find a community here and a place you can call home.

1.3 Extract 3

Thank you very much for that, Patrick.

OK, as Clare said, I'm Sarah Wilkes, and I'm the programme coordinator for the day. I'd just like to take a moment to explain a couple of changes to your programme. Ah, if you could please turn to page 3 of your programme ... Ah, the talk on 'Life in the UK' at 3 p.m. will be in Room 7A, not 8A as advertised. That's room 7A. Secondly, the information session on work and visas has been moved from lecture hall 2 to lecture hall 1 – it's a bit bigger, so there'll be plenty of room for everyone. And finally, the afternoon walking tour of the campus will begin at 4.30 p.m., fifteen minutes earlier than advertised. Oh, and there's also an error with the opening times of the library information centre. On Monday to Thursday it's open until 9 p.m., but on Friday it closes at 8 p.m. So, if you could please note that down ... Otherwise, everything in the programme should be correct. So it just remains for me to say enjoy your day and please approach one of the staff if you need help at any time ...

1.4 Extract 4

1 Hello, I'm Kate, from Student Affairs. We mainly deal with issues like accommodation, and we can help out if you need information on counselling services offered by the university. The Student Affairs offices are located on level 2 of this building and we are open from 8.30 to 5.30, Monday to Friday.
2 OK ... I have an announcement about access to the library. Due to some building work the library will be closed until next Thursday. It will open again at 9 a.m. that morning.
3 If you're planning to travel by bus or take a train anywhere, you should think about getting a student travel discount card. This gives you twenty per cent off most fares. The discount cards are available from the Student's Union. Just ask someone at the main desk for an application form.
4 It's important that you have access to a doctor during your time at the university, so please make sure that you register with the University Medical Service. Their offices are in the Taylor Building. That's the one opposite the Student's Union. The Medical Service staff would prefer it if all students could register before the 28th of September. Thanks.

1.5 Extract 5

A So we're ready to take questions now. Can I just ask you, before you ask your question, to just give your name first. So lots of people with their hands up – yes ....
B Hi, my name is Jack, from China. I'd like to know ... Is there free internet access everywhere on the campus?
A Not absolutely everywhere, unfortunately. But we do have wireless in most main areas ... certainly in your room, in the Student's Union, in the library, and also in your department building. But you will need a separate password for that.
B OK. Where can I get more information about that?
A You need to ask your tutor or the administrator for your department. ... Yes, at the back ...
C Hi, my name is Bogdan, from Bulgaria. How do I take books out of the library? Can you borrow them? I mean, like in a normal library?
A What subject are you studying?
C I'm studying biochemistry.
A OK, well, as far as the main library is concerned you can borrow up to ten books on your card.
C And journals?
A No, you can't take journals out of the library. They're mostly online. But your department also has books and journals and you can arrange to borrow those for short periods. ... Any more questions?
D Yes, my name is Frederick. What time's the last bus from town?
A About 11 p.m.
D What happens if you miss it?
A Well, there are city night buses which run all night.
D And is the university bus free or do you have to pay?
A Yes, it's free if you have a student bus pass.
D How do I get one of those?
A You need to get a form from the Student's Union and fill it in.

Unit 2

2.1 Extract 1

Today we're going to look at a slightly different area of mathematics, but one which continues to be relevant and important in many contexts – banking, programming, sending military information ... So, today's subject is cryptography – that is, the art of writing and solving codes. And first, we're going to focus on some of the processes involved in creating codes, and then we'll look at the work of cryptographers – these are the people who make and break codes.

2.2 Extract 2

OK. So, let's look at some simple codes to begin with. Now, the most basic type of code is known as the substitution cipher. Let me clarify a bit here. In cryptographic terms, a cipher is another word for a code. And what we mean by a substitution cipher is when you create a code by replacing each original letter in a text with a different character. An early example of this is the Caesar cipher, which replaced each letter of the alphabet with the letter three places further down the alphabet: so A was replaced by D, B was replaced by E, and so on.

Now, every substitution cipher uses a key. The key is the component which tells you what you need to do to create the code. For example, in the case of the Caesar cipher, it tells you how many spaces the letter has been moved along. If you want to have a more secure code, you can regularly change the key that is used.

Over time, substitution ciphers became more complex. Cryptographers started to use not just one key, but many different keys in a message. And this raises the question, if the cryptographer uses many different keys in a single message, how can anyone break such a code?

Well, one method is to use a crib. A crib is a type of answer key. This is usually part of the decoded text that someone has already found or has worked out. When you have a crib, you can use it to guess the meaning of the rest of the ciphertext. Just to clarify, a ciphertext means the coded message. So if you guess, for example, that the characters E-F-B-S in a letter represent D-E-A-R, the word 'dear', then using those letters as a starting point, you can work out what the key is.

So for the very simple example that I gave you before this lecture ... the answer is ...

2.3 Extract 3

... But without a crib, complex substitution ciphers were very difficult to break. However, this changed in the 9th century, when the Arab philosopher Al-Kindi focused on complex ciphers. Al-Kindi's method for breaking codes was called 'frequency analysis.' He realized that, in any language, different letters appear with a certain frequency. In English, for instance, the letter E accounts for 13% of all letters in a text. Other letters, such as X and Z, are much less frequent.

Each letter also has a different personality. The letter Q, for example. It's a comparatively rare letter, it's almost always followed by a U ... well, in English, anyway ... and it's often placed at the beginning of a word. So to break the code you simply have to match the personality of each character in the cipher text to the same personality in the regular alphabet.

2.4 Extract 4

A How was your Maths lecture on Tuesday?
B It was interesting, actually. We looked at cryptography – it was about how ciphers are made and some of their uses.
A Ciphers?
B Yeah. A cipher is another word for a code.
A You mean like computer codes, HTML, that kind of thing?
B Er, no ... not exactly. It was about the history of code-making. Codes that people have used to send information to each other in letters or codes for government documents. We looked at pretty much everything ... from substitution ciphers to more complex codes.
A Right ... What's a substitution cipher?
B A substitution cipher is when you replace the original letters in a message with other characters.
A Like using Z to mean A, that kind of thing?
B Yes, that's right, but most codes aren't quite that simple ... because each substitution cipher can use more than one key.
A Er, I don't get that. Can you explain what a key is?
B OK, well ... The key is the component which tells you the operation to perform to create the code. Like moving a letter a certain number of places.
A Oh, right. So I guess if you use one substitution cipher, then that might make Z mean A, but, like, another cipher could make Z mean E.
B Yes, exactly. The thing is that without a crib it's almost impossible to break a code that uses a lot of keys. A crib is a type of answer key that tells you how to convert the ciphertext into a message that can be understood.
A Sorry, what does ciphertext mean?
B Ciphertext means the coded message. Whatever you wanted to keep secret in the first place.
A OK. Interesting stuff. Did they recommend any books on it?

Unit 3

3.1 Extract 1

OK. So, we've looked at the subject of ethics in sport, in quite a lot of detail. What I'd like to do now is to summarize some of the main points we've covered. So, first, we looked at the distinction between gamesmanship and sportsmanship. What is the difference between them?

Well ... gamesmanship, if you remember, is the principle, the idea, that winning is the most important thing. Winning is everything. You do whatever you can to win. And it's also the idea you're only guilty of doing something wrong if you're caught. And it happens in all sport. So an example of gamesmanship is deliberately injuring an opponent or faking an injury, pretending you're hurt when you're not. Another example is using performance-enhancing drugs in cycling; or in football, maybe unfair play, like wasting time when your team is winning. So gamesmanship is what most people consider to be unethical behaviour. But it's important to remember that the people who practise gamesmanship don't always think they're doing something wrong. They think it's the responsibility of the referee to enforce the rules. So if the referee doesn't catch them, they're not breaking the rules.

OK, how is sportsmanship different? Well, sportsmanship represents a more ethical approach to sport. It's based on the principle that the goal is not just to win, but to win by keeping to the rules. So, to win with honour, if you like. And like gamesmanship, you find sportsmanship in all sports. Sportsmanship is often more associated with amateur sport ... in other words, when people are doing a sport because they love it, not because there's a lot of money involved. With sportsmanship the belief is that the competition is important, but the most important thing is to practise that sport in an environment of honesty and respect. So, what does that mean exactly?

3.2 Extract 2

We looked at four principles of ethics in sport:

So firstly, fairness. Fairness in sport is defined as following the rules. That doesn't just include the participants, the players. It's also important the officials apply the rules fairly too. So in football, if you commit a foul ... an example of a foul is touching the ball with your hand ... then you should admit it. Maybe get a yellow card. If someone else commits a foul, the referee should apply the same rules, treat them the same – so they get a yellow card too.

Secondly, integrity. Playing sport with integrity means that you play the sport in the correct spirit, in the spirit of honesty. Sometimes this doesn't happen. For example, when two football teams know that a draw, like a one-all or a two-all, will mean they both qualify for a competition – so neither team tries to win the match. They play for a draw. That is not playing with integrity – in fact, it damages the integrity of the sport.

Thirdly, respect. Respect is polite behaviour towards someone – or something – that you think is important. So behaving to them as you would like them to behave to you. So in sport, you should show respect for your opponent, and for the rules of the game, but also respect for the referee, respect for supporters, the people watching, and so on.

Lastly, responsibility – being responsible for your behaviour on the field and off the field. This is important in contact sports such as rugby, where you could really injure an opponent if you play irresponsibly.

This last point is important because ethics in sport is related to ethics in general – in society, in everyday life. The negative behaviour of sportspeople, particularly role models such as famous footballers, has an effect on the behaviour of other people in society, especially children and young people. And of course, the ethics of society also has an effect on the behaviour of sportspeople. OK. So, are there any questions?

3.3 Extract 3

Well ... Gamesmanship, if you remember, is the principle, the idea, that winning is the most important thing. Winning is everything. You do whatever you can to win. And it's also the idea you're only guilty of doing something wrong if you're caught. And it happens in all sport. So an example of gamesmanship is deliberately injuring an opponent or faking an injury, pretending you're hurt when you're not. Another example is using performance-enhancing drugs in cycling; or in football, maybe unfair play, like wasting time when your team is winning.

Secondly, integrity. Playing sport with integrity means that you play the sport in the correct spirit, in the spirit of honesty. Sometimes this doesn't happen. For example, when two football teams know that a draw, like a one-all or a two-all, will mean they both qualify for a competition – so neither team tries to win the match. They play for a draw. That is not playing with integrity – in fact, it damages the integrity of the sport.

This last point is important because ethics in sport is related to ethics in general – in society, in everyday life. The negative behaviour of sportspeople, particularly role models such as famous footballers, has an effect on the behaviour of other people in society, especially children and young people. And of course, the ethics of society also has an effect on the behaviour of sportspeople. OK. So, are there any questions?

3.4 Extract 4

1. Yes, you mentioned drugs, but there was a word which I didn't catch. Performance ... something?
2. What does that mean?
3. I'm not sure I understood what you said about gamesmanship. Do some people believe this is a good approach?
4. Could you just repeat the part about ... fairness?
5. And referees and officials are the same thing? Is that right?

3.5 Extract 5

Presenter ... Ok. So, are there any questions?
Student A Yes, you mentioned drugs, but there was a word which I didn't catch. Performance ... something?
Presenter Oh, performance-enhancing drugs.
Student A What does that mean?
Presenter Well, enhancing means increasing or improving. So performance-enhancing drugs will make you perform better, make you faster or stronger. Of course, not all drugs enhance performance, but some do.
Student A Can you spell that?
Presenter Yes, E-N-H-A-N-C-I-N-G.
Student B I'm not sure I understood what you said about gamesmanship. Do some people believe this is a good approach?
Presenter Yes, that's right. They believe in winning at any cost.
Student A Could you just repeat the part about fairness?
Presenter Yes, fairness means participants or sportspeople following the rules. And the officials applying the rules to everyone.
Student B And referees and officials are the same thing? Is that right?
Presenter Well, not always. It depends on the sport. An official is anyone in a position of authority and the referee is the main official in a sport such as football or basketball.

3.6 Extract 6

My field of study is Environmental Science. A very important concept in this field is, um, sustainability.

What is sustainability? Well, ah, it's the idea that you use resources in a way which meets your needs today but also your needs tomorrow.

What does that mean? Well, for example, it means that if you cut down a tree for wood today, then you should plant another tree for your wood in the future.

Sustainability is a very important concept in environmental science and in economics because resources are limited and the world population is growing.

So, um, ... are there any questions?

Unit 4

4.1 Extract 1

So today we're going to be looking at food production and consumption globally, and some of the issues affecting production and consumption in different parts of the world. As you know, and as we've discussed before, there are huge differences in the amount and the quality of food available to people across the world, depending on which part of the world they live in. So, we have a situation where many developed countries, Western countries like the USA and Canada and Australia, have more food than their populations need. A lot more food, in fact. And at the same time we also find that in the developing world there are countries which don't have enough food to feed all of their population all of the time. So, examples of these would be parts of Asia and Africa, countries like Bangladesh, Sudan, and Ethiopia. And as a result, in these countries there are situations in which the population suffers from hunger, from malnutrition and, in the worst cases in recent history, from starvation. So, in this lecture I want to examine some of the reasons for this imbalance in food distribution and why it's such a serious issue for all of us.

4.2 Extract 2

So, let's look first at the historical background. This graph compares world food production and world population growth in the forty years between 1961 and 2000. In the 1960s, there was a lot of concern in the West about population growth. It was thought that the world population would increase faster than food production, and that therefore, there would be a reduction in food supply globally – there would be less food, basically. But, in fact, as you can see, the opposite happened. Both food production and the world population increased, but the growth in food production was actually greater than population growth. And this was because of a number of factors, but mainly it was because of better technology and because farming methods became more efficient than in the past.

4.3 Extract 3

However, as the graph shows, this trend was not the same everywhere – there were regional variations. This data comes from the Food and Agriculture Organization of the United Nations. Here we can see a breakdown of food production by continent over the same period, 1961 to 2000. You will notice that there are significant differences. So in Asia, for example, food production was higher than in Latin America. And in Latin America, it was similar to North America. But in Africa, food production actually went down over the same period, as you can see. So why was food production in Africa not as high as in other parts of the world?

There are quite a number of complex reasons why Africa was not as productive as other countries during this period. But the main reasons were, firstly, a series of droughts, where there was no rain for extended periods of time, and without water of course, food production was badly affected. And the second reason, it must be said, was poor planning in terms of managing food supply and distribution. The consequence was that many African countries had to import food from other parts of the world. And in fact, even today, the amount of food that Africa imports is bigger than the amount it exports. But this is expensive, and in countries that did not have the money to import enough food, people went hungry.

4.4 Extract 4

According to figures from the American Association for the Advancement of Science, we produce enough food for every person on the planet to consume an average of 2,790 calories a day. So why are there still so many problems in terms of food supply? Why do we still see large parts of the world suffering from hunger and malnutrition?

Well, one problem is distribution. You can see clearly from this table that the consumption of food per person is lower in some countries than in others – much lower, in fact. In the USA, the average person consumes 3,830 calories per day. Some consume more, some consume less, but the average figure per person is 3,830 calories. That's more than enough. In Eritrea, it's only 1,530 calories per day. Less than half as much. And it should be noted that these figures include food that is wasted or thrown away. OK, these are extremes, but they show clearly, I think, the extent of the imbalance.

So, how do we solve the problem of this imbalance? An obvious answer is to distribute the excess food produced in richer countries to the poorer countries, but unfortunately it's not as simple as that.

4.5 Extract 5

OK. So today I'm going to talk about the cost of food and fuel, and some of the effects that rising fuel prices have on food production and consumption. Let's look first at some historical background.

Ah, this chart compares the relationship between oil prices and the price of food. You will notice that the two trends are similar – especially when we look at sharp increases during times of oil shortage.

Ah, OK, so let's take oil first. As you can see from the graph, oil prices increased at a faster rate in 2006. But then, if you look here, you can see an increase in food prices where they began to follow the trend.

OK, ah, let's look at this in more detail. Here we can see a table showing the main food commodities. Again, you can see the sharp increases in cost that are similar to increases in fuel prices …

Unit 5

5.1 Extract 1

Good morning. Today I'm going to talk about environmental change and its effect on different societies throughout the ages. First of all I'll give you an overview of what is meant by 'environmental change', when related to a civilization. This will be followed by a short case study about Easter Island, in the South Pacific Ocean. Then we'll go on to look at two very different points of view on how to address environmental concerns. And then I want to look at the implications for future societies.

OK, so the success of a civilization is closely linked to its environment. Evidence for this can be found in the failure of certain past civilizations, societies which failed because of environmental factors. Examples of this are Easter Island, the Mayan civilization of Central America, and the early Norse settlers in Greenland … All of these in the last one thousand years.

Several environmental factors contributed to the collapse of early civilizations. These included problems with the soil – for example the ground was too wet to grow crops in. Secondly, poor water management – when not enough fresh water was available, or the water that was available was not drinkable. And then also the introduction of non-native species of animal – in other words, animals that the settlers bought with them, and which then had an effect on the native species. There was also more pressure on the things that could be used for survival – food, water, and so on. And as the civilizations became more established, and the population grew, there was increased demand for resources – often leading to overhunting or overfishing.

5.2 Extract 2

In most cases, it's likely that more than one factor caused this collapse, this failure of a particular society because of changes to the environment. This is certainly the case with Easter Island, the Polynesian island famous for its stone statues. According to early researchers, the people who settled there changed the environment by cutting down many of the native palm trees and clearing the land to use for agriculture, for farming. This seems to make sense – as we know, there was a lot of farming on the island, and removing trees certainly affects the local environment. But when archaeologists examined the area in greater detail in the year 2000, they also found the bones of thousands of rats buried in the ground. Now there were no rats on Easter Island before the settlers came. They arrived with the settlers, in their boats. Modern archaeologists believe that the rats also contributed to the rapid destruction of the palm trees by eating all of the seeds, the palm nuts. So there were several things happening which had an effect over time …

5.3 Extract 3

In recent times, with more modern civilizations, other environmental dangers have emerged: chemical pollution, energy shortages – so, not enough energy – and of course climate change. I want to look at two different views on how we can tackle these problems facing our environment and our civilization, two different stances on the situation: the technocentric view and the ecocentric view. The technocentric view is that nature is there to benefit us, to benefit humans. As the Earth's most important species, we humans are in charge. According to technocentric thinkers, if there is a shortage of food or energy resources, people often look for a technological solution. In this way we can continue to grow economically. So in their opinion, economic growth is a good thing.

The ecocentric view is that the Earth is here for all species, not only for humans. Ecocentric thinkers believe it is a mistake to think that we can manage nature. In their view, nature is complex and we still don't fully understand it.

So ecocentrics believe that it is our responsibility to protect nature and to preserve existing ecosystems … as much as possible. Lastly, they say that resources are limited, so we must only use what can be replaced. I'll stop there for a moment so we can briefly discuss these two opposing views …

5.4 Extract 4

Tutor So, now that you've had some time to think about yesterday's lecture, it would be useful to just recap on some of the key ideas. Sarah, could you comment on the two stances presented in the lecture – the ecocentric and technocentric views?

Sarah Well, OK … It seems to me that the technocentric view is probably right. We're always being told that technology can have a positive effect on environmental needs. For example, forty years ago people thought that we couldn't grow enough food to support the global population. But in fact, with new farming methods we've increased food production.

Joel Yeah, I agree with that. I think that we're going to see a lot more use of technology to deal with the environment. You know, to solve issues like climate change by capturing carbon. And we'll get better at using technology to find new ways of doing things, like getting more minerals out of the Earth by deep-water drilling. That's just an example, but I mean, now we can get oil out of places like the Arctic that were impossible to reach, even twenty years ago.

Hasan Yes, but there's a limit to the Earth's resources, that's what the ecocentrics are saying. I would argue that you have to balance economic growth with the use of resources. We can't just go on using the same amount of oil and gas – it's not sustainable. There have to be controls. I mean, these are finite resources.

Sarah No, I don't agree. We're already seeing that technology increases access to oil reserves. Why not other resources, too? And why shouldn't people in the developing world have the same opportunities as people in developed countries?

Unit 6

6.1 Extract 1

... So today we're going to be looking at graphene. Graphene is a material that you all will have heard of, I'm sure. It's been in the news a lot recently, and it has some remarkable properties which we're going to look at in some detail. I want to cover the history of graphene and briefly outline how it's produced. But just to start, what actually is graphene?

Well ... graphene is the name given to a sheet of graphite which is only one atom thick. And as you know, graphite is a form of carbon, with a layered structure. And graphene is only one layer thick. So that's the first thing to note – that it's an incredibly thin material. And because it's so thin, it's very flexible, but also extremely strong and chemically stable. It's also highly conductive. That is to say, it conducts heat very effectively. So it has a lot going for it.

Graphene was first 'discovered' by the German chemist Hans-Peter Boehm and his team in 1961, but it wasn't developed further until the beginning of this century, so around 2000 / 2004. A number of scientists had recognized the potential, the possibilities of graphene. One of them was the physicist Andre Geim of Manchester University in the UK. His vision for the new material was to use it to make foldable computing devices – computers or smartphones with screens that you could bend and fold. His thinking was that this would have significant benefits from a commercial perspective because using graphene you could produce a flexible smartphone or tablet that is almost unbreakable. Which is pretty amazing when you think about it.

6.2 Extract 2

Historically, graphene was difficult to isolate. It wasn't until 2004 that Andre Geim and his team discovered a simple way to produce it. The technique they used is known as 'mechanical exfoliation'. What they did was, they began with a 25mm thick piece of graphite and started to split it horizontally, to make it thinner. So this process involved repeatedly dividing the graphite, layer by layer, until only one layer remained. Now, Geim's technique is very successful at producing small amounts of high-quality graphene. However, for many businesses mechanical exfoliation is not really satisfactory because it's very difficult to manufacture large quantities of graphene using this process. In practical terms, it just takes too long to produce graphene in this way.

6.3 Extract 3

More recently, a research team at Northwestern University, in the United States, have begun to use a different method for developing graphene. They hope to produce larger quantities of graphene using a more industrial process, so that it can be used to create new products. The Northwestern process involves breaking down graphite chemically in a liquid solution. What the researchers did was to add graphite to an ethanol-based liquid, so an alcohol-based liquid. And they observed very small, very thin pieces of graphene beginning to flake off from the graphite. They then mixed these graphene flakes into printer ink and put the ink into a normal inkjet printer. From a commercial perspective, this represents a much better solution. It means that industries can print graphene electronic circuits onto any surface: a flexible plastic screen, pieces of clothing, paper, and so on. I mean, imagine, for example, a large screen that can fold like a map into something you could put in your pocket ...

6.4 Extract 4

1 The aim of the study was to examine the different properties of precious metals, for example, silver and gold.
2 Professor Shackelford has a Ph.D. in materials science from the University of California.
3 Most students have studied four years of science already, that is to say, physics and chemistry.

6.5 Extract 5

Right, OK, so this morning I want to talk about a material, a building material, from a range of perspectives. The material I've chosen is something that we see every day. It affects the way we travel, the way we work, and the cities that we live in. It's probably all around us at this very moment ... So, I'm talking about concrete. Technically, concrete is defined as 'a composite material of water and coarse granular material embedded in a hard matrix'. And of course, it's something that we are all familiar with.

Historically, it has been the main building material for large-scale construction. In fact, the earliest large-scale users of concrete were the ancient Romans – both the Coliseum and the dome of the Pantheon in Rome are actually made of concrete. Although it was used less after the end of the Roman Empire, construction work in the mid-18th century was often influenced by Roman design, and this helped concrete to become popular again.

Today, concrete is, by weight, the most widely used man-made material. The largest sector of the concrete market, ready-mix, is worth approximately $100 billion. So, in that respect it's been commercially very successful.

In practical terms, concrete is a versatile substance - you can build quickly with it, it's strong, and it lasts a long time. For example, the Assyrian Jerwan Aqueduct, which is made of waterproof concrete, was built in 688 BCE.

There are, however, some environmental impacts. Producing and transporting concrete uses a lot of energy. It also uses a lot of water, which we all know is a precious natural resource.

And finally, there's the question of what it looks like. A lot of people would say that visually, concrete isn't very attractive. And it's true that many concrete buildings are not very beautiful to look at. I mean, look at the university library for a start ... But perhaps that says more about the architects than the building material.

Unit 7

7.1 Extract 1

In today's lecture we're going to look at the significance of personal names in different cultures. First, we need to define our terms. What do we mean by terms like 'family name' or 'given name'? After that, we'll look in detail at naming traditions in two specific cultures: firstly, one of the tribal groups of Native Americans in the United States, and secondly, the Han tradition of naming in China. Finally, we'll see how these two examples relate to the wider question of the significance of names in society.

So, what do we mean by personal names? Well, personal names fall into three very broad categories. One, family names or surnames – such as Schmidt, ah, Gonzalez, Mandela, Jarvis. Two, given names or first names – Thomas, Catherine, Maria, Ahmed. And then middle names, which some cultures use more than others. The main focus in this lecture will be given names – taking into account social, historical, and cultural perspectives. But first, just a brief word about surnames.

7.2 Extract 2

Surnames, or family names, are the names that show that a person belongs to a particular group. This could be a family group or tribal group like the MacDonalds in Scotland. Or it could be a geographical group .... people who come from the same village or region.

The names Da Silva and Da Costa in Portuguese, for example, refer to people who live in or near the forest or near the coast – *silva* means wood; or forest in Portuguese – *costa* is coast. Surnames can also refer to an occupational group – so names like Carpenter or Baker. A carpenter is someone who makes things from wood, a baker is someone who bakes bread. So in the past you maybe had a man in a village called John and he was the man who made the bread for the village, so he was known as John the Baker, John Baker. In many cultures we also find patronymic surnames, surnames taken from the name of the father. There are many examples of patronymic names in northern Europe and Scandinavia, such as Eriksson (son of Erik) in Swedish, or Ivanovna (daughter of Ivan) in Russian. In modern society, surnames have become very important for administrative reasons, but compared to given names, in most countries they're a relatively recent phenomenon. So for example, in the Netherlands and Japan surnames were not in common use until the 19th century.

7.3 Extract 3

Given names are a much more ancient tradition than surnames, and these are what I'd like to look at now. The question for sociologists is not just what influences parents to choose a particular given name. It's also interesting to examine how the choice of name influences a person's character or their prospects in life. So, I've chosen the example of the Apache, one of the major Native American tribal groups in the south-western United States. I've chosen the Apache because names have a particular significance, a particular meaning, in their culture.

Traditionally, Apache men – like this guy here, ah, this is the Chiracahua Apache Geronimo – Apache men were named after a particular trait of their character or a particular thing they had done, perhaps an act of bravery. Until one of these things became obvious to everyone, the child was simply called 'boy'. So among the Apache, we find given names like 'Always ready' or 'Strong swimmer'. So Geronimo was what the Americans called this man, but his Apache name was something like Goyahklay, which means 'one who yawns'. And these names could change during a person's life according to the development of their character or to significant events in their lives.

7.4 Extract 4

OK. Let's look at naming traditions of Apache women. Now, the women in Apache culture were named in the same way as the men – that is, after a character trait or significant action. Some women could also be named after things in nature, things familiar to the tribe, so for example, something like 'Morning Star' or 'Bird Singing'. However, the main difference between men's and women's names in Apache culture was because they had different lives, different roles in society. So for Apache women life was more domestic, and so they had fewer significant events in their lives. And the names they were given reflected this.

7.5 Extract 5

So, I'm going to be following up on last week's lecture. I'm going to summarize the main points, and I also have some references, um, for further reading about the topic.

OK, today I'd like to talk about names, and their cultural importance. Uh, I'm going to explain briefly the significance of personal names and then I want to focus on surnames and their historical role. Ah, as we heard in the lecture, in the past surnames usually told you one of four things about the person: number one, um, what tribe or family group a person belonged to; number two, where they came from; three, what their father's name was; or finally, what job they did.

OK, so, um, after discussing examples of these names in Scottish culture, I'd like to talk a little bit about the importance of *by-names*. Now, by-names are names taken by people in some parts of rural Scotland where there are so few traditional surnames, um, that a large number of people are called the same thing. For legal reasons, and to make it less confusing, many people are given an official name, um, and an unofficial name, so the listener can understand which person called ... for example, John Sutherland ... er, they know which John Sutherland is being referred to.

OK, um, and then finally, in my conclusion, I'll explain why nowadays the meaning of names is less culturally important, but names are more important for, um, administrative reasons: for voting, for work, for travelling to other countries, and so on.

Unit 8

8.1 Extract 1

The title of my presentation is *The Mariana Trench: Geography and Exploration*. So, first of all, what is the Mariana Trench? Well, it's a deep underwater valley, a break in the Earth's crust, about two and half thousand kilometres long. It's the deepest part of the world's oceans. At the deepest point, a place known as the Challenger Deep, it's eleven kilometres below the surface of the Pacific Ocean, near the island of Guam. This is approximately 2,400 kilometres east of Manila in the Philippines, which you can see here, on slide 1.

OK, there are about twenty similar trenches in the world's oceans. They're formed when two plates of the Earth's crust meet and one is forced under the other.

There are several reasons that scientists explore these trenches. One is to find micro-organisms that could lead to new discoveries, for example in medicine. Another reason is to examine the rocks and hopefully learn more about why earthquakes and tsunamis take place. And lastly, to maybe find new species – because it's possible that there are forms of life down there that no one has ever seen before, which is very exciting.

Although they have sent men to the moon, up until now the very deep ocean has still not been explored properly. The depth of the Mariana Trench was measured by British scientists in 1875 using a rope and again in 1951 using an echo-sounder. But it was only recently that people actually went down into the trench itself.

8.2 Extract 2

The oceanographer Jacques Piccard and US Navy Lieutenant Don Walsh made the first expedition to the bottom of the trench in 1960. They used a US navy bathyscaphe, the Trieste bathyscaphe. That's a bathyscaphe there ... Up to then, most deep-sea diving vessels had been bathyspheres – small round steel containers that were lowered from the ship onto the seabed by a cable. A bathyscaphe has no cable. As you can see in this picture, it has a bathysphere at the bottom for the crew, but above it there's a large float. The float is filled with gasoline. This is let out and replaced with sea water when the bathyscaphe has to descend into the water. To return to the surface the bathyscaphe also has iron ballast – so, heavy weights – which is dropped to make the vessel lighter and help it ascend ... to get back up to the surface.

The system worked perfectly. However, when the Trieste finally reached the bottom of the trench, the crew had used almost half their air supply. The descent had taken five hours. They only stayed on the bottom for about twenty minutes and then ascended again. While they were exploring the trench, the crew noted that the seabed was soft and featureless. They also reported seeing a flat fish, but this was later disputed by other scientists.

8.3 Extract 3

The Trieste bathyscaphe reached the Mariana Trench five hours after it had begun its descent from the surface. However, whilst it was descending, one of the windows in the vessel cracked under the intense pressure. The two crew members were concerned about this and so they reduced the time they had originally planned to spend on the bottom. When they had completed a quick observation of the environment, they returned to the surface.

8.4 Extract 4

Tom presented an overview of the earliest expeditions to the Mariana Trench. I'd like to tell you about a more recent high-profile exploration of the same area. Despite all the scientific interest in the trench, there haven't been many expeditions. This is mainly due to the huge costs involved in getting so far below the surface. So, as we heard from Tom, the Trieste explored the region in 1960. The next expedition took place on the 26th of March 2012.

The person who undertook this descent was the film director James Cameron, whose most famous film is probably *Titanic*, made in 1997. He went down alone in a new type of deep-sea vessel that used special foam for flotation and had engines to power it. He also took with him more scientific equipment than the earlier expedition. The purpose of his journey into the deep was to confirm what the Trieste had seen, and to find out as much as he could about the deep-sea environment. Once Cameron had reached the bottom, he was able to explore the sea bed. He spent two and a half hours there, recording information using digital cameras. While he was driving around on the seabed, he also observed that the terrain was soft and flat, but unlike the previous expedition he saw no fish, only small crustaceans – creatures like shrimps or prawns.

So these two expeditions were mainly about proving that people could reach the bottom of the deep ocean. However, the pictures that James Cameron took while exploring the trench have been made into a 3D film called *Deepsea Challenge*. Cameron has said that he hopes this will inspire other potential explorers, just as the photographs of the Trieste's journey had inspired him as a child.

Unit 9

9.1 Extract 1

I'd like to talk today about a condition known as synaesthesia and its possible causes. Now, synaesthesia attracts a lot of interest because scientists believe that understanding why it occurs could help us understand how our brains process sensory stimuli.

Synaesthesia is a condition where our senses – sight, smell, taste, and hearing – appear to be mixed up. So, rather than just hearing music or tasting food or seeing numbers on a page, a person with synaesthesia – a synaesthete – experiences an extrasensory response to a stimulus. So for example, ah, when they hear a musical note, they might also see a colour. When they hear a particular word, like 'book', they might at the same time get a taste of something completely unrelated, like chocolate. When they see a number on a page, they might at the same time see in their mind a certain shape or colour. Most synaesthetes find these associations pleasant rather than unpleasant. Because of this, synaesthesia is not considered an illness.

9.2 Extract 2

Serious synaesthesia only affects one in 2,000 people, but it has been suggested that we all have a tendency to be synaesthetic. This raises two important questions. Is synaesthesia due to a physical difference? Or do people become synaesthetic because of environmental factors?

Now, some psychologists believe that synaesthesia develops in children when they're growing up because the taste and sound associations that synaesthetes describe often come from things in their childhood: the pleasant taste of sweets or the unpleasant taste of vegetables that they had to eat; um, the songs they learned at school or the music that they repeated when trying to learn the piano.

However, there are other psychologists who believe that synaesthetes make these unusual associations owing to a physical difference in their brain structure. The suggestion is that ... their brains are cross-wired so that when they receive a signal, more than one part of the brain is activated. OK? When they receive a signal that normally activates just one part of the brain, another part of the brain is also activated. This theory has been tested with neuro-imaging, where the brain is scanned and the activated sections of the brain 'light up' on the screen when they are stimulated. Some scans have shown different parts of the brain lighting up. But others have not. So, in fact the results of neuro-imaging have been inconclusive. It seems that there is both an increased and reduced sensitivity ...

9.3 Extract 3

1 Synaesthesia attracts a lot of interest because scientists believe that understanding why it occurs could help us to understand how our brains process sensory stimuli.
2 Most synaesthetes find these associations pleasant rather than unpleasant. Therefore, synaesthesia is not considered to be an illness.

3 Is synaesthesia due to a physical difference? Or do people become synaesthetic because of environmental factors?
4 However, there are others who believe synaesthetes make these unusual associations owing to a physical difference in their brain structure.
5 The suggestion is that their brains are cross-wired so that when they receive a signal, more than one part of the brain is activated.

9.4 Extract 4

Tutor OK, I'd like to follow up Wednesday's lecture on synaesthesia and its probable causes. I want to expand on some of the ideas that were discussed and also touch on your reading from last week – so we can explore some of the practical applications of neurobiological study. OK? Sound good? Right. Before we start, are there any questions?

A Yes, er, in the lecture Dr Ellis said that synaesthesia was a 'pleasant' condition. But I'm not sure why people think that. Surely it must be very confusing ... and quite annoying sometimes.

Tutor Well, I think in some cases it might be, but from most of the case studies and extensive evidence from interviews and questionnaires, it seems that the majority of synaesthetes actually find their condition a positive thing.

A And also, I didn't understand if people can have more than one type of synaesthesia at a time. I mean, can more than two senses be mixed up?

Tutor Not usually, no. But there are many different kinds of two-sense synaesthesia.

B Can you tell us what the most common types are?

Tutor Well, the most common variant is what is called grapheme-colour synaesthesia. This is where people see letters or numbers in particular colours. Because we already know quite a lot about the visual system and its neurological effects, grapheme-colour is certainly the most studied form of synaesthesia.

B Does anyone know why that's more common than other types? Is there a reason?

Tutor Good question. It could be that the grapheme-colour is just the most reported form, but there are some studies which suggest that it's because of other factors ...

9.5 Extract 5

My presentation is about narcolepsy. Narcolepsy is a condition which affects the brain's ability to control the normal sleep-wake cycle.

Narcolepsy affects one in every 200 people, so it's a relatively rare sleep disorder. It can affect people of all age groups.

People with narcolepsy – narcoleptics – are unable to sleep properly at night and they tend to fall asleep during the day. The key symptom of narcolepsy is called ES, or Excessive Sleepiness.

Narcolepsy is a big problem for sufferers because interrupted sleep causes tiredness, problems with concentration, and it can cause hallucinations – where people think they're seeing things which aren't there. These hallucinations usually happen in the transition between sleeping and waking.

The exact causes of narcolepsy aren't known, but it may be due to a chemical imbalance in the body.

9.6 Extract 6

My presentation is about narcolepsy. Narcolepsy is a condition which affects the brain's ability to control the normal sleep-wake cycle.

Narcolepsy affects one in every 200 people, so it's a relatively rare sleep disorder. It can affect people of all age groups.

People with narcolepsy – narcoleptics – are unable to sleep properly at night and they tend to fall asleep during the day. The key symptom of narcolepsy is called ES, or Excessive Sleepiness.

Narcolepsy is a big problem for sufferers because interrupted sleep causes tiredness, problems with concentration, and it can cause hallucinations – where people think they're seeing things which aren't there. These hallucinations usually happen in the transition between sleeping and waking.

The exact causes of narcolepsy aren't known, but it may be due to a chemical imbalance in the body.

Unit 10

10.1 Extract 1

So we are looking today at new trends in tourism – how tourism has changed in recent years, due to economic, social, and environmental factors. And how these perspectives are shaping the way that we view travel – and travellers.

Now, the first thing that I want to discuss is the growing trend in what is called 'responsible tourism'. Air travel is becoming cheaper and easier, the number of people who want to travel is increasing, especially from emerging economies like China. So, the tourism business is booming. But this puts a lot of stress on the environment and it raises a number of issues, which responsible tourism tries to address.

Now, responsible tourism can be defined as tourism which minimizes the negative economic, social, and environmental impacts on the host country. It should also make positive contributions to the conservation of the country's natural and cultural heritage. And in addition, responsible tourism should benefit the local people by involving them positively in the tourist industry and ensuring that they're paid fairly.

So responsible tourism has three main aims. First of all, to reduce the amount of energy resources consumed in global travel. Second, to protect the local communities from the negative impact of mass tourism. And thirdly, to limit the amount of overseas travel.

10.2 Extract 2

In response to these three main aims I want to argue that responsible tourism has several key principles. First of all, a responsible tourist should understand the place they are visiting – its culture, its economy, and its politics – and show respect for these things. Tourists do this when they read a guidebook before they visit a country. It's a simple enough thing to do, and it's something which prepares travellers for interacting with the culture they are going to visit. Knowing what to wear at a religious site or how to greet someone politely – this shows that the tourist is aware of the cultural difference and that they're interested in observing it.

Responsible tourism also means supporting the local economy. So, for example, rather than staying in a hotel owned by a multi-national corporation, a responsible tourist will stay in a hotel run by local people. And use local guides, or services wherever possible. And, I would argue that this is the most important factor in responsible tourism, because any money they spend, any income which enters the local economy in this way, has a better chance of staying in the local economy, and supporting local growth. In addition, responsible tourism means being aware of your impact on the environment. Renting a bicycle rather than a car to visit the surrounding area is an example of this. Another example might be using a company that doesn't waste resources, like a hotel that only washes your bath towel and bedding when you ask them to.

10.3 Extract 3

Responsible tourism may involve different practices in different places. But I would argue that the most important thing is the attitude of the traveller, the respect that the traveller shows to the people and environment that they are visiting. By showing this respect, both the traveller and the host can benefit from tourism: the host benefits economically because more tourism brings more money into the region. And the traveller, well ... the traveller benefits from knowing they're making a positive contribution. They get that 'feel good' effect. Furthermore, by showing respect, the traveller creates the conditions where he or she can get closer to the culture of a particular place. The more you respect a culture, the more likely it is that you'll get closer to it and see parts of it that outsiders don't usually see. And increasing our knowledge of different cultures is, after all, one of the main purposes of travel and tourism.

10.4 Extract 4

1 Responsible tourism has several key principles. First of all, a responsible tourist should understand the place they are visiting – its culture, its economy and its politics – and show respect for these things.
2 Responsible tourism also means supporting the local economy.
3 In addition, responsible tourism means being aware of your impact on the environment.
4 The traveller benefits from knowing they're making a positive contribution. They get that 'feel good' effect. Furthermore, by showing respect, the traveller creates the conditions where he or she can get closer to the culture of a particular place.

10.5 Extract 5

Tutor So that completes my summary of last week's lecture on responsible tourism ... Does anyone have any questions or need anything to be clarified? Elena, you have a question?

Elena Yeah, there are a few things that came up that I'd like your view on. At the end of what you were saying, ... you said that an important argument for responsible tourism was because it was the best way to get closer to other cultures. I understand why you say that, but actually I don't agree with the premise of your argument. Because, I don't think most people travel to learn about other cultures. They travel to sit on a beach or relax by a swimming pool.

Tutor There is some truth in that, yes, but even people who go on beach holidays can be responsible tourists. You can be a responsible tourist and still enjoy yourself, I think. Ah, Carsten?

Carsten OK, so, the problem I have with the responsible travel argument is that, in the end it's saying just don't go on holiday at all. Don't fly, don't go abroad, just stay at home. You know?

Tutor Well, I realize that it might look like that – the anti-holiday argument. But actually, responsible tourism encourages travel. Although you could argue that it just has to be the right kind of travel. Going on holiday in your own country is one kind of responsible tourism, but it's not the only kind.

Carsten OK. Yes, I see what you're saying. Although I'm not convinced.

Oxford source material used in this course

The reading, writing, and speaking skills modules of *Oxford EAP* include extracts from the following source material published by Oxford University Press. For more information about any of these titles, please visit: **www.oup.com**.

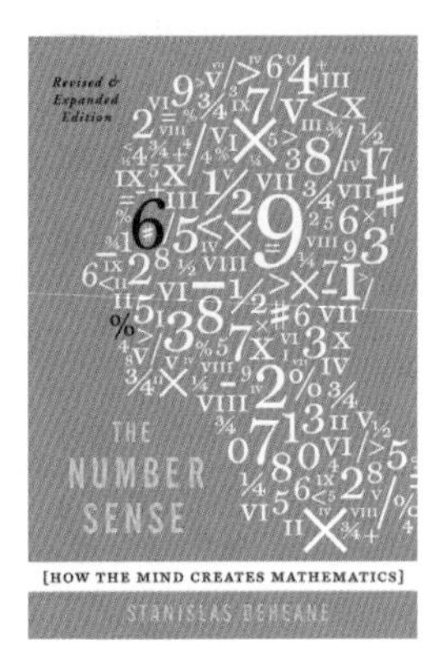

page 027
The Number Sense

page 040
IB Business and Management Course Companion

page 055
IB Psychology Course Companion

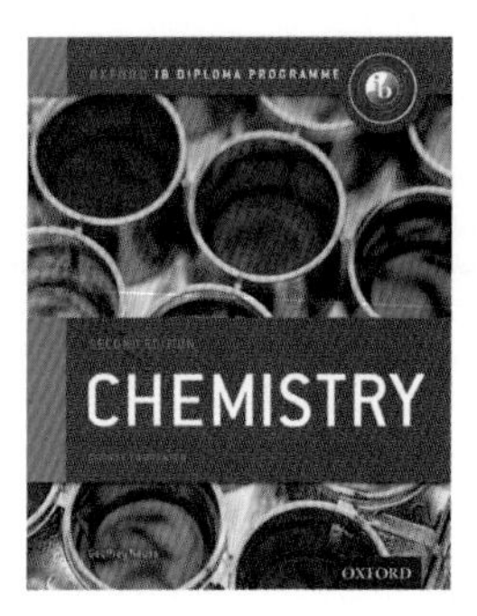

page 083
IB Chemistry Course Companion

page 096
IB Theory of Knowledge Course Companion

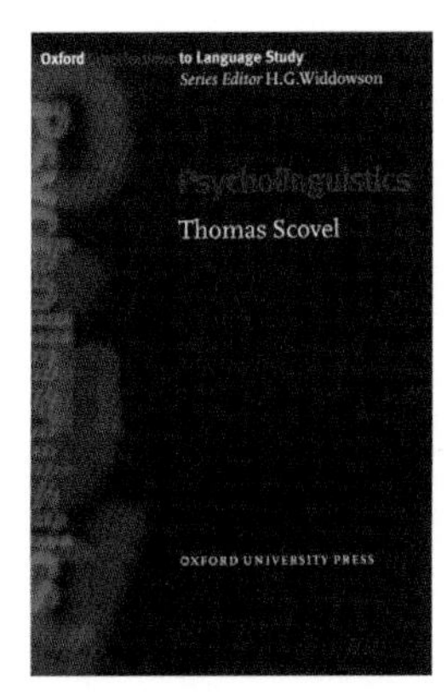

page 102
Psycholinguistics: Oxford Introductions to Language Study

page 103
How Languages are Learned

page 110
IB Physics Course Companion

page 125
IB Biology Course Companion

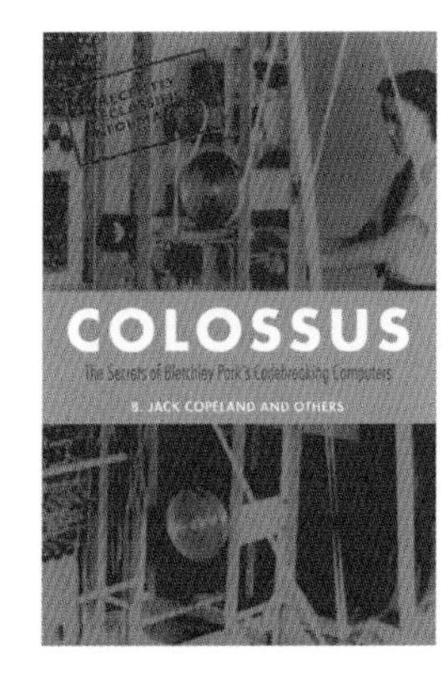

page 169
Colossus

page 171
IB Geography Course Companion

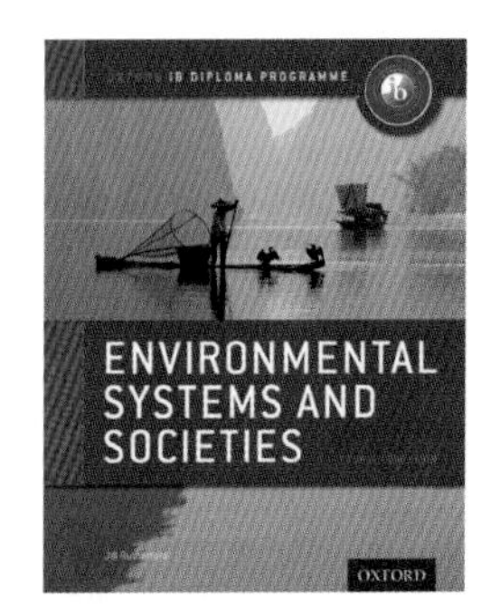

page 174
IB Environmental Systems and Societies Companion

Great Clarendon Street, Oxford, OX2 6DP, United Kingdom

Oxford University Press is a department of the University of Oxford. It furthers the University's objective of excellence in research, scholarship, and education by publishing worldwide. Oxford is a registered trade mark of Oxford University Press in the UK and in certain other countries

First published in 2015
2019 2018 2017 2016 2015
10 9 8 7 6 5 4 3 2 1

ISBN: 978 0 19 400208 0

Printed in China

This book is printed on paper from certified and well-managed sources

ACKNOWLEDGEMENTS

The authors and publisher are grateful to those who have given permission to reproduce the following extracts and adaptations of copyright material: p.029 Figure from *The Number Sense: How the Mind Creates Mathematics*, Revised and Expanded Edition by Stanislas Dehaene, Oxford University Press (2011), redrawn from "Subitizing: An analysis of its component processes" by George Mandler and Billie J. Shebo, *Journal of Experimental Psychology*, Vol 111 (1). Reproduced by permission of Oxford University Press and American Psychological Association. p.051 Figure adapted from *IB Environmental Systems and Societies Course Book* by Jill Rutherford (Oxford University Press, 2012). Data taken from FAOSTAT. World Agricultural Production (dataset). Reproduced by permission of FAO. p.055 Extracts from *IB Psychology: Course Companion* by John Crane and Jette Hannibal (Oxford University Press, 2009), copyright © Oxford University Press 2009, reproduced by permission of Oxford University Press. p.069 Adapted extract from "Out of sight, out of mind: workplace smoking bans and the relocation of smoking at work" by Odette Parry, Stephen Platt and Carolyn Thomson, *Health Promotion International*, Vol 15 (2) pp.125–133. Reproduced by permission of Oxford University Press p.083 Extracts from *IB Chemistry: Course Companion* by Geoffrey Neuss (Oxford University Press, 2007, copyright © Geoffrey Neuss 2009, reproduced by permission of Oxford University Press. p.096 Extracts from *IB Theory of Knowledge: Course Companion* by Eileen Dombrowski, Lena Rotenberg and Mimi Bick (Oxford University Press, 2013, copyright © Eileen Dombrowski, Lena Rotenberg and Mimi Bick 2007, reproduced by permission of Oxford University Press. p.139 Extracts from *IB Business and Management: Course Companion* by Paul Clark, Peter Golden, Mark O'Dea, Phil Woolrich, John Weiner and Jorge Olmos (Oxford University Press, 2012, copyright © Paul Clark, Peter Golden, Mark O'Dea, Phil Woolrich, John Weiner and Jorge Olmos, reproduced by permission of Oxford University Press.

Sources: www.wikipedia.org

The publisher is grateful to the following for their permission to reproduce photographs and illustrative material: Alamy p.8 (© Caro), 18 (© James Osmond), 22 (© Jim Batty), 24 (© Art Directors & TRIP), 55 (© Gary Cook), 66 (jeremy sutton-hibbert/cut trees), 69 (© Radharc Images), 74 (© Universal Images Group Limited), 95 (© GL Archive/Geronimo, © The Protected Art Archive/Apache women), 98 (© Ville Palonen/Moroccan storyteller), 128 (© Chad Ehlers/bungee jump, © Jeff Rotman/shark diving), 134 (© NASA Archive), 136 (© Craig Lovell – All Rights Reserved); Corbis p.26 (Wally McNamee/Olympiad), 85 (© Wally McNamee/gold miners), 98 (© Leah Warkentin/Design Pics/teacher reading), 107 (© Bettmann/Bathyscaphe Trieste), 110 (© NASA/JPL-Caltech); Getty p.29 (J. B. Spector/Museum of Science and Industry, Chicago/Chronoscope), 36 (Jason Hawkes/The Image Bank), 39 (Universal Images Group), 41 (Universal Images Group), 64 (Mario Tama/Getty Images News), 65 (Danita Delimont/Gallo Images/Norse settlement, Greenland, Bruno Morandi/The Image Bank/Mayan Pyramid, Mexico), 66 (Jim Richardson/National Geographic/Easter Island aerial view), 79 (Vincenzo Lombardo/Photographer's Choice/Graphene), 85 (Isifa/Getty Images News/gold bullion), 98 (AFP/puppeteer), 113 (Malcolm Park/Oxford Scientific/white dwarf), 116 (Richard Allenby-Pratt/arabianEye), 138 (Lucas Schifres/Getty Images), 144 (Marc Lester/Anchorage Daily News/MCT); NASA p.113 (red giant), 114 (ESA/V. Beckmann (NASA-GSFC)); Oxford University Press RF p.12 (Digital Vision), 13 (Alamy), 19 (Shutterstock), 26 (Shutterstock/clock/Superbowl XLV), 37 (Getty/football red card), 50 (Shutterstock), 54 (Moodboard/swimming, Getty/basketball, Shutterstock/football/running/cycling), 65 (Shutterstock/Easter Island), 66 (Shutterstock/rat), 72 (Getty), 82 (Ingram/cells, Shutterstock/periodic table), 86 (Alamy), 88 (Ingram), 92 (Getty), 96 (Getty), 100 (Shutterstock), 106 (Getty), 120 (Getty), 124 (Shutterstock/peanuts, Alamy/EpiPen), 128 (Kzenon/job interview), 143 (Shutterstock); Rex Features p.16 (Rex), 109 (Keystone USA-ZUMA); SPL p.29 (American Philosophical Society/James McKeen Cattell), 44 (University of Durham/Simon Fraser), 78 (Science Picture Co), 79 (NREL/US Department of Energy/Aerogel, Pascal Goetgheluck/Gecko tape), 82 (David Parker/prism), 87 (Sheila Terry), 122 (Mehau Kulyk), 124 (Colin Hawkins/sneezing woman), 131 (CDC); Oxford University Press covers p.40, 175.

Lecturer and presenter portraits by: Mark Bassett p.9, 23, 37 (man in glasses), 52, 65, 79, 81, 93, 108, 121, 135

Illustrations by: Peter Bull p.80, 107 (Mariana trench, bathyscaphe), 117, 125; Richard Ponsford p.27, 29, 30, 32, 33, 51, 53, 60, 61, 83, 107 (map), 163, 165.

Cover photograph by: Gareth Boden.

Design by: Richard Ponsford.

The authors and publisher would like to thank the following individuals for their valuable advice and assistance in developing the material for this course: Asmaa Awad (University of Sharjah, United Arab Emirates), David Bozetarnik (Sharjah Women's Higher Colleges of Technology, UAE), Jim Echelberry (University of Fukui, Japan), Fatos Ugur Eskicirak (Bahcesehir University, Istanbul, Turkey), Ana Silvia Ferreira (São Paulo University, Brazil), Jeff Gibbons (King Fahd University of Petroleum & Minerals, Dhahran, Saudi Arabia), Claire Graham (Sino British College, Shanghai, China), Yakut Ilyas (Meliksah University, Kayseri, Turkey), Professor Narahiko Inoue (Kyushu University, Japan), Tanisaya Jiriyasin (University of the Thai Chamber of Commerce, Bangkok, Thailand), Alev Küçük (Eastern Mediterranean University, North Cyprus), Jill Newby (Foundation Institute, University of Nizwa, Oman), Gary Pathare (Higher Colleges of Technology, Dubai, UAE), Adrienne Radcliffe (RMIT University, Ho Chi Minh City, Vietnam), Gordon Reisdorf (Konan University, Kobe, Japan), Lynne Robinson (Petroleum Institute, Abu Dhabi, UAE), Walaiporn Tantikanangkul (Chiang Mai University, Thailand), Kate Tindle (Zayed University, Dubai, UAE), Bob Wenn (Abu Dhabi Men's College, UAE).

Special thanks to: Edward de Chazal and Richard Storton